LEAVING THE HALL LIGHT ON

*A mother's memoir of living with her son's bipolar disorder
and surviving his suicide*

MADELINE SHARPLES

Dream of Things
Downers Grove Illinois USA

First Dream of Things Edition, July 2012.
Published by Dream of Things, Downers Grove, Illinois USA
Originally published in hardcover by Lucky Press LLC in 2011.

Dream of Things provides discounts to educators, book clubs, writers groups, and others. For more information, visit www.dreamofthings.com, write to customerservice@dreamofthings.com or call 847-321-1390.

Sharples, Madeline.
    Leaving the hall light on : a mother's memoir of living with her son's bipolar disorder and surviving his suicide / Madeline Sharples.
       p. ; cm.
       ISBN: 9780982579480
1. Manic-depressive persons--United States--Biography. 2. Manic-depressive persons--Family relationships. 3. Suicide victim--United States--Biography. 4. Mothers of suicide victims--United States--Biography. I. Title.

RC516.S53
616.89/50092--dc22   2012942154

Permissions: I would like to gratefully acknowledge the writers whose quotes I use in this book. I made an exhaustive search to determine whether previously published material included in this book required permission to reprint. In the case of any errors, I apologize and will make a correction in subsequent editions.
The following authors, their agents, and publishers have graciously granted permission to include excerpts from the following: *Operating Instructions*, by Anne Lamott, Anchor Books, 2005: Random House deemed the excerpt falls within the realm of fair use in the U.S., Canada, the E.U, and the open market.
Bel Canto by Ann Patchett, copyright © 2001 Ann Patchett. Reprinted by permission of HarperCollins Publishers.
"Slip Slidin' Away" by Paul Simon, copyright © 1977 Paul Simon. Used by permission of the publisher: Paul Simon Music

Cover Photo: Madison Poulter
Book Design: Janice Phelps Williams

For the loves of my life
Bob, Ben, and Marissa

I could not have gotten through this without you.

And in memory of
Paul Ian Sharples

December 31, 1971 to September 23, 1999

Poem Credits

Leaving the Hall Light On—The Muddy River Poetry Review (2009)
under title, "What Is Loss?"

Mania—Survivor Chronicles (2010)

The Last Night—Memoir (and) (2009)

Thursday Morning—Memoir (and) (2009)

Years, Months, and a Day —unFold (2010)

My Jazzman—Survivor Chronicles (2010)

The Bully—Didi Hirsch Survivors after Suicide Newsletter (2006)

Buddha—Survivor Chronicles (2010)

Lunch excerpt—Perigee Publication for the Arts (2009)

Making It Hard—ONTHEBUS (2004)

Aftermath—The Compassionate Friends newsletter, We Need Not Walk Alone (2001)

The Dreaded Question—Survivor Chronicles (2010)

Demolition—Perigee Publication for the Arts (2009)

Black Bomber—The Great American Poetry Show Volume 1 (2004)

Today I Saw You on the Hill—poetsespresso (2010)

ACKNOWLEDGMENTS

It is so exciting to have this new and updated edition of *Leaving the Hall Light On* published. That it happened so quickly is really quite amazing. Thank you to my new publisher, Mike O'Mary of Dream of Things, for that. Mike almost immediately agreed to republish my book, and he has been so generous with his advice, editorial skills, and marketing prowess. I feel my association with Mike was meant to be. Thank you Mark Shelmerdine, my friend and mentor, who recommended I contact Mike. When I found out I needed a new publisher I called on Mark immediately. He has been my go-to person for everything related to publishing since I first began this journey in 2009.

I also thank Keith Alan Hamilton who asked everyone he knew to help me find a publisher – and believe me he knows a lot of folks. Keith has also touted my work on his Hamilton Gallery site. Another big thank you to Doreen Cox, not only for recommending her own publisher to me, but for blasting the Twitter stream with tweets about my book. My social networks friends have shown their support and love over and over throughout my publishing woes and successes.

Putting my book together in the first place took a village. I was very fortunate to have had the help of many talented writers and friends in conceptualizing and organizing my book, reading, and editing its many drafts, and providing photography, word processing, and general advice and encouragement: Marlene Clark McPherson, Elizabeth Isenberg, Sita White, Lollie Rogana, Larry Ziman, Paul Blieden, Madison Poulter, Ed McPherson, and Maria Guzman.

Thank you to my husband Bob for his patience and for giving me the space to pursue my writing dreams, to my son Ben for his praise and encouragement, and to my daughter-in-law Marissa who is always ready to toot my horn.

I must also thank the many reviewers who have posted such glowing remarks on the Amazon and Barnes and Noble websites, and on their own blogs. I think their enthusiasm is the reason Mike and so many others are rallying around this book. Thank you all so much.

LEAVING THE HALL LIGHT ON

May 1973, at Grandma and Grandpa's piano

When I held Sam alone for the first time..., I was nursing him and feeling really spiritual, thinking, please, please God, help him be someone who feels compassion, who feels God's presence loose in the world, who doesn't give up on peace and justice and mercy for everyone. And then a second later I was begging. Okay, skip all that shit, forget it—just please let him outlive me.

Anne Lamott, *Operating Instructions*
Anchor Books, 1995

February 1997, playing piano at his dad's sixtieth birthday party

CHAPTER ONE

S
ometime during the night or early morning of September 23, 1999, my twenty-seven-year old son Paul walked out of his dark bedroom in his bare feet, entered his bathroom, and closed and locked the door behind him. Still wearing the white, long-sleeved shirt and khaki pants he had worn to work the day before, he went to the far side of the room, stepped into the bathtub, closed the sliding glass shower door, and sat down in the tub. Using a box cutter, he slashed both of his wrists. Then he slashed his throat and bled out into the tub.

That seemingly painless and swift act—it took approximately thirty to forty seconds for Paul to die—brought our tight, average suburban family to the depths of despair. My husband, Bob, age sixty-two at the time and a successful aerospace engineer for most of his professional life, had to touch the cold, lifeless body of the child he deeply loved. Our second son Ben, age twenty-five, two and a half years younger than Paul, was in San Francisco performing with his fellow classmates on the main stage of the American Conservatory Theater and almost ready to receive his masters degree in fine arts in acting. His brother's death was almost the end of his dream. Though I had struggled through the years of Paul's bipolar disorder highs and lows, I, then age fifty-nine and retired from the aerospace industry as a proposal expert, was writing grant proposals for non-profits, active in my community, and enjoying life with my friends, my gym, my book clubs, and walks along the beach. I was also an avid journal writer and beginning to take an interest in creative writing. Though I was healthy, the stress of Paul's illness kept me thin.

Because writing was a constant in my life, I felt compelled to write the story of my oldest son's life-and-death struggle with his bipolar illness (also called manic depression) before the memory faded. I could never forget those few months in the spring and summer of 1993 when Paul had his first mental breakdown—or crackup as he called it—and the years of worry, weight loss, rescue attempts, and grief ever since. And, I don't ever want to forget. I want to remember everything about him—how his fingers trickled up and down the keyboard as he played the piano; his dark blond hair cut close to his head in a buzz; his passion for second-hand plaid shirts, washed out jeans, and Doc Marten oxfords; his appetite for burgers and steaks, pizza, and ice cream; his brilliance with all things related to computers; his wonderful ability to write and draw; and his obsession for order and regimen in the way he treated his belongings.

Even after all these years reminders are everywhere—his room in our home that I've turned into my office; his piano that no one ever plays, still up in the family room; our living room where he used to wrestle with his dad and brother before it was furnished; the downtown Manhattan Beach Starbucks where he liked to sit outside; the Manhattan Beach pier; the hundreds of photos either on display in our home or scanned into our computer; his books and records packed away in boxes in our garage, and things I couldn't possibly part with—his black bomber jacket, his poems and short stories, his photos, anything in his handwriting, his CD collection, and, of course, recordings of his original compositions, now on CD and on my iPod courtesy of his best friend from high school.

The doctors told me it wasn't my fault when my son was diagnosed with bipolar disorder. They said this disorder, caused by a chemical imbalance in the brain and triggered by stress, usually hits young people in their late teens or early twenties, like Paul who had just turned twenty-one. One day he was perfectly fine, playing the piano at his grandmother's eighty-fifth birthday party. Two weeks later he was calling us up every few minutes, writing all over his walls with a blue felt-tipped marker, saying people were lurking in doorways out to get him and poisoning his food and cigarettes.

He was no longer able to sit still long enough at the piano to play a song through from the beginning to end. Was he acting like a crazy person or someone high on drugs? At first we didn't know which.

But deep down I felt guilty. Why hadn't I seen the signs? Why didn't I take better care of him? He was my son. I should have known how to protect him from the danger he was in. I didn't know then that I had no control over what happened to him. I could only care for him the best I could. I couldn't spoon-feed him like a child anymore. He didn't allow it. He was an adult, and he controlled the outcome. Even so, my feelings of guilt have never gone away.

From the time he was born—in fact even before he was born—Paul was special. He presented himself feet first. All the Lamaze classes my husband and I attended went by the wayside when the doctor kicked Bob out of the delivery room and performed a Cesarean section. Paul was stubborn even in utero—he wouldn't come out the natural way.

September 1972, nine months old

When I finally was allowed to see and hold him twenty-four hours after the delivery, I was the first to notice that both of his hands were deformed—the middle and ring fingers of both his hands were stuck together. I was in so much shock as I held him and peered into his face that I couldn't keep it in focus. His face seemed to recede and disappear as I held him in my arms. My worst fears and bad dreams had materialized. My child was born with a deformity. What had I done to cause that? As was the hospital's custom with Cesarean deliveries, he had been thoroughly examined by a pediatrician and observed in an isolette around the clock for the first twenty-four hours of his life. Yet no one who had given him his initial exam noticed. When I looked at his fingers, I started screaming, and Bob took off down the hall to get the doctors to reexamine him. If they had missed something so obvious as his webbed fingers, what else did they miss?

Throughout my pregnancy we had never let up on our fears about how our child would turn out. I would be over thirty at the time of the birth and in the early 1970s that was considered old to have a first child. I had already had two miscarriages, and Bob was the father of a Downs Syndrome child born from his first marriage. I was also under a lot of stress, mostly caused by my mother's jealousy. She couldn't stand that Bob and I were happy; she couldn't stand the attention I was getting while I was pregnant, she couldn't stand that I didn't need her anymore, and she couldn't stand that she had no control over me anymore. Whenever we spoke on the phone, she picked a fight. One time when I was about six months pregnant with Paul, I called my parents from a pay phone to check in during our return trip from a weekend at Big Sur. I was happy and relaxed from our trip, and we wanted to drive through to our home in Riverside rather than stop and see them in Beverly Hills. I stood in the phone booth at a gas station for at least half an hour with Bob waiting in the car while she told me how disrespectful and inattentive I was. "You left us all alone while you were away having a good time," she yelled. I finally yelled back, "If something is wrong with my baby it will be your fault." As a result she, too, was very worried about how Paul would turn out. She had a vested interest in him being born perfect. He was except for the "funny finger thing"—as we began to call his deformity.

Otherwise, Paul was diagnosed as a healthy baby, and we immediately fell in love with him. He was so easy. He nursed well and slept well in between feedings. From the beginning he was the love of Bob's life. He would hold Paul in his arms and constantly talk to him. He'd hold him close to the pictures on the wall and tell him their stories as he described the books, the chairs, the kitchen items, his parents, his grandparents, and the wonderful future we wanted him to have. This child was loved, and the doctors reassured us his fingers could be easily fixed—a simple surgery, they said, when he was older.

The word "simple" was the understatement of the century—at least to us. At age two Paul was in surgery for over eight hours to separate the two fingers with perfectly normal bone structure on both hands and remove skin from his groin area to build the webs in between his fingers. He was barely conscious when he was rolled away in his hospital crib with the high bars all around. I wanted to go with him, to be there with him at least up to the surgery room, but there was no way. In those days, hospital rules were so insensitive that they didn't allow for the needs of the little patients or their parents. Then we sat all those hours in the waiting room—my dad was with us—and we didn't move until we knew he was safe and in recovery. And still we weren't allowed to see him until after he was out of recovery and fully conscious. Unfortunately, it was during the four-hour recovery time that all the damage was done.

"Mommy, I can't move my fingers," were the first words I heard when Paul was brought out of the recovery area. I was devastated to see him this way. I had only done what I had thought best for him in the long run, but at the moment I felt I had made a terrible mistake. And, maybe so. The happy-go-lucky little boy was now gone. Still beautiful, still bright, and immediately agile with all his little fingers once his casts were finally removed, but he was never the same again.

The happy, smiley boy who had embarked on that surgery with full trust in us and confidence that his adored Dr. Lane (he said, Dr. Yane) would separate his fingers just like we fixed his broken toys—in an instant—just like that, awoke to find both his hands and arms up to his elbows in heavy casts so he wouldn't do any damage to the one hundred stitches the doctor had sewn in each hand. Before the surgery he was able to suck those fingers. Now he was cut off from that security "blanket" cold turkey. Before the surgery he went to anyone. He was a child full of trust and love. Afterward he had a list of fears: pictures of clowns, people with masks on Halloween, Santa Claus, and old men with beards. These things would trigger hysteria. Fortunately, those fears were finally allayed once he started watching Sesame Street. He would shriek with laughter at the fuzzy monster puppets that spoke to him in a language he could understand and learn from.

The only explanation for his fears that we could think of was his half-conscious state during the recovery and that the doctors and nurses all wore surgical masks in the cold, sterile atmosphere of the recovery room. I wasn't allowed in. I wasn't allowed to help him. For the first time I wasn't in control—except that I had allowed the surgery. I knew we had to get his fingers separated, but maybe we should have waited until he was older when he could better understand the procedure and the aftermath. Had I known how long the surgery would take, had I known beforehand he would have to wear such debilitating casts for so

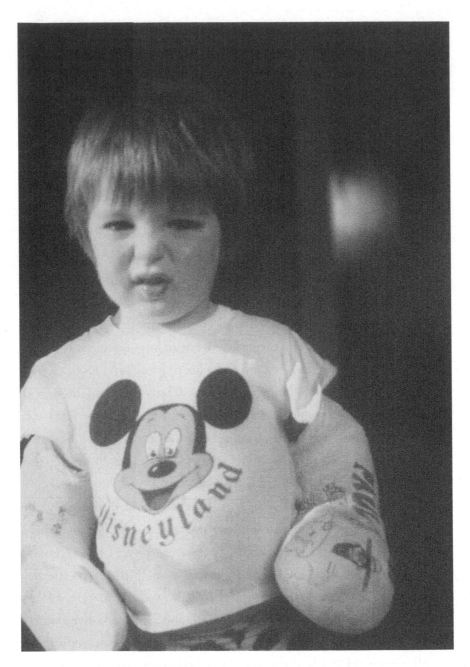

February 1974, with casts after finger surgery

long, I might have decided to wait. Even the doctor had misgivings. He said that had he known the procedure on both hands would take eight hours, he would have done one hand at a time.

I, at least, was allowed to stay with him the night of the surgery, though both of us hardly slept. He would not allow anyone but me to touch him. "Mommy will do it," he said, whenever a nurse came to change a dressing or give him a sip of something to drink. I sat up with him on my lap through the night.

That incident was the first of many traumas that Paul suffered during his terrible twos, perhaps precursors to his bipolar diagnosis nineteen years later. Very shortly after the surgery we moved to a house we purchased in Manhattan Beach, California. Later that year his brother Benjamin was born. The first time Paul saw Ben, he quickly remarked, "He's already had his surgery," thinking that all little babies are born with funny fingers. And soon after, one of his favorite people, my father, was diagnosed with cancer of the bile duct system. From the time Paul was a baby, my dad loved to take care of him whenever he got the chance. He would feed him juice or water from a bottle (not milk since I breast-fed Paul until he was fifteen months old), take him for buggy rides, readily change his diapers, and proudly hold him on his lap as Paul, with an adoring look on his face, gazed up at him.

My dad had encouraged us to have Paul's hand surgery sooner rather than later. He would lie down with Paul for their afternoon naps and he could see Paul trying to pull his fingers apart. He worried that he would try to separate them himself. Once Paul asked for a screwdriver (he said "foogiver") so he could open his fingers. We were all worried that he would harm himself unless we acted quickly.

After my dad had bypass surgery, he couldn't be Paul's playmate and caretaker again. "Why doesn't Grandpa play with me anymore?" Paul asked when we would visit, and by the time Paul was three and a half, his grandpa was gone. Paul missed him and he never forgot him. They were alike in many ways. My dad was short; so was Paul—not quite five foot nine inches. My dad was small boned; so was Paul. Otherwise they didn't look alike. My dad had dark skin and dark hair and big brown eyes. Paul was pale with dark blonde hair and amazing blue eyes rimmed with dark lashes. But like my dad, Paul was gentle with little children. They were both quiet and inward. They both loved to read and listen to music. And Paul walked fast like him.

Looking back, I think a couple of other events in Paul's life were warning signals about how he would turn out. One was his strong re-action to Bob's possible job transfer to the East Coast. Paul was so adamant about not wanting to go, about not wanting to leave his high school, jazz ensemble, and his life in Manhattan Beach, that we went to family therapy for help. The rest of us were okay with the move—including Ben—but Paul couldn't be placated. While in therapy the doctor recommended that Paul take a series of psychological tests. These showed he was slightly depressed, but both Bob and I and the doctor didn't see that as a major problem. Maybe we were sticking our heads in the sand, but we chalked the depression up to his being a fifteen-year old who wasn't getting what he wanted. The job transfer never hap-pened, and although Paul was elated at the news, he continued with the psychologist for about a year on his own.

The second event started when Paul was seventeen. He met a thirty-two-year old divorced woman at a party given by his high-school jazz teacher and began a full-fledged love affair that lasted about two years. Instead of crying rape, we tried to end the affair by urging him to attend college in New York City at the New School jazz program in place of one of the California schools that had offered him admission. And in enthusiastic agreement, he entered as a freshman in August 1989. By the summer after his sophomore year the affair was over, but not with-out a lot of pain for him. He acted like an adult while he was inside the relationship, but when she decided to end it he was like a hurt little child. And I could do nothing to help him through it.

It is so hard for a parent to say what impact a first love has on a child. It appears that Paul matured greatly with respect to the opposite sex, but the effect of that love affair on Paul's later approach to and choice of women stayed with him for the rest of his life. He really didn't know how to behave in a give-and-take relationship with women. I always thought the affair was a major stressor and trigger to the onset of his first manic episode in 1993 when he was living in New York City.

Still, I was shocked that Paul had bipolar disorder. When the doctors asked me if my family had any history of mental illness, I said no. But, after thinking about it, I realized that he had the family curse. He would have to live a life faced with the mood swings I had seen in my mother and uncles. And I felt guilty because I kept thinking Paul went crazy because of my genes. I couldn't get that out of my mind.

Paul's bipolar disorder diagnosis was based on a combination of my family history, his age and artistic bent, lab tests to rule out drugs, brain scans, and his response to the antipsychotic and mood-stabilizing drugs the doctors prescribed. The cruelty of this illness is that he, like other manic-depressives, liked the highs so much he refused to stay on his meds once he was stabilized. Consequently, it took more episodes, the breakup of his last long-term love affair (not the older woman he fell in love with when he was seventeen), the loss of all his friends in New York, and the inability to stay focused enough to play the piano for more than a few minutes at a time before he finally understood what havoc his mania caused in his life and in the lives of those around him. But that didn't deter him. From the beginning of his illness he was edging toward his destiny.

I couldn't help feeling guilty, and I know I shouldn't have, for his illness and its effects. But seeing what had happened to my beautiful boy, hearing his constant babbling about how his food and drinks were poisoned and that the Mafia was out to get him, seeing his vacant, glazed-over eyes, I couldn't help it. My stomach was in turmoil. I couldn't eat. I couldn't sleep. I couldn't think about anything else. Every few minutes I would break down in tears. Even with a new discovery by scientists at the University of California at Irvine that two genes on chromosome eighteen are involved in manic depression—one gene helps the brain cells receive chemical messages, and the other has to do with the body's hormonal response to stress—I still blamed myself and my family's history for our misery.

When Bob and I decided to have children we never imagined that a mental illness could appear in one of our children—our son Ben shows no signs of it—and had we known would we have done anything differently? I doubt it. We didn't connect my grandmother and uncles' mental health to anything our family had to worry about. We didn't even know what manic depression meant in those days.

The doctors didn't seem to know enough about it to treat Paul properly when he was diagnosed. Most of the drugs he took were hit or miss, experimental. The recurring theme was: "Let's try this and see if it works." He had side affects from Lithium, the usual drug of choice for his illness, so he was prescribed Depacote. And as he still had side affects and delusions and hallucinations, he was given new medications that we now know can cause teenagers and young adults to have suicidal thoughts. Who knows if those drugs caused Paul to commit suicide? I do know he abused his drugs. He took them, he stopped taking them, he took them sporadically. He never was consistent. Could that abuse of his medication have caused his suicide? We'll never know.

I do know one does not have control over manic depression or of someone who has it. One does not get it because one is bad or selfish or their mother didn't raise him or her right. One gets it when some chemical in the brain goes out of balance—most often when a person is just approaching adulthood—and as a result that person and the persons around him are never the same again.

And now the literature says that heredity is definitely the cause of bipolar disorder with researchers getting closer to the genes that cause it.

I know all of that rationally, and still I look at the fat smiling Buddha on my office shelf and think about Karma and the guilt I have always felt about my role in the breakup of Bob's marriage. (His former wife had just had a beautiful little boy badly damaged with Down's syndrome, and Bob was intent on seeing me and being with me.) He had wanted to leave her before she got pregnant, but stuck it out throughout her pregnancy. I was attracted to him as soon as we met. He was extremely articulate about almost anything, and he was so sexy. We had lunch together several times and then went out on our first date the night of March 11, 1967. We fell in love that night. We still think of it as our real anniversary. We married three years later. But at what cost? In my mind, guilt and bad Karma.

In my least rational moments I believe the bad Karma took away my son in exchange for me taking Bob away from his former wife. I tell myself over and over that he would have left her anyway. But that doesn't assuage my guilt. It doesn't absolve me of what happened. It doesn't bring Bob back to his former wife or Paul back to me. Losing Paul was our punishment; I irrationally think that when I am down in the deepest doldrums. Women have stolen husbands away in the past but didn't lose their sons as a result, but I bet they lost something else. Something else very dear to them. And that doesn't matter to me at all. I lost Paul. That's what matters. I lost Paul.

And then I bring myself back to my rational self and my work on healing, getting over it, and really living a complete life without him. Someone recently said, "There is no healing from a loss of this kind, there is only getting used to it." Parade Magazine recently reported cancer patients saying, "Patients won't go back to normal after cancer. But they can find a best new normal." Both statements are true for me. I'm getting used to living a life without Paul, living a life after my loss. I am moving on in so many ways, such as in the poem I wrote just one year after his death:

One Year

It's a year, they say,
time to stop mourning for your dead son,
get on with your life.
Okay, I will, I reply.
Look—I work, I work out, I write, I travel,
I read, I go to movies, I make love, I eat out,
I enjoy the company of friends.
And—I nurture myself with new hairdos,
makeup, massages, and manicures.

After all, Paul took his own life a year ago
He didn't take mine
At least not completely.

What they don't know is
my life now is just playacting
meant to fool others as well as myself
into believing that I can move on
and begin to live my life again.

I'm fully aware that my life is filled with diversions—going to the theater, the opera, the movies; reading one book after the other, traveling on weekends and for weeks at a time, and having dinners out with friends. Playacting meant to fool others as well as myself into believing that I can move on and begin to live my life again? Maybe. But, this playacting is doing the trick. I used to spend a lot of time wondering what would happen if I let it all hang out and finally quit work, and lived without all the crutches I've set up for myself? I hung on to the crutches for a long, long time—over ten years—and I've finally let the biggest one go. I retired from my job in aerospace in April 2010, and I'm doing very well working on my own now. I've made a life for myself as a writer. But more about that later.

Before I move on, I want to explain the title of this book, *Leaving the Hall Light On.*

At first I believed—my magical thinking—that if I left the hall light on, if we didn't move away from our house, if we didn't change our telephone number, Paul would know how to make his way back. Paul would know we were still here waiting for him. For a long time I waited for that familiar sound of his Volvo coming into the garage, the sound of the door from the garage slamming as he entered the house and went down the hall to his room, the sound of him walking around the house at night, the sound of the door opening and closing as he went in and out of the house. In fact, for a while I thought I heard those sounds. And for a long time I left most of the things in his room and closet alone for fear of removing his presence there. For a long time I refused to give away his things in case he would need them when he came back.

Once those sounds in my imagination and my magical thinking fell away, my need to keep the hall light on became another one of the things that helped me get through it. We left the hall light on for him when he was home. I just couldn't break that routine.

And while that was all going on Bob and I had a push-me, pull-you interaction about it. Bob always had a habit of turning off all the lights before he went to bed. Since he usually went to bed after me, I would wait until he got into bed. Then I'd get up and turn on the hall light again. And mind you that was a trek across the living room and down the steps of our tri-level house to the garage entry hall on the ground floor where the office that Bob and I originally shared, the guestroom, and Paul's room (that became my private office) were. Sometimes we'd go back and forth on this several times in one night. If he forgot his glass of water he'd get up and turn the light off again. If he needed a certain vitamin from the kitchen cabinet, he'd get up, go into the kitchen to get what he needed, and then go down and turn the light off again on his way back to bed. And, if I fell asleep before him, I'd wake in the middle of the night and go back down to turn the light on once more.

Once in a while I'd ask him to leave it on. If he asked why I'd give him the lame excuse that I needed a light on to guide me through the house when I left to go to the gym in the dark of the early morning. Sometimes he'd buy that. Most of the time he'd forget and turn off the light.

Gradually though, say in the last two, three years, leaving the hall light on became less and less important. That I could leave it off night after night meant I was healing. And it also meant that I was over the magical thinking stage of my grieving process.

Leaving the Hall Light On

I lose my keys or sunglasses
and find them in my hand all along.
I lose my little boy in the department store
and he pops out squealing with laughter
from under the clothes display,
I lose important papers
and find them
in the stack of other papers on my desk.

I didn't lose my son, Paul.
Paul is dead.
Death is forever.
There's not a chance of finding him.

The light I've left on in the hall for him
every night since he died
doesn't show him the way back home.
There are no more piano gigs out there for him.
The Sunday paper entertainment guide
doesn't list his name at any jazz club.
He can't join the young guys at the Apple Genius Bar
and help people solve their computer problems.
Paul would have loved that job.
He was made for that job,
but he checked out too early.
The new meds and surgery for manic depression,
the new information about mental illness
are not for him.

Why do people refer to death as loss?
Maybe just to encourage
people like me.
Maybe just to keep me looking for him.
Maybe so I can pretend he's still out there.

Maybe that's why I long to mother
the strong young men at the gym
who hardly notice me
and the bright ones at work.
They are the right age.
They have the same look.
They have the same appeal.

Every time I see a young man
with close-buzzed hair,
well-worn jeans,
a white t-shirt, and a black jacket,
sitting outside of Starbucks,
sucking on a cigarette,
every time I see a skinny guy
walking fast across the street
carrying a brown leather bag over his shoulder,
I look to make sure.

CHAPTER TWO

I hung up the telephone and looked down on the street from our hotel window. The snow was coming down in big clumps and swirls that, even from twenty-two stories above the sidewalk, I could tell was beginning to stick.

"He'll meet us at the Russian Tea Room at one," I said. "He picked that restaurant because he wants to see how much of our money he can spend."

Bob was on the bed doing the daily crossword puzzle. How he could be so focused and calm at a time like this was beyond me. I was pacing the room, worrying that Paul would not show up, looking out the window, watching as the snowfall got heavier and heavier, hearing the laughter of the maids as they rolled their carts down the hallway, and feeling so trapped and like such a failure. We were both sleep-deprived from our flight to New York from Los Angeles and our unsuccessful intervention attempt to get Paul to agree to let us take him to a hospital the night before. But Bob didn't seem to be fazed by it. He just lay there putting one letter after the other into those little white boxes while I couldn't concentrate on anything else but Paul and my nervous stomach.

As soon as we arrived in New York, Bob and I, along with my sister's husband, who flew in from Oregon to help us, and a few of Paul's friends, met at Paul's one-room fourth-floor walk-up apartment. We each tried to persuade him to go into the hospital, and then we sat on his futon bed staring at each other not knowing what else to do or say. Paul would hear none of it. He chain-smoked. He sat down at the piano and started to play a tune. After a minute or two he got up, paced around the room, talked and tried to explain the scribbles he had written with a felt-tipped blue marker all over his apartment walls, doors, and ceiling, and then he'd go back to the piano and play for a minute or two again. His words didn't make any sense, his eyes looked wild, he was unshaven and in a dirty shirt. He couldn't play a whole tune from beginning to end. He left for a while with his band partner, Tom, who thought a walk and a talk might persuade him; he talked again with our brother-in-law, but those talks failed too. By two in the morning it was clear to all of us that our hastily conceived plan to convince him to willingly go into the hospital had totally backfired in our faces. And he wanted us out. He practically pushed us out the door. He wouldn't listen to any of us. He flat out refused to go. And even though he had agreed to meet us today, I wondered if he would really show up. What was going though my mind was whether I would ever see him again. It was easy to disappear in New York City. My son was young and vulnerable and now sick. Anything could happen to him.

Looking back on our intervention fiasco, I despaired that nothing was going to get through to him. Everyone in his room that night thought he was on drugs, but we didn't know for sure. I didn't know what the affects of drugs even looked like. But if he was on drugs, I knew I had to keep trying to get him into some sort of rehab.

Just two weeks before he had been home in Manhattan Beach playing Happy Birthday on the piano at my mother's birthday celebration, and he was perfectly normal. He was calm, loving, and talked easily to everyone. For the two nights he was with us, he slept easily in his childhood bedroom, and kissed and hugged me when I said goodbye to him at the airport. Now he was someone I didn't know anymore. I couldn't talk to him. I couldn't reason with him. Clearly he wasn't happy to see me in New York trying to tell him what to do. In just two weeks he had become another person. It all seemed so hopeless.

At least he had agreed to meet us for lunch.

Bob finally set his pencil down on the bedside table and discarded the newspaper. He got out of bed and walked into the bathroom to get ready to leave for our lunch date with Paul.

Though the snow was falling harder now, the lines of yellow cabs inching and honking their way up the street convinced us to walk to the restaurant. It was so cold and dark outside that it looked like early evening rather than the middle of the day, and within minutes we realized how ill-prepared we were for this kind of weather. Neither of us had hats or boots, and our lined raincoats were inadequate to shield us from the wind. My coat kept flapping open and I had to clutch at the slick material to keep it together. We held onto each other to keep from falling on the wet and slippery sidewalks. Bob protectively had his arms around me. Besides being exhausted, I needed holding and nurturing myself. I was so frightened and desperate I was hardly equipped to help my son.

Finally we reached the Russian Tea Room's familiar revolving door. The room was as I remembered it from the many times we'd gone there after the theater when we visited Paul at school in New York. And many times Paul had gone with us. The bar area was on the right of the entrance and a cloakroom on the left, and then a long walk into the dining room. A row of oak and leather booths took up one side of the dining room. The walls and the waiters' jackets were Russian red.

After checking our coats the host escorted us to a table in the middle of the large, brightly lit room. It was full. People dressed for business were chatting, ladies lunching were gabbing and laughing, and I sat in this posh scene in a pair of faded jeans, an old velour top and a pair of flat, brown, lace-up shoes with lug soles. I wore no jewelry except for a wedding ring and almost no make-up. I felt so embarrassed. Bob looked a little more presentable. In our haste to leave Los Angeles the day before he had had the good sense to pack a decent pair of slacks and a sports jacket.

But when I was packing, I thought we were going to New York to take care of Paul, not to gad about in fancy places. I didn't think it mattered how I looked, and it didn't. But for some reason when I saw Carol Channing and Lauren Bacall chatting away in stylish suits in the booths directly to our right, I was more distressed. While my life was unraveling and scraggly, others were dressed to the nines and laughing as if they didn't have a care. I couldn't stand it.

Bob and I spent a few minutes reminiscing about the happy times we'd spent in this room, the vodka Bob liked to drink, and my fascination with "people watching." With still no sign of Paul, we decided to order lunch—our first meal since our flight across country the day before. While Bob sipped on his ice-cold vodka, he ordered a bowl of seafood chowder, an entree of seared tuna over fresh spinach with garlic-mashed potatoes on the side, and a glass of Merlot to wash it all down. I asked for a green salad with some grilled chicken on it and a bottle of Pellegrino water with lime.

The drinks and food arrived. Bob ate heartily, I picked at mine. My stomach was in knots, churning—acting as it always does when I'm under stress—and we tried to devise another plan of attack if Paul would ever show up. But, we kept going around in circles. We really had no idea what to do.

Finally, I saw Paul at the entrance checking his jacket. He spotted us and slowly made his way to our table, moving his mouth constantly. He seemed to stagger as he walked. He was as thin as a scarecrow. His face looked haunted. His eyes, glassy with deep black shadows underneath, couldn't stay focused. What had happened to my beautiful son with the chiseled features—high full cheeks, a square jaw line, and clear blue eyes? Just two months earlier when he was home for the Christmas holidays, when we celebrated his twenty-first birthday on New Year's Eve, he looked so healthy. When he was home just two weeks ago, he seemed fine except for a bit of a cold. How could the affects of little sleep and food have changed him so quickly? Even so, he had tried to make himself look presentable. His clothes were clean. He wore his usual baggy jeans, a long-sleeved green and brown striped heavy knit T-shirt I had bought for him at one of his favorite shops in Hermosa Beach, California, and his brown, thick-soled Doc Martens oxfords. And, he was clean-shaven.

He was babbling as he sat down at our table.

"I've got to be careful what I eat. They're poisoning my food and cigarettes. They're putting drugs in my drinks," he said as he sat down opposite from me. He picked up the menu, opened it, closed it, and quickly put it aside. Who was poisoning him? If he was on drugs he surely was taking them himself.

"I can't stand the sirens. I want to go south where it's warm. Help me rent a car. I want to go to Florida." I knew what he meant about the fire engine and police alarm sirens. Their sounds were everywhere—especially in this weather. But the last thing I would do was rent him a car and help him go to Florida. He was in no condition to drive.

"I've got to find a drummer for my gig tonight. That's why I'm late. I had to make some calls. Where's the phone?"

He started to get up, but changed his mind and sat down heavily in his chair. One of his forks fell under the table, and he got down on his hands and knees to retrieve it. When he sat down again, he began to tap his fingertips wildly on the table.

"I took a cab here—left a twenty dollar tip," he said, not looking us in the eye.

He couldn't keep his body still. His fingers on the table and his foot under the table kept time with his racing mind. Where was he getting the money? We were supporting him. How could he have enough money to pay for his food and rent and still tip a cabbie twenty dollars from what we were giving him while he was in school? Was he selling drugs? I didn't ask these questions out loud. My mind was racing too.

The waiter came back to take his order.

"You order for me, Mother." The waiter looked at me. "Order the same thing you're having. That's what mothers are supposed to do, order for their sons," he said with a wry smile on his face. It was as though he were trying to act normal, but having a very hard time keeping himself together. "I'll have what you're drinking too," he said. I asked the waiter to bring my son the same thing I was having.

When Paul's Pellegrino water came to the table, he wouldn't drink it because the bottle was already opened. He loudly called the waiter back to our table and asked him to bring him another and open it in his presence. The waiter was gracious and didn't question Paul's request, but, whether I imagined it or not, I saw from the expression on his face that he sensed something was wrong. I also might have imagined the people at the tables nearby staring at us. Was I being paranoid, imagining things? I don't know. All I knew for sure was something was very wrong with my son, and I had to figure out a way to take care of him—quick.

When Paul's food finally came, he hardly ate a bite. He couldn't concentrate on eating anymore than he could concentrate on playing the piano.

Finally I couldn't stand the babbling and Paul's behavior and our inaction any longer. I rummaged in my purse for a piece of paper. I tore off part of an old envelope and wrote on my knee out of Paul's sight, "Let's get a cab and take him by force to St. Vincent's"—the only hospital I could think of—and passed the note under the table to Bob. (I still have that scrap of paper.) Bob immediately got our check and asked that the desserts he had just ordered for himself and Paul be packed to go. Once Bob paid the bill, we maneuvered Paul toward the coat-check room, and, after we all got our coats on, over to the door. He resisted getting in a cab with us probably knowing we were up to something.

"Come on, we'll give you a ride back to your apartment," I lied. Bob took hold of him and somehow got him through the restaurant's revolving door and out in the street.

"I'll walk. I want to walk in the snow. It's fun. I can make snow-balls," he said. The doorman hailed a cab and I got into the front seat. The cab driver looked toward the street in front of the restaurant and saw Bob practically pushing Paul toward us.

"This is not an ambulance. You've got to get an ambulance driver to handle him," said the cab driver.

"I'm his mother," I screamed over and over. "You've got to help me! I'm his mother! You've got to help me!"

Bob managed to open the back seat of the cab and push Paul inside, and with the promise of a large tip and the boxed desserts from the famed restaurant we had so conspicuously departed, I got the cab driver to relent and take us to St. Vincent's.

Bob kept a firm hold on Paul during the ride to the hospital while Paul clutched the back of my seat so tightly I could see his white knuckles. He kept edging himself toward the door and trying desperately to talk his way out of what we were doing.

"I'm all right. Leave me alone. I can take care of myself." Bob and I gave each other a look, promising each other we had to be strong and not give in to his pleas and desperation.

"If I go south, I'll be okay. I've just got to get out of New York."
And, as the snow flew around us as the cabbie drove us over the icy
streets, I didn't blame him for wanting to leave and go south.

But Bob arms were tightly around Paul's shoulder. We were determined. We were acting like kidnappers, kidnapping our son to try to
get him fixed, trying to cure him of his demons. Taking him this way
was the only thing we could think of to do.

Paul was still resisting when we arrived at St. Vincent's emergency
entrance. Luckily, as Bob and the cabbie were trying to get Paul out of
the cab, five police officers who were standing in the driveway inter-
vened and forced him inside. Something in Paul's behavior—his resist-
ance, his holding on to the cab door for dear life—seemed to alert them
to our trouble. We didn't ask the police for help, but they knew intu-
itively that we needed it. By the time I walked through the crowded
waiting room, talked to the receptionist, and was ushered inside, he was
already handcuffed to a gurney in a private holding room, waiting for
a doctor to see him. An armed police officer was stationed outside his
open door. I peeked in and then turned away. I couldn't face him like
that. At least not yet.

Bob and I went to the waiting area, cried, and looked out of the window as this March 1993 snowstorm, that looked more like a blizzard than
a light spring sprinkle, played havoc with the streets of New York City.
And we waited for word from the doctors on call in the emergency area.

Blizzard in B

It is mid March, 1993,
and a bitter blizzard blows in.
Some predict
the century's biggest.

Flakes of snow swirl in gusts to the sidewalk.
Cold slaps our cheeks,
pushes through our clothes
as we cling to each other,
walk through the cavern
at the feet of New York's skyscrapers.
The sirens set our teeth chattering
as impatient cabbies honk,
inch their way up the streets.

Yet, we trudge forward
uncertain of what
we will discover when we arrive.
A more foreboding blizzard, perhaps,
blows through our boy's broken brain.

The next morning as I was on my way to meet the doctor assigned to our son's case, I passed by Paul's room and saw him off his gurney, still handcuffed to it, walking it around the room. I kept going. I couldn't stop. I couldn't talk to him. I was barely able to look at him that way.

The doctor and I sat in a conference room so tiny that only a desk and two chairs—one on either side of the desk—fit inside. The walls were white like the rest of the walls I had seen in the hospital—sterile, uncaring, and cold. Not an environment conducive to supporting families in distress.

She sat across from me in her doctor's white jacket with her blonde hair pulled back in a ponytail. She was both professional and sympathetic. Her soft eyes, her smile, and her warm handshake showed me she was concerned. I was a mess—stomach in a turmoil, pale, unwashed hair, no make-up, bloodshot eyes from hardly any sleep, and wearing the same plaid flannel shirt and grubby jeans I had worn for days. We talked for a few minutes more while she tried to assure me that committing Paul was the right decision. I kept hoping Bob would appear. He had gone off earlier to settle some of the hospital's financial demands. For the time being I was on my own.

"Is he a danger to himself?" she asked, getting down to business. She began writing on a form.

"Yes," I said. I tried to read what she was writing, but it was impossible to read upside down.

"Is he a danger to others?" I didn't know. I just knew what I had to say now.

"Yes," I said, and looked up at her. Was she going to save us? Could I rest my faith in her? I didn't know the answer to those questions either. I only knew that this is what I came to New York for. I was finally getting my son admitted to a psychiatric hospital. I had to resort to kidnapping to do it, but I was willing to do anything it would take.

This was my first experience with the words "danger to himself, danger to others," and at this point I didn't realize how important those words would become in Paul's treatment or, for the most part, his lack of treatment. Mentally ill adults in our society are protected from hospitalizations against their will unless there is proof they are a danger to themselves or others, and time and time again Paul escaped being hospitalized by proving he was not, simply by how he looked and responded to a doctor's or a police officer's questions.

She shoved the form in front of me. "Will you sign?"

With my hand shaking so much that I could barely hold a pen, I signed, committing my twenty-one-year-old son to the locked mental ward at St. Vincent's Hospital in New York City.

"We're going to admit him and do some tests to determine if he has schizophrenia, schizoaffective disorder, manic-depression, post-traumatic stress syndrome, or is suffering from the effects of drugs," she said. And she said she doubted his behavior was caused by drugs.

Her words knocked the air out of me. I had been so sure that his behavior of the last few days was related to drugs, that it could be cured. I had never considered he was mentally ill. But, how would I have known the difference? I had no idea what a person on drugs or suffering from mental illness looked like. Somehow I knew a drug problem could be treated but I thought being mentally ill lasted a lifetime. Whether my thoughts and preconceptions were accurate or not, I was about to learn a lot more about mental illness in the days and years to come.

"Do you have a history of mental illness in your family?" she asked. I looked out the window behind her. The snow had stopped, but the wind was still blowing "Yes," I said, "my mother told me stories from the time I was a little girl about my grandmother. She had a nervous breakdown—my mother called it—when her oldest daughter, my mother's sister, died from uterine cancer. She was hospitalized and given electric shock treatments."

But I had never seen her behave any way other than a wonderful, little old lady who wore black lace-up oxfords and her long white hair wound up in a bun and pinned to the back of her head with huge, gray, plastic hair pins. She signed the cards and letters she sent to me, "your loving grandmother." Just weeks before she died in her sleep of a heart attack, she was jumping up and down in my bedroom because she was so happy to be visiting us.

"Also two of her sons, my uncles, had to be hospitalized a time or two," I told the doctor. In good times one uncle spoke five languages, remembered stories of his childhood in Lithuania and Russia, and told the corniest jokes to anyone who would listen, but when he got depressed he didn't know where he lived or who he was. My other uncle had a booming voice and a brash demeanor on his good days. When he would come to visit us in Chicago from his home in the east, he would take my brother and me out of our beds even if we were down for the night and throw us up onto his shoulders. He'd bounce us around for a while and then tell us to go back to sleep. I was scared to tears but always looked forward to his visits. Later on, his highs gave way to deep depressions. He'd sit staring at the walls, hardly speaking, and worry for no reason that he had lost all his money.

"I think my mother has some form of mental illness," I said. "Some days she can be higher than a kite, talking nonstop, reveling in everyone's attention. And on others she just sits, staring off in space, unable to open her mouth. I never know which mother I will encounter when

I call her—the friendly mother or the one ready to pick a fight." The doctor wrote furiously on her pad.

"Was she ever hospitalized?" she asked.

"No," I said, even though I've thought on more than one occasion that she definitely belonged in a mental ward. Her mood swings drove me nuts. She was like a child in a lot of ways, given to temper tantrums if she was criticized or didn't get her way. Even my father complained about the way she behaved.

"What about you?" she asked. I looked down in my lap and folded and unfolded my hands. They were sweating even though I was cold.

"Oh, I'm okay," I said. "I've never had bouts of mania or very deep depressions, but I have had my share of worries and phobias—the freeway, flying, cancer, high places, fast cars." On the outside I always seemed calm and with hardly a care; my head and stomach knew otherwise.

But I really didn't know what I was talking about. I asked her what the symptoms were for the mental illnesses they were testing my son for. She said she suspected he was bipolar. He was exactly the right age—early twenties for its onset. The manic manifestations—unusual euphoria, fast talking that made little sense, lots of energy, and the need for little sleep—were all signs I had seen in just the last few days. He could also show extreme irritability or intrusive behavior. But she also warned me that the majority of people with bipolar disorder are in the depressive state most of the time, losing interest in things and activities they once enjoyed. And because I shared with her his recent paranoia, she said a bipolar I diagnosis was most probable. People with bipolar I experience psychotic symptoms such as hallucinations or paranoia; whereas people with bipolar II have less severe manic symptoms and can still function normally throughout the day.

She also said he would be monitored for schizoaffective disorder, with symptoms such as changes in appetite and energy, beliefs someone on television was speaking directly to him, little concern with hygiene and grooming, trouble concentrating, either a very good or very bad mood, and disorganized speech, false beliefs, hallucinations, and paranoia. Though schizoaffective disorder was ruled out during this first hospital stay, several years later his last psychiatrist gave him that diagnosis. To me bipolar I and schizoaffective disorder looked very much alike.

She did not tell me then what I later learned—that bipolar depression could lead to thoughts of death and suicide. However, she also gave me some hope. Though bipolar disorder is a lifelong condition with no cure, with proper treatment the symptoms can be managed. She said I had done exactly the right thing in bringing him into the hospital.

She finished writing and tried to assure me he would be in good hands. "We'll initially give him antipsychotic medications so he can calm down and get some rest and later start him on a regime of lithium," she said. "He'll be with young people, and there's even a piano on the ward."

She got up and took my hand. I felt a slight squeeze, and I thanked her and left the cramped conference room and walked down the hall to Paul's brightly lit temporary room in the emergency ward. The doctor seemed to know her stuff, but I wasn't really comforted. I had misgivings about what I had just done and was worried that Paul would resent me for it. And I did it without Bob's support. He was still in another part of the hospital working out financial details.

The officer at Paul's door gave me the high sign that it was okay to go in. I hesitated, worrying that he wouldn't want to see me. He was still handcuffed to a gurney but was now back on it, trying to open a carton of milk. He looked so pale and pathetic in his hospital gown. And though he was still babbling, he was much more mellow than when I had seen him just an hour before.

This didn't look like my son who just weeks before had had so much going for him—one more semester before getting his BFA in jazz music at the New School, lots of piano-playing gigs, and a lovely girlfriend. His words said he didn't want to recognize me as his mother either.

"I don't want to talk to you," he said in a clipped flat tone I had never heard before. "You're not my mother. My mother would get me out of here." I just stood there for a few minutes, taking it all in. Neither of us said anymore. And then I left him like that. With my eyes flooding over, I walked to the lobby to wait for Bob and looked out to the parking lot. It was snowing again, harder than ever. Great gusts were falling from the sky, covering the ground with about two inches.

I needed Bob to hold me and warm me from the chill while we decided what to do next.

November 1994, playing at his cousins Stephanie and Mike's wedding
(Paul Blieden reimaged photo)

CHAPTER THREE

By the time Paul entered his fourth year of college in September 1992, he was well on his way to being a viable jazz musician. However, he talked as though he was disenchanted with the New York City jazz scene. Although he was successfully making it professionally as a performer (a goal he had had for at least the last six years) he was concerned about the cut-throat competition and the difficulties of being in the business. Even so, he formed a group with Tom, a bass player from his class and a couple other musicians, and they played in small neighborhood venues in lower Manhattan. Paul kept a list of fill-in players if someone from the group couldn't play—just like the list he neatly printed in a little notebook of all the tunes he knew how to play. Even though Paul was an artist, he was meticulous and well-organized about his things—he kept everything just like new—and his schedule. He maintained a calendar, tracked his earnings and spending—that this recordkeeping abruptly stopped on February 23, 1993, was the first clue that something was wrong. And he never blinked when it came to asking for work—just like he was always able to ask for the toys, books, electronic equipment, music recordings he wanted as he was growing up. He could talk to anyone intelligently, ingratiate himself to them, charm them—he was always adept at talking to people no matter their age, even as a child. So he was the logical choice as his jazz group's manager. Plus, because he had worked a lot of jobs during high school and college, he was the most experienced.

A few days before his first manic break (I'll call it episode) in February 1993, he played three successive gigs with some older musicians in Brooklyn, rather than with his own group, and had not slept for at least two nights in a row. He also drank heavily during these performances. However, he was elated with his success, playing in a crowded nightclub with other performers he didn't know and being widely and strongly accepted. He was so stoked he told Bob and me that he intended to petition the New School to graduate in June even though he would be five units short so he could move on with his career.

We think that burgeoning jazzman lifestyle of little sleep, little food, and lots of booze, and the heroin-overdose death of one of his classmates sent Paul over the edge. Even though I had encouraged him to follow his dream, I always worried about the musician's lifestyle. He had always lived on the other side of the clock—up in the night, composing his music of the night as the phantom of the opera did—and asleep in the day. But right before his first episode he hadn't slept for days. Perhaps his own concern about living that kind of life and the worry about having a steady income once he was out of school and on his own also aided in his downfall.

He became so sick that even he didn't know what was wrong. He wrote all over the walls, ceiling, and doors of his apartment that people were poisoning his food and drinks, his clothes were strewn all over the place, his dishes were stacked up—all behaviors so foreign to the orderly and neat guy he normally was. When I first saw this scene in early March 1993—right after finding out about his crazed behavior—and the wild look in his eyes, I knew something was terribly wrong with my son. I was scared that I didn't know how to fix him, that no one would know how to fix him. I didn't yet realize that as a result of this first manic episode, his life as a viable musician and promising and talented young man had stopped forever.

In between his manic episodes—he had three significant ones starting in March 1993 and ending with his death in September 1999—he had bouts of sanity when he could compose something or play a gig, but that didn't last. For the most part, he played in fits and starts. He'd get a gig and show up sometimes and sometimes not. He taught a couple of young students for a while and dropped them. His last public performance was at a reunion of his high-school jazz ensemble group in December 1998, almost a year before he died, at a local jazz venue in Los Angeles. At that time he put together his last CD, a Christmas music collection, for his on-and-off girlfriend, Janet, the woman he loved until the end of his life. It was inspired by a gig he had playing background music at a Manhattan Beach Christmas party. The last music he composed was also for Janet—a half-hour melody to accompany her yoga practice. It is haunting, melodic, and simply beautiful—as if the music is coming from a dream, though I know better. It came from the music he constantly heard in his head.

Mania

Intoxicated, euphoric,
exhilarated, with visions
of power without bounds,
Paul is like Superman.
He climbs, he circles, he races,
he floats above reality

until paranoia removes all
semblance of his sanity.
Then he sees demons lurking in alleyways and
imaginary Mafioso poisoning his drinks and cigarettes
as well as the world's water supply.
He is left to wander, pace,
click door latches as he goes in and out
of the house and up and down the stairs.
While he babbles unintelligibly, imperceptibly,
he keeps time to his internal orchestrations.

The voices he hears echo like violins
ever louder, faster, discordant
until a cacophony of drumbeats
and a tintinnabulation of scraping symbols
pound his brain.
He looks for an exit
where none exists.
There is no escape, no way out
except death
and eternal silence.

LEAVING THE HALL LIGHT ON ~ 51

EPISODE ONE

Both Bob and I sensed a difference when we talked to Paul on a Sunday evening in late February 1993. In our separate conversations we asked him if he was "on" something. Even though he told us a new woman, Maria, was in his life and that she was with him then, it didn't explain the eerie and far-away sound of his voice—as if he were at the end of a long, dark tunnel.

"No," he said, "I'm not on anything. I'm just high on music and love."

Then four days later, we got an early-morning call—before eight o'-clock Pacific Time—from Janet—who was at that time Paul's former girlfriend in New York (but one he would go back to over and over). She spoke to Bob—I was already at work—to warn us that she and Paul had spent some time together again and that something was wrong with him. "He was taken to two mental hospitals this week," she said, "but he's managed to quickly get himself released." She said she had seen him earlier that day but described him as incoherent, angry, and trying to find a way out of town—he wanted to get someone to help him rent a car to go to Florida. She gave Bob the name of the doctor from New York's Beth Israel Hospital who had seen Paul the day before.

When Bob arrived at work, he found me and called me into his office. For the first time in our professional careers we were working on the same proposal to obtain a work contract from the Republic of China on Taiwan to build them their first satellite. That our desks were in close proximity made it easy for us to communicate. Never did I think we would need this proximity because of a family crisis. We immediately called the doctor at Beth Israel. "I suspect Paul is on drugs, possibly co-caine—at least that's what Paul told me," he said. He had had a two-hour conversation with Paul, and even though the doctor thought his main problem was substance abuse, Paul was very evasive about his situation. "He asked me for some names of treatment centers and I gave him several referrals, but I eventually had to release him at his request," the doctor said. The doctor had no reason to hold him. Paul did give him Janet's name as someone he trusted and who cared about him, and the doctor advised Paul to go to her. Janet said he did.

"Paul came to my apartment around seven that night after his release from Beth Israel. He was very upset, very paranoid," she said. She thought he was grieving over his friend and classmate Bill's death from a heroin overdose and that Paul was possibly exhibiting drug-withdrawal symptoms.

"He told me that many sinister things were going on in New York City—that jazz players in the clubs he worked in were putting heroin in his drinks. He was convinced heroin was getting into his body—possibly because of the shock of Bill's death from an overdose of heroin," Janet said.

Over the next four hours Janet calmed him down and fed him some pasta. He told her that an Italian woman, Maria, was living at his apartment and that Maria was insecure and didn't trust anyone, and that she hung out with some pretty dark, strange people. Around eleven that night he went to sleep on Janet's bed.

"When he woke at about four-thirty in the morning," she said, "he was even more crazed than when he had arrived the night before. He was cursing, saying everyone in New York is doing heroin, that everyone around him is crazy. He verbally attacked me and savagely criticized my photography, when just a few days before he had complimented it. He developed an evil-sounding laugh and then stared at me in a frightening way," she continued.

She said he began to shake and his breathing was labored and abnormal. "I became so frightened I called 911. The police came with an ambulance and took him to St. Vincent's Hospital emergency room."

Once again, Paul said he didn't want to be held and was let go before being examined by a doctor. He took a cab and left in a fit of anger.

Following this, Janet contacted Paul at his apartment, and he began talking about the Chinese and their role in the heroin trade. Paul's mind connected Bob's recent business trips to Taiwan with his paranoia of being poisoned by sinister forces in New York. He was very angry with Janet for calling the cops on him and feeding him "poisoned pasta," and he hung up on her. That's what prompted Janet to finally call us. And I was glad that she did. I liked Janet very much and was thankful that she was back in Paul's life—even if they were just beginning to renew their friendship. She later became our lifeline to Paul and eventually his lover again. I was happy about that too—hoping that one day she might be my daughter-in-law.

Then we called the director of The New School jazz program where Paul was studying. The director said that when they had told Paul his buddy Bill had died that weekend from a heroin overdose, Paul sat down in a chair in the office and started talking nonsense non-stop— as if he was trying to understand what he had just been told. The director said Paul then talked about his own drug use—saying over and over that the mafia was slipping drugs in his drinks and cigarettes. That would be the mantra that he repeated to his friends and us. We continued to believe the drug part until we knew what really was wrong with him. Paul later confirmed to us he had learned of Bill's death around noon from one of his professors, describing the professor's words as: "Oh, by the way, I heard Kitty (Bill's nickname) is dead. I've got to go to lunch." Paul was furious at his insensitivity. When the director noticed how the news of his friend's death affected Paul, he called the Student Life office and got the assistant dean to come over. She and another teacher walked Paul to Beth Israel Hospital and left when Paul went in with a doctor. The director also said Paul made them promise not to

call us. Since Paul was over twenty-one, the director was not obligated to do so.

We assumed, like the doctor at Beth Israel and Janet, that Paul was on drugs, and we feared that he would leave town. We also feared that he would overdose like his friend, Bill. So within thirty minutes we decided Bob would go immediately to New York and arrange to bring Paul home. I would stay behind to talk to doctors and hospitals about admitting him to a rehab facility. Little did we know how hard it would be to implement this direct course of action or to find out what was wrong with our son.

By the time we devised this plan, Paul had already called us three or four times within a two-to-three-hour period—our first taste of the constant and obsessive phone calls that became a part of his new personality. Bob persuaded him to stay in New York until he got there and to meet him at the airport. With that, Bob left. I broke the news to our son, Ben and told him we wouldn't be visiting him at Berkeley that weekend as planned. Instead, he came home to be with me.

Throughout that first weekend we never veered away from our initial thought that this was some kind of episode related to drugs. Through a recommendation from our assistance program at work, I called the Del Amo Hospital in Torrance, California, to arrange to have Paul admitted as soon as he arrived in Los Angeles.

"You ought to have him dried out in New York for a few days before you try to bring him home," the hospital official said, giving me the first indication that getting him to consent to our course of action might be harder than just willing it to be so. And he hadn't even met Paul yet.

"Oh no," I said. "My husband is on his way there and will bring him right back with him. So I need a place for him tonight." I was so confident, so sure of myself and of our plan.

"Well," he continued. "I've seen this kind of behavior over and over, and people on drugs or whatever is going on with him are not so easy to control. Your husband may have a difficult time getting him on a plane. Does he have some kind of sedation he can give him?"

At this point I had no clue about how any of this worked. And, as I gradually learned, I became less arrogant and confident about what we could do on Paul's behalf. Unfortunately, I became an expert in things I didn't want to know anything about very soon.

But in that first conversation I refused to admit we'd have any trouble. I had tunnel vision. But then again what did I know? How could I know?

"No," I said. "I'm sure we'll be able to get him here today." I thought I was so smart and efficient about how I was handling things on this end, and everything seemed to be going as planned in New York City— at least for the first few hours.

Paul was at the airport when Bob arrived, but was acting strange, looking stoned, talking about almost nothing else but that heroin was being put into his drinks. Maria, his new girlfriend, came with him but they had had some kind of fight.

"Pay no attention to that person. I don't know her," he said, shivering. He said he was very cold. Bob and Maria were not. Bob gave Paul his jacket to wear. After Bob got a rental car he and Paul dropped Maria off at Paul's apartment and eventually had something to eat at around one in the morning in Greenwich Village. They then checked into a Hilton hotel about three. Paul at first agreed to stay there with Bob, but soon after they got to the room, he announced he was leaving. Because he was quite agitated and was prepared to fight to get away, Bob just let him go. He was gone about two hours. When he came back, he and Bob talked, or rather Paul talked for almost two hours on the same paranoid subjects he had been repeating over and over for the last several days, until Bob got him to lie down and go to sleep.

When he woke, Paul agreed to go to California with Bob, and Bob arranged for them to leave on a late-afternoon flight. They then drove to his apartment. Maria was still there, and he asked her to get him drugs and to come to California with them. Instead, Bob got Maria to give him Paul's keys and to pack up her stuff. They dropped Maria off at a friend's apartment on the way to the airport.

Bob called me with the news that they would arrive in Los Angeles that evening. I was elated and so proud of what we had accomplished that I drove over to the Music Center to exchange some opera tickets, stopped at a favorite deli on Fairfax Avenue to have some chicken and rice soup, and bought lots of bagels, sweet rolls, and lox in preparation for both of my boys' arrival. On the way home, I picked up Ben at the airport.

When Ben and I got home later that afternoon, and I listened to the latest news from Bob on our answering machine, my heart sank. Bob had called from the Newark airport saying Paul wouldn't get on the plane. He was too afraid he would "wig out," and he left Bob standing in the check-in line. He ran away from Bob, went back to the Hertz lot, attempted to steal a car, and was arrested by the Port Authority police. When Bob saw him next he was in the back of a squad car with his hands cuffed behind him. Eventually, Hertz agreed not to prosecute if Paul would go home to Los Angeles with his father and get treatment. Even so, Paul refused to go to California with Bob. They fought and Bob let him go again. Bob returned home by himself the next morning so that together we could try to figure out how best to help our son.

Chicken Soup

I sit in the deli on Fairfax this afternoon
and remember that day years ago
when I went there
for the same bowl of chicken and rice soup.
Soon Bob would bring Paul
home from New York, I thought.
We would take him to the hospital,
and all would be well.
I even bought lox and bagels and chocolate-chip
sweet rolls to celebrate their homecoming.
Only later did I find out
that Paul ran away at the airport
and wouldn't be coming home that day
after all.

After Bob returned we spent the next two days calling everyone we could think of in New York who might know what had happened to Paul between the time he played Happy Birthday to his grandmother on his piano in Manhattan Beach and now, two weeks later and in the midst of something we didn't understand. We contacted his teachers, his friends, and the doctors who had seen him the previous week and who had tried to persuade him to be hospitalized. Then we decided to both go back to New York and try to get him admitted into a hospital there. We left first thing on Monday morning—Day Five, March 8, 1993. As mentioned earlier, my sister's husband, our brother-in-law Tom, also flew in from Oregon and met us at the Newark, New Jersey, airport. Tom and Paul always had a special relationship because of their love of jazz music. He cared very much for Paul and was willing to help us any way he could.

After we took Paul by force from the Russian Tea Room and committed him to St. Vincent's psych ward, the doctors told us his condition was more than just drug-induced. They said, at first, that it could be a brief reactive psychosis as a result of stress from school, his late-night music gigs, and his friend's death. However, after a few days we got a more definitive diagnosis—bipolar disorder (also called manic depression) with test results showing *no traces* of drugs in his system.

I couldn't stand it. I thought a drug problem could be treated. I didn't understand mental illness. I didn't like what I was hearing. I was frightened. I didn't think mental illness was something that could be cured. Of course, I really didn't know if a drug addiction could be cured either. I didn't know anything about either. All I cared about was getting Paul fixed. I wanted my beautiful boy back—the one I knew and loved.

This Paul, the one I was interacting with now, was a new person to me, and I didn't know how to behave toward him. I didn't know how he would react from one minute to the next. I feared for my own sanity.

I couldn't stop crying. I was a mess. If I had known at this point that this was the beginning of seven years of hell and uncertainty, followed by all the years of grief, I don't think I would have been able to cope with it.

Also, seeing him in that hospital ward, shuffling up and down the corridors wearing shoes without shoelaces and pants without a belt—those things, taken away because he might harm himself with them, broke my heart. He looked like a zombie, wearing an old, frayed bathrobe over his clothes to keep warm. He was being fed the antipsychotic drug, Haldol, which made him raise and lower his arms unconsciously. He had no control over them. All he seemed to care about was the next cigarette break. He wore a cigarette behind his ear as he waited and paced until he could have his hourly smoke.

After a few days on a mix of antipsychotic and anti-mania medications, Haldol and Lithium, he began to look and feel better. Janet came to visit and he greeted her warmly. He began to think of her as his savior, no longer angry at her for calling the police and telling us about his behavior. And to our great relief, Maria just disappeared from his life.

In his normal charming way, he persuaded us to help him get discharged. We consulted his internist who was regularly talking to Paul by telephone, and he agreed. He would monitor Paul's progress and dispense his necessary medications. We also, at Paul's prodding and the internist's advice, went back to California. As our flight was leaving JFK, I cried hysterically. How could I leave my son so alone like that? Though he appeared better at first, I knew we weren't out of the woods yet. And I was right. Within hours of his discharge he behaved erratically again. He refused to take his medications, he cleaned out his bank account—another symptom of manic depression is excessive spending—and he took an immediate dislike to the psychiatrist his internist sent him to when the internist quickly realized he couldn't handle Paul either. This new psychiatrist called us with much concern about Paul's condition. He said he should still be in the hospital on heavy tranquilizers, that his psychosis was drug induced (he was wrong about that), and that the lithium was useless. He assured us that he could get Paul back into the hospital without us being there.

About a week later, after talking to Paul several times a day—he called at all hours babbling, not knowing or caring whether we were listening or not—and learning that he had verbally abused his friends such that they'd have nothing more to do with him—we talked to his psychiatrist and literally begged him to get Paul hospitalized again. "I won't do it on hearsay—yours or Janet's (who was also calling him)," he told us. But he did agree to call Paul and get him to come to his office. He was successful and arranged an appointment for the next day. Janet spent the night with him before his appointment and managed to keep him calm—so calm that this was the first night in almost a week that we weren't disturbed by a call or two from Paul.

As planned, Paul kept his appointment with the psychiatrist but arrived late and threatened to harm him physically. Still, he got Paul to fill prescriptions for two more heavy-duty antipsychotic drugs, Trilofon and Cogentin. Later that day, Paul called Bob and me at work—literally screaming on the phone—threatening and being verbally abusive to us as well. We got the psychiatrist on the other line, and he asked us to find out where Paul was calling from and to keep him talking, which in his condition wasn't hard to do. We determined he was at home, and the psychiatrist sent the police to pick him up and take him to Bellevue. I was completely distressed at the abusive and aggressive way Paul was behaving. This was so unlike him. More and more I realized I didn't know my first-born son anymore. Manic-depression and the prescribed antipsychotic and anti-mania drugs had turned him into a different person. My Paul was a gentle, sensitive, and quiet-spoken person who had never threatened anyone.

The psychiatrist felt that the psychiatric ward at Bellevue Hospital was the best place for Paul. It had a young adults program in a locked ward run by a psychiatrist who had trained with him, Dr. Phil Hala-mandaris. We spoke with the doctor almost daily and he took excellent care of Paul. Janet was very impressed also. She visited Paul frequently. At the doctor's advice, we stayed home in Manhattan Beach.

Paul stayed at Bellevue for three weeks and was prescribed a regular regime of Lithium (Bellevue determined he indeed had bipolar disorder) and antipsychotic medications upon his release. In April 1993, he was so much better that he was able to go back to school and salvage ten units of the semester. However, even though he could go to classes— probably because of his determination to show he had beaten his demons and because of Janet's continued support—the lithium caused terrible side effects: nausea, trembling, and the inability to concentrate on his music. But he stopped his aggressive behavior. He was back to being gentle Paul again.

When the semester was over in June 1993, he returned home to Manhattan Beach, very depressed and complaining of hearing voices in his head. His doctor here prescribed Depakote for his mania and Prozac for his depression—her answer to the side-effect inducing drugs he had been on in New York. And she was right. The side effects subsided, but the new drug regime caused him to sleep away most of the summer.

June 18, 1993

Paul is morose, depressed, sick,
living like a hermit,
holed up in his room,
awake when I sleep,
he sleeps when I am awake.
I hear him prowling in the night,
in and out the door,
quietly moving through the house.
I can't imagine his pain,
what it must be like to be him.

We didn't bother him about his sleeping habits that summer. We were concerned but as long as he was eating we let him live by his own schedule. We just wanted him to get well, and to that end we soothed him the best we could. He liked to come into our room and lie down on our bed as we massaged his back. That seemed to calm him. I also gave him an aromatherapy diffuser filled with oil called Inner Peace. I showed him where to apply it, and I know he used it regularly, carrying it around with him to the end of his life.

One day in August he announced he felt better. He started eating normally, he talked to us without acting delusional, he said the voices had calmed down, and he began to play the piano again. He also started going to an all-night coffee shop in West Los Angeles where a lot of twelve-steppers hung out, and he got a gig playing piano there several nights a week. Janet also came to visit him. I felt encouraged. He seemed to be a normal person again. His Manhattan Beach doctor seemed to have finally found the right prescriptions to keep his disease at bay. My only reservation—and this was a big one—was that as soon as he began to feel better, he told us he would only promise to stay on his medications until he got his college degree. He hated how he felt on the drugs. He didn't like feeling calm and even-tempered. He liked the manic highs that he thought stimulated his creative juices, and he was determined to get those highs back.

In late summer 1993, he returned to the New School in New York City and finished his last semester of college. He graduated with a Bachelor of Arts degree in jazz music in January 1994 but refused to participate in any ceremony. He received his degree certificate in the mail. Then Paul kept his promise to stop taking Depakote and Prozac. He told us that he had talked it over with his doctor in New York who advised him to be on the lookout for signs of the return of mania. He said he also had a supply of Depakote to take in an emergency. Dummy that

I was, I believed him. We found out much later that his doctor had agreed to no such thing. In fact, his doctor had warned him that if he went off his medications he would eventually be back in the hospital.

EPISODE TWO

During the next twenty months Paul appeared to be keeping his manic behavior in check. Although his relationship with Janet was on-again-off-again, he held a part-time day job doing market research for a Chicago-based company that sold banquet space. He went to fifteen mid-town Manhattan hotel lobbies five days a week to collect information from their video monitors about what organizations were holding meetings in the hotels that day. He recorded his findings on an audiocassette, typed the results of his research into his computer each Sunday evening, and e-mailed the results to his employer.

By November 1995 he began to enjoy a rise in his success at hustling music gigs in New York City. We helped him buy an electronic keyboard and amplifier. And, in his characteristic business-like way, he made lists of places in the East Village and in Greenwich Village where he could play, either on an existing house piano or on his portable keyboard. He acted as he had before his first episode, making the contacts and landing several jobs, some with sell-out crowds. He was determined, and he felt proud of his accomplishments.

As winter came on, Paul was working several jobs simultaneously—his day job collecting hotel banquet data, playing weekly gigs at nightclubs in lower Manhattan, and his weekly daytime gig accompanying a dance class at Columbia University.

When he said he felt fatigued because he had to work in the cold outdoors so much—something that never bothered him in his healthy days—Bob and I advised him to try to sleep and eat more. Even though we kept hoping that the bipolar diagnosis was wrong, that Paul had finally and completely recovered, we still worried that the great increase in stress associated with his demanding work schedule, the cold weather, and having been off his medications for the last twenty months would bring back his manic behavior. Paul, also worried about having another manic episode, went back on his medications a couple of times for short periods because he felt some symptoms returning. During this period the greatest threat to his stability was the instability of his relationship with Janet. It was falling apart again.

By early December 1995, I felt as though my life had turned another corner, and I was back down the road to hell again. Paul told us about his bouts with "shallow" mania, but that he was trying to control them with good food, more sleep, medication, and sporadic appointments with his doctor. I was hopeful that this would be successful until we got another phone call from Janet to report that he was delusional and paranoid again.

By mid-December our lives turned upside down. Paul got so bad in New York that we brought him home—at his request. When he arrived, I was horrified when I saw him—he was gaunt with staring eyes that seemed to stare at nothing—a "flat affect" the doctors called it. I fed him immediately, and he ate as if he were starving.

His escapades, or flights of fancy as he called them, while he was with us were bizarre. Most notable was when he stole our Mercedes and drove to Berkeley planning to stay at his brother's apartment while he was away on his winter holiday break. He didn't have the keys to the apartment. And when he realized that and decided to return home, he couldn't remember where he parked the car. He checked into a hotel for the night and called us to tell us his dilemma.

"Just stay put," Bob said. "I'll be there first thing in the morning [Christmas day] to help you."

By the time Bob got there, he was gone. And no one, not even Janet, heard from him for the next twenty-four hours. Yet, Bob, with the help of the Berkeley police, found the car almost immediately.

Paul finally emerged the next morning in an Oakland jail. He had been arrested for climbing a fence at the Oakland airport and running around on an unused runway. He said he was trying to find a bus that would take him to New York and to Janet. Luckily the district attorney and the judge took pity on him. He was released into our custody after two nights in jail and with his promise to continue with his manic and psychotic medications and psycho-pharmacologic help. I felt that seeing a psycho-pharmacologist—a psychiatrist who only dispensed drugs—was not the optimal solution because Paul needed talk therapy as well. But the judge's admonition was better than nothing. In the end, it didn't matter what I felt. Paul didn't keep his commitment to the judge anyway.

The following week he stole our Volvo. He left at two in the afternoon on New Year's Eve day (his birthday) and was finally picked up by the police at nine the next morning on New Year's Day for speeding just outside of Boise, Idaho—with no more than fifty cents in his pocket and a lightweight sweatshirt to protect him from the twenty-degree temperature outside.

The arresting officer had him checked out at the local hospital, and again Paul talked his way out of being committed. Again he was declared not to be a danger to himself or to others even though he drove to Boise at speeds averaging over seventy miles an hour the entire way. The officer dropped him off at a local truck stop where Paul called us by pay phone. He explained he was trying to get to New York but somehow lost his way.

This time we arranged for him to come home by plane, but the following weekend while Bob was in Boise retrieving the car, Paul surreptitiously packed his clothes and the rest of his things and booked himself on a cheap flight with money from a back paycheck. He told me he was going the night before and I agreed to take him to the airport for his flight back to New York. He arrived there at the outset of one of the biggest blizzards in New York's history.

Besides the fast driving—another manic behavior—up and down the West Coast, he walked enormous distances around Los Angeles, sometimes coming home with his feet blistered and bloody. His erratic, selfish, obsessive behavior taught me more about a Paul that I never knew existed—that he was a liar and a thief. I could not trust anything coming out of his mouth to be true. This was a Paul I didn't like at all.

I didn't know if his lying was a by-product of his illness or just his current way of life. "I lie to get what I want," he said. He also said he lied so he didn't have to face the real issues. For instance, he refused to tell his doctors the truth about his delusions and the voices in his head because of his fear of being forced into a mental hospital. This lie caused him and us great discomfort. Had he told the truth early on to his first doctor, I think the outcome of his stay in Manhattan Beach would have been very different. He would have been hospitalized with his medications administered by someone else instead of him being allowed to take his medications when he pleased. He would have been declared a danger to himself and to others had he told the truth about how he really felt— and especially the fact that he was hearing voices in his head. Because he was an adult the doctors and the police, whom we had called on several occasions, would not take our word, which was exactly what he wanted.

Within weeks Paul was so sick we brought him back to California again. He needed to be alone, he said, where it would be quiet, where he could hear himself think. He tried to convince us to let him go camping on his own or take a powerboat out into the middle of the ocean or travel down to Mexico. He wanted to get away from civilization. There was no way we could support this, so he left on his own—with a hug. As I pleaded with him not to go he assured me he'd probably be gone for one night—that's all the money he had, and he was true to his word. He called the next day after sitting up all night in a Denny's restaurant in Ensenada, and said he'd be back by bus from San Diego at four in the afternoon. When I picked him up at the bus station he was very depressed and disillusioned.

One morning in mid-March 1996, he said, "I'll be back in a couple of hours," as he again kissed and hugged me, and that was the last anyone heard from him for two and a half days when he finally left a message for Janet. Once I got over my initial frenzy and fears of another disappearance, I remembered that he had talked about taking a trip on a Greyhound bus. I checked the bus schedule and found one that left Los Angeles each evening at six and arrived three days later in New York City. Sure enough, three days after he left me with that kiss and hug in our kitchen in Manhattan Beach, he called Janet from a room at the YMCA in Harlem. All he had with him was a change of shoes and socks and a light jacket. I don't think he even packed a toothbrush.

After his initial symptoms and diagnosis in March 1993 until December 1995, Paul was seen by a total of four psychiatrists. From the time he arrived home in Manhattan Beach in mid December 1995 until he left in mid March 1996, he saw another psychiatrist who prescribed a regimen of three drugs: Depakote for the mania, Risperidol for the psychosis and Klonopin for relaxation and sleep. But, he took the Depakote only as much as he thought he needed it, not the amount the doctors prescribed. He took the Risperidol and Klonopin sporadically. We tried to make it easier for him to take his pills. We laid them out for him on the kitchen counter according to the times of day he needed to take them, we bought him his favorite ice cream so he could sprinkle one of the medications over it, and we were home almost constantly watching over him. But we couldn't shove those pills down his throat—something I thought of doing many times.

Bob and I tried to placate ourselves by thinking that we had done everything we could. We were in a hopeless situation. We couldn't control Paul. We couldn't help him. We felt like our hands were tied behind our backs—and by him. Paul was the driver here—it was all up to him. We were out of touch and out of control at his choosing. All we could do was hope for the best, that somehow he would integrate what everyone had been telling him for so long—that he had to get help and that he was the only one who could do it. His survival and recovery were up to him.

His being back in New York was not the answer. He was still in the same manic episode that had brought him home in December, and he had no doctor, no job (he quit the data-gathering job before he came to Manhattan Beach), and only a few weeks left on his rent so he would soon need to move out of his apartment. He had money for food—but that was it.

He had been rejected by his New York friends—Tom, his music partner; Ray, an older friend who took him under his wing for a while, and finally, Janet. Tom couldn't rely on him to show up for their gigs. Ray thought he'd burn down their apartment because he kept leaving the stove burners lit, and Janet just couldn't stand his erratic behavior toward her. On some days he was happy to be with her, on others he was morose. She couldn't count on the stability of his mind. He was paranoid again and truly believed the bad guys—whomever they were—were out to get her as well as him. She was just more comfortable being his girlfriend from afar, communicating either on the phone or through his letters. I've seen many of them and the letters, besides being beautifully written, are like prose poems and very loving and soulful. From his writing I know he truly loved her, as if she were a dream fantasy that had no chance of coming true.

We also had better communication when we were away from each other. For some reason he could tell the truth about how he was feeling over the phone. When he was home with us, instead of communicating—except on rare occasions—he hid in his room.

So when he went back to New York City in March 1996, I greatly feared for his life. In the past I had said Paul was too selfish to commit suicide, but I was beginning to doubt that conviction too. I couldn't reach him by phone most of the time when I called—it was a time before either of us had cell phones—and I only had brief and sporadic reports from Ray and Janet. I had no idea what his frame of mind really was.

The vicious cycle was continuing. Janet loaned him sixty dollars and again said she wouldn't see him unless he went to the hospital. Ray actually took him to St. Vincent's and even got him in the door and talking to a doctor. But the doctor gave him an option—go into a hospital in New York or California. Given the option, Paul would certainly not stay at St. Vincent's even though it was the only way Janet would deal with him. He chose to come back to California.

We threatened him that, if he left again, he would be on his own. How many cross-country trips could we keep paying for? How many flights of fancy could we endure? And it wasn't even the money. We were willing and happy to spend the money if it helped him, but at this point we couldn't rely on anything we did to be successful. So the real trick was making those threatening words stick.

"You must follow the doctor's orders or you can't stay with us either," I said. That was the first time I ever threatened like that, but even though I said those words, I knew I was as weak as hell where he was concerned. I knew I couldn't kick him out on the street. I knew that he was really sick, and over and over I realized I couldn't make him better. All the mothering, loving, caring, and nurturing in the world could not cure him. He needed way more than I could ever give him. I tried to be strong, I tried to protect myself, I tried to be whole for Bob and Ben. Even as I said those words to Paul, I knew I would never abandon him.

So, I thought positively. He was coming back—his choice again; and I still thought he had more of a chance to get well with our support here, than alone, abandoned by his friends, in New York.

He kept his word and returned home to us in April 1996 and went into the hospital right away—Del Amo, the one I had hoped he'd go into at the onset of his first episode over three years before—and he seemed to get along fine there. He stayed for a week, and by the time he came out he was much subdued and on a regular medication routine. However, his behavior was still erratic. He prowled around the house, walking in and out of the front door. He had no interest in finding a job and talked constantly about going back to New York. He was trapped, and he knew it. And I was frustrated and angry. So much so that I accepted a two and a half month consulting job in Houston, Texas—just to get away. I needed some space, and I took the first opportunity that came up.

Coincidentally, in August 1996 Paul was offered a six-week contract to play keyboard in a band accompanying the Ringling Bros. Circus at the Texas State Fair, through his friend and former piano teacher Stuart. He would be in a group of five, first rehearsing for two weeks in

Florida and then going to Dallas for four weeks of half-hour performances three times a day. This news was a mixed bag for me. I was happy
and very proud of him. I knew he'd do a great job playing the music, yet
I was worried that he couldn't keep himself together. This was the first
time he would be on his own since his release from the hospital, and if
things went as he planned, this gig would afford him the money and
freedom to return to New York. To me this was the true test—would he
be able to manage his medicine on his own? One plus was that he would
return home in late October 1996, and we could assess his condition
then. But, as soon as he took the job, he warned us, "I'm planning to
move back to New York City in November." As much as I wanted to see
him back on his feet and on his own and financially secure, I feared for
him. I kept asking myself, could he really make it on his own?

I had hoped that he would make it so successfully in California that
he would decide to stay. Not in my house for sure, because it was so
hard to see the way he lived, but somewhere close by where I could keep
an eye on him. When the Dallas job came through, he had just been
hired to play once a week at a new restaurant in West Hollywood and
was doing a gig for tips at Universal City. His contacts really came
through for him in California. That had never been the case for him in
New York.

But I had to let go. I had to give him his wings. And when all was
said and done, we were all so much better off when he was gone. I knew
that unless he could accept being in California, and not always longing
to be back in New York, he and we could never be happy. His presence
only brought a toxic gloom over all of us.

Paul got home from Dallas in October 1996, before I was finished
with my Houston assignment. And because of that I feared he'd be gone
before I returned. But he surprised me. He picked me up from the air-

port looking good and behaving quite amiably. "I've got a room in Ray's apartment," he immediately told me. "I'm leaving in two weeks."

We asked him to give someone power of attorney in case he hit bottom again, but he refused. He wasn't willing to give us the power to have him declared a danger to himself and to others that would justify admitting him to a mental hospital. He still wanted to control his own destiny. However, he did agree to see his doctor to get another prescription for his meds so he would have a supply on hand until he had a new doctor in New York. I was impressed that he was being responsible. He was tying up loose ends. He wasn't doing anything precipitously. He was planning things out before acting—contrary to the way he had behaved so many times before in the past year. Could I really believe that this miserable chapter in our lives was finally closing? He even thanked us for our support—something he rarely did once he got sick. That he and Janet were speaking again could possibly have been a reason for his more rational behavior. That was a good reason. One I was happy to accept.

However, as Paul's departure date got nearer, his behavior became erratic again, and I got angrier and angrier. He stayed behind the closed door of his room or paced the floors at night once he thought we were asleep, he participated very little with us as a family, and he felt no compunction about asking us again for the six hundred-fifty dollars we supposedly "owed" him for a musical instrument he had recently purchased. His asking was nothing new. He always had his hand out even when he was well. He loved getting us to buy things for him, yet since he worked while he was in college and afterward while he was stable, he was also able to afford most of the things he needed. I also must say that while he was well, he returned the favor with thoughtful cards and gifts for us—a little blue glass vase, a book of Matisse cutouts, mother-of-pearl earrings, a pretty scarf, a vintage recording of Dylan Thomas' "A Child's Christmas in Wales" that Bob wanted. He was always generous to us when he had the money. Plus in the old days he could be attentive and thoughtful. He liked that I worked out and kept in good shape; he immediately read with pride my essay that was printed in our local newspaper; and after my visit with him for a few days the year before he got sick, out of concern for my safety, he sat with me at Union Station in New York until my train for Washington, D.C. arrived. So this one-way me, me, me behavior was new. It was selfish without any give-backs and very grating on me.

And as a result my reaction was new. I immediately took umbrage with the term, "owe." We didn't owe him a dime. Actually he was into us for about ten thousand dollars—money we'd spent on his air travel, doctors, hospitalizations, telephone calls since his arrival here the year before. (Because he was no longer a student he was no longer covered by our insurance at work. Besides benefits for mental illness didn't come close to covering all the expenses involved had he been insured.) I resented his thinking we owed him. I didn't want the money back. I never thought of his owing anything to us, but I wanted respect and appreciation and civility from him—none of which was forthcoming. His illness made him more selfish than before.

I should have been glad that he was going. Ben and Bob were. Yet I felt that New York was so toxic for him, I feared for him. No, I didn't want to have him living with us indefinitely—he was much too difficult—but I wished he could find another place to go. Even though he and Janet were talking again, she also was fearful of his return. She was afraid his crazy days would be repeated. We were all afraid of that. Would he abandon his resolve to stay on medicine and stay focused once he was on his own again? He did okay during his time in Dallas, but there he was working every day. He had to stay well. Once in New York, with no regular work and no one to check up on him, I wondered if he would be able to keep it together. I wondered how he thought he'd be able to pick up the pieces again in New York now that all the friends he made at school there had deserted him. I felt he had a chance in California. He had friends in the music business here. His music teacher who got him the Dallas gig, his former jazz ensemble teacher from high school, and our piano tuner were all looking out for him and trying to find him work, but he rejected them all. I thought he could have had a place of his own in Hollywood or Hermosa Beach. He rejected that idea too. He had to go back to New York—the place that was so bad for him, the place that brought out his darkest fears—that the mafia was lurking in doorways, ready to pounce at any second, poisoning his food and drinks. He had forgotten all that. He was optimistic that he could make it there. And, Janet was there. He had to be where she was whether she welcomed him or not.

I couldn't stand myself. I couldn't stand how I was feeling. I should have been optimistic and wishing him well. But no, I didn't see good things for him. I saw poverty, struggle, and possible homelessness unless he really looked at his mental condition and resolved to get himself well. But, I knew Paul couldn't do that. He'd continue lying to himself; telling himself that he could get by on his own. He'd remain his morose, dour, and mentally disabled self until he ran himself back into the ground again.

And I was tired of the subject of Paul altogether. It made me feel uptight, constantly sick to my stomach, and depressed. I thought maybe once he left the brightness of our lives would appear again. Maybe we could live freely without the constant feeling of walking on eggshells. We were so out of control. Sure, we made progress. He seemed somewhat recovered—at least right then. But, at such a huge expense to everyone.

Bob felt the day-to-day experience of living through Paul's behaviors drowned out the fear and worry we felt and replaced it with frustration and anger. Whether he was living in New York City and they conversed on the phone or he lived with us in Manhattan Beach, he was a difficult person to get along with. He was a taker, selfish, and sometimes nasty when pressured. Bob also discovered that Paul had an on-going difficulty with Janet and was not particularly nice to her, even though they were lovers. Apparently, his medications produced unwanted sexual challenges for him such as the inability to orgasm and undesired mental displacement in his creative process. He never agreed to adopt a long-term course of medication. Rather he most often chose to self-medicate with marijuana and other substances. That, and his habit of blowing off psychiatrist after psychiatrist were a great source of that anger and frustration in Bob. Bob always feared the worst. He would ask him at times of relative rationality, "Do I have to worry about you?" Paul's response to Bob was always the same, "Leave me alone."

Ben, on the other hand, was scared because he didn't understand what was wrong with Paul. He, like Bob and I, didn't know how to help him, and he worried, rightly so, that Paul might be suicidal.

Ben began to feel very uncomfortable interacting with Paul, and he didn't like seeing all the pain Paul caused us. He was angry with Paul for being so selfish, self-absorbed, insensitive, unkind, and inconsiderate of others. Ben resented him when, in his rational moments, Paul assumed he knew who Ben was and what Ben should do with his life when Paul really didn't know what he was talking about. "Don't be an actor," Paul told Ben, "it's too hard." Ben felt guarded around Paul, and he hated it.

Even though he had much concern for Paul and his mental health, Ben wasn't sorry to see Paul go back to New York City again. And I didn't blame him. That's how I needed to feel. I could go on living my life again without the constant shadow of Paul over me. But, for that feeling I paid the price in guilt. He was my son. How could a mother feel that way?

Once he was away, I knew the worry and fear would lessen—just as when he went to summer camp or away to college. When the boys lived at home I couldn't go to sleep until I knew they were safely home after a night out. When they were away, those thoughts never entered my mind. When Paul finally left, I gave some of my worry and fear to Ray and Janet. I let them have the responsibility. I believed that I had done all I could. I was through at least for the time being.

EPISODE THREE

Paul was in New York for less than four months when he was out of control again. He was off his meds, he didn't have a job, he lied to us that he was going back to his first and most effective psycho-pharmacologist, his roommate wanted to kick him out, and we received a letter from Janet telling us his behavior was so crazy we had to get him back to California immediately. By January 1997, he was in a full-blown manic state again. Ray and Janet tried to get him into a hospital there but failed. Bob went and actually talked him into going into Bellevue, but he only stayed for three days. Then he decided he'd rather come back to California and go into the small hospital in Palos Verdes he had been in two or three times before. We agreed and brought him home again in April 1997, with the admonition that he had to go into the hospital immediately upon his return.

As usual an immediate hospital admission was a slippery proposition. Even though he had promised, he refused to be admitted. Then he vacillated between going into the hospital in Palos Verdes and the

University of California at Los Angeles Neuropsychiatric Institute. So when he first arrived, his behavior was no different from how it had been at the height of his other manic episodes, and as a result my mood mirrored his. When he was crazy, I was at my wit's end. At one point I was so frustrated with his behavior and his equivocation about going into the hospital, I wrote the following words in my journal:

> *I feel as though the boy I raised has already died. He is not my son but some other person altogether. I'm living with a stranger—a selfish, irresponsible being who is using me up. I told Bob yesterday I'm tired of it. And I don't know how to stop the cycle. And, I can't save him. In fact, the way I feel now, I don't want to. I just don't have the energy and maybe not even the love.*

With Paul being home my moods were a mixture of pain, worry, fear, and a deep sadness. But I finally began to figure him out. At first I just couldn't understand why he went off his medicine, but then I decided—not knowing if I was right—that he just didn't want to grow up and take care of himself. If he stayed sick, he'd be cared for—given room, board, and spending money. Why would he want to give that up?

Ben was in grad school up in San Francisco, so we didn't have to worry about Paul getting in his way when Bob and I finally concluded that we had no choice. He was our son, our responsibility. We agreed that we could never turn him out into the streets. No matter how painful his being back with us could be, we would take care of him for as long as he needed us to.

When he arrived, he looked very thin, with his hair long and his face unshaven. But his eyes didn't look as wild as they did when he came home in December 1995. He seemed nervous. He kept going in and out of the house over and over again—either out the front door or out on the deck.

Almost as soon as he walked in the door, he began talking about taking a plane back to New York to pack up all his stuff and send it back here. I kept thinking he wouldn't be here long. As soon as he got some money, I knew he'd go back. And with that realization the most I could conjure up for him was hate. I was full of hate for my own son. I wasn't supposed to feel that way. But I couldn't help it. I felt as if he had drained all the love out of me. When his manic behavior turned to a deep depression, I felt more useless and frustrated. I wanted to help him get out of his depression and I didn't know how.

I tried to let him be, let him come to me if he wanted something, but that didn't work for me either. I needed to help him somehow. And, I became crazed and worried that he might commit suicide. I don't know where that came from. He had never threatened it—at least not to me. But, I was so worried. When he'd go to sleep in the middle of the day, I was never afraid that I'd wake him as I walked by his room. I was only afraid that I couldn't wake him. Was I irrational? I don't think so. I had a right to that fear. I kept wondering if he was degenerating before my very eyes.

One day at the height of his depression I finally confronted him. He came up to the kitchen—wearing the same clothes he'd had on for days, still unshaven, still not showered. He began to eat some chips. I called him into the family room and turned off the television set.

"How much have you eaten today?" I asked.

He looked at me sheepishly. "Not much," he said.

I sat there thinking for a few minutes and finally came out with it. "Do you want to get well?"

Surprisingly his reply was yes.

"So you need to eat and then go downstairs and shower and change your clothes," I said those words as forcefully and as clearly as I could. And, guess what? He did it all. He made himself two salads accompanied by other nibbles and wolfed down his food as if he had been starved. Then he showered and changed clothes. I just couldn't stand it any longer. I had to finally say something. I gave him a little prodding—and I let him know someone was watching and caring. Nagging didn't work. He never responded to that. Showing that I cared seemed to work.

Even so, he was nowhere near getting better. In fact he was worse. The delusions and paranoia took over his mind, and we couldn't get through to him. We were at a total loss about what to do except to force him into a hospital for a long, long time. Maybe even forever. Maybe he needed electro-shock treatments. Yet, to do any of this felt next to impossible. Unless I could prove he was a danger to himself and to others I could not get him admitted. His doctors were no help. The care from his doctors and from us did not work.

After failing to get him into University of California at Los Angeles's Neuropsychiatric Institute—his choice—we finally got him to go back to the small psychiatric hospital in Palos Verdes where he spent a week the year before.

At times I felt like I was losing my mind. My imagination ran rampant. Once I found what looked like a drop of blood on my office carpet. Later, while I was in the middle of a relaxation sequence at the end of an aerobics class, my eyes flew wide open, my stomach started cramping and churning, and my mind imagined Paul dead and buried. I saw him attempting suicide by slashing his wrists; I saw more blood in his sink, down the hall toward his bedroom, and all over his room. All this stemmed from what I thought was a tiny spot on the carpet that I never verified was blood at all.

His moods controlled mine. When he was most manic, I fluctuated between worry, anger, and frustration. I felt so out of control. He couldn't stay still and I couldn't stand it when he paced back and forth, going up and down the stairs, into and out of the house, mumbling and babbling to himself. It was my sign that he was in a very bad way. He had no control over this restlessness and nervousness—called akathesia—it had to pass on its own.

That I could do nothing to help him killed me. If I tried to talk to him, he usually barked something back or just ignored me. He only wanted to be in his own head, conversing with the voices he had inside there.

It was at these times that I felt so used. He was dominating our lives. He was holding us hostage. We had to do everything his way. We couldn't argue with him. And I felt he had no concern or interest in us. He asked a question and when I tried to answer he just rolled his eyes. He couldn't care less. He wasn't interested in what we had to say unless it concerned his demands on us. I just couldn't stand it anymore. I wanted so much to be rid of him. He was tearing us apart.

I would ask myself, why couldn't I be the kind of parent who just let go completely? But the answer to that is easy. He was my boy. I couldn't let go of him—like how I still feel about him now. Even though his episodes were costing us thousands of dollars and more in emotional costs, as Bob and I had agreed, we were there for him no matter what. There was no way out. I, too, wanted to run away, but I stayed for my boy.

I had to learn to leave him alone as much as possible. I learned the best way to behave was to wait for whatever mood he was in to pass and not to believe most of what he said. As I thought more and more that this person who was living in my home had no feeling for me, that he just wanted to take from me, I learned to remove myself from him physically and emotionally as much as possible.

From that point on, Paul never lived anywhere else except in our house in Manhattan Beach until he died. He went back to New York, once with his father to pack up and ship all his things back here, once with both of us to go to his grandmother's funeral, and once on his own two months before he died to see Janet for the last time. That visit was the kiss of death for him. I think it was then that Janet told him it was finally over. After he came back in April 1997, he never talked about moving back to New York again.

He went into the hospital twice during the early part of his last two and a half years, and by the time he came home the second time, he calmed down quite a bit. He took a computer course at the University of California at Los Angeles—he was computer savvy from the time he was a little boy—and then with the help of our cousin Larry, got a job as a troubleshooter for an Internet service provider. Bob and I also hired him to develop a CD of the proceedings of a conference we were producing for the University of Southern California School of Engineering. His work was so meticulous I was afraid we'd miss our deadline because he insisted on changing things up to the last minute. In the end, his work was a complete success.

When he seemed better, I had high hopes for his recovery and the realization of his dream to settle down and marry Janet. There was actual talk of her moving here, but in the end, that turned out to be just that—talk. During the last two and a half years of his life his relationship with her was on and off, off and on. That's how it was throughout their seven years together. Yet his life and his moods had to do with how things were going with her. If things were going well, he was happy and okay. If things were going poorly, he was morose. Her problem with him had to do with his illness and his continued abuse of his medication intake. He just couldn't stay on them for long, and when he became manic, he'd take his meds to stave off another mental episode. As soon as he felt better he'd stop again.

Janet just couldn't stand that. She needed him to be stable. She saw him crazy and out of control too many times. She couldn't commit to leaving her life in New York, leaving a perfectly good job, and a good rent-controlled apartment for a guy who didn't love her enough to stay on his meds. She loved him. I truly believe that. But she knew she could never live with him.

No one could. And, as we found out later, neither could he.

July 11, 1997

He lays
in the fetal position
in the shrouded corner of his room,
not reading,
not listening to music,
not eating,
not talking.

Sometimes he goes outside,
sits on the still patio,
and watches
the smoke
from his cigarette
swirl to the sky.

Back to his cell
he shuts the door
and finally sleeps.
I've no fear
of waking him
only of being
unable to wake him

I live one minute at a time
and wonder
how will it all end.
Will he and I ever be free?

CHAPTER FOUR

I almost had angry words with Paul the night before he killed himself. But something held me back. We spoke calmly even though I was upset and angry at him for blowing off his doctor's appointment and refusing to make another. Bob nagged him for not taking hold of his life and turning it around, and all he got were rebuffs. So I didn't nag that night. I didn't have anymore nagging in me. I didn't have anymore anger in me either. I only had love and worry and sadness.

But, what if I had nagged and gotten angry or said something different that night? Would it have triggered something else in him? Maybe he wouldn't have killed himself that night. Maybe I could have gotten him to call his doctor. I should have been more aggressive with him. Instead we just had a casual conversation. I did not want to upset him and did not want him to leave until the conversation was over.

The Last Night

How could I have known
it would be the last night? A night
like all the others:
the low creaking groan
of the garage door,
tires screeching to maneuver
into the narrow place,
the roar of the engine before silence.
Then slamming the door,
my son, sweeps down the long hall,
calling out hello in his deep friendly voice.
I startle as I hear his heavy strides
pass my door,
I call out to him.
Returning, he enters my room—
standing, staring, looking more calm
than I've ever seen him.
His blue eyes like sapphires
fringed with thick dark lashes
never leave mine while we speak.
My lips kiss his cheek
cool as alabaster.
I marvel at his smile—lips
barely turned up not showing his teeth.
He looks like the angel
he will soon become.
He has already found peace.
Only I don't know it yet.

I go over and over that last conversation in my mind. What could I have said that could have prevented his suicide? What did I say that caused it? Even though I know in my heart of hearts that I didn't cause it, I feel so much guilt about what wasn't said and what was said that could have made him take his life that night.

It was about six in the evening when I heard him open the door from the garage. He was arriving home from work at the usual time. He said, "Hello," and I called to him to come on in as he walked by my office and down the long hall to his room. I hadn't seen him for a day or so because I had been observing Yom Kippur and attending a break-the-fast dinner—something he never liked to participate in even when he was well—so I was eager to at least say hello. He went into his room first and then came back to my office.

He looked good, well rested even after a day at work, but he was quiet. And I wondered why I had been so worried about him. He was holding down a job and had recently been promoted to manage several people at the office. Every day he drove back and forth into the heart of Los Angeles without any mishaps, and he came home around the same time every evening. The only thing I should have been concerned about was how much time he spent alone in his room after he came home.

"Paul, you've cut your hair. I love it," I said. His hair was in its usual quarter-inch buzz. He buzzed it himself. It made him look clean. He had a nice round head—no bumps, just a smooth fuzz of dark blonde hair all around his head. He didn't have to buzz it because he was growing bald like some of the young men in our family. No, he had a full head of thick hair.

For years he had long hair, sometimes flowing down his back and sometimes pulled back into a ponytail. In the early 1990s he had his hair styled with a shock of it spilling over onto his forehead and over one eye. That haircut made him look very handsome—in fact we took family pictures that show his hair that way. I always think those were his most handsome days before he got sick and before the medications' effects puffed out his chiseled cheekbones and chin. I don't know why he decided to buzz it, but I never cared about what my boys did with their hair. They could shave it off or dye it purple. I never found that important enough to make an issue of. Anyway, he looked good with the buzz.

"Thanks," he said as he stood opposite me, leaning against Bob's wooden desk. I was sitting at my computer trying to figure out a label-making system. I turned my chair around to face him.

"Are you going to see Janet soon?" I asked. I knew I was being a little pushy asking this question, but I was hopeful that things were better between them. I would have loved to have Janet visit soon. He was another person when she was around. We saw more of him, he was more talkative, and it made him so happy.

"No, I don't think so," he replied. "Why?" He showed no reaction. No smile. No frown. He just looked at me calmly in the eye.

"Oh, I thought you were since you usually buzz your hair just before you see her."

I was encouraged by his haircut. In his worst depressive episodes he wouldn't shower, he wouldn't shave, and he'd let his hair and sideburns grow. Tonight he was clean-shaven and well kept. He had on khakis and a white long-sleeved business shirt and his brown Doc Marten shoes—the clothes that he had worn to work that day.

I wonder if that was a stupid thing to ask. Maybe he was trying to get over Janet and my questions brought it all back to him. Could that question have made him go ahead and take his life?

I changed the subject and told him about the computer program I was having trouble with. I was trying to make labels to put on a big mailing Bob and I were doing for a small engineering company. But my computer skills were far inferior to Paul's.

"Maybe you'll help me with it," I said. Paul could always solve my computer problems. He'd work on them at night and in the morning I'd find instructions about what to do that he had hand-written out. He didn't write in cursive. He always meticulously printed out the instructions step by step on a piece of paper torn out of his notebook. Even a grade school kid could follow them.

He only nodded his head, acknowledging my request for help. But he didn't give me a commitment.

"Well, you look great," I said. "Let me give you a kiss."

He leaned down so I could kiss his cheek. I didn't get up from my chair and take him in my arms. I just sat there and kissed his cool, smooth cheek. He stood back up, looked at me briefly, said nothing else—no good night, no good-bye, no nothing—and in an instant he was gone. He walked down the hall to his room and shut the door. And as soon as he left, I felt we had unfinished business.

During this last conversation I had briefly mentioned to Paul about reading some of our cousin Yael's essays. Because he and Yael were close, I thought he'd like to read her stuff too. So after he left the office and walked into his room and shut the door, I noticed that I hadn't given him the pack of essays. I picked them up off my desk and walked down the hall to his room. I could tell from looking under the door that his room was dark, and I decided not to disturb him. Instead, I shoved the papers under his door, thinking he'd get up in the night and pick them up and read them. He read many of my suggestions. Probably the last two were Schlink's *The Reader* (ironically about a young man's affair with an older woman) and Irving's, *A Widow for One Year*. Paul was always a voracious reader.

Afterward I kept thinking how could I have let him walk away from me and go into his dark room? I only kissed his cool, pale cheek. I should have hugged him and told him how much I loved him. He needed hugging, touching, and a serotonin jump. He wasn't being touched enough, so he lacked the serotonin that touching and close relationships provide. Hugs from Bob and me could have helped. Another back massage. Why didn't he ask? He said it made him feel better and helped him sleep. He also needed a loving visit with Janet. For sure that would have saved him.

But he had been so distant that last night I was reluctant to push him any further. I didn't want to push my luck. I didn't want the kind of rebuff that Bob had experienced when he tried to talk to him during the past few weeks. He would call out to Paul and Paul would yell back, "Don't bother me," and then slam the door to his room. At least I got a chance to talk to him as short as the conversation was. At least I have that. Anyway, there was no way for me to know I would never see him again. It was a normal conversation, not a "Goodbye-I'll-never-see-you-again" conversation. Maybe Paul knew it was the last time, but he sure didn't give me an indication that it was.

I keep going over that last night again and again. What more could I have said to him to keep him with us longer? I still think about not hugging him that night. Why didn't I hug him and tell him I loved him before he left the office? Why didn't I knock on his door and give him the papers and talk to him about them? We could have talked some more. I could have hugged him. Maybe the hug would have been enough to stop him—at least that night.

When the police went through his room the next day, looking for clues: a note, anything, they found the papers still on the floor and listed them on their evidence sheet. My son's possessions were listed on an evidence sheet. No son's things should ever be on an evidence sheet. He never picked up Yael's papers. I wonder if he even saw them as he left the room in the night to go into the bathroom. Did he have to step over them? Did he step on them? Did he have to step over all the clothes that were on the floor? I thought about that too. I wanted to know everything he did that night—every move he made, every feeling he had—even though I know I never will.

In the end, I didn't know the signs. I stuck my head in the sand. I didn't keep my eyes and ears and mind open. My worry wasn't enough. My living in the same house with him, my being there, my talking to him, my pleading with him to go to the doctor, none of it was enough. I needed to stroke him, and hug him and kiss him more. He needed that so that he knew that I loved and cared about him. With the cool, calm, and disconnected way I acted that last night he probably thought I didn't care an iota about him. I let him slip away. Mothers shouldn't let their sons slip away.

Suicide is the destiny of most people—especially young men—with bipolar disorder, according to Kay Redfield Jamison in her book, *Night Falls Fast*. In reality, there is probably nothing I could ever have done or said to prevent it. The more I have come to know about manic-depressive illness over these last few years the more I have come to know I could never have stopped him. Cop out or not, that's the reality of it.

The Look

(inspired by the film "Revolutionary Road")

She looked toward him
from the counter
and offered him a glass of orange juice
freshly squeezed.
She was fully dressed in blouse and skirt
and little wedgie shoes,
Her makeup was perfect.
Her long blonde hair just so.

She then invited him to sit down
at the table.
"Scrambled or fried eggs?" she asked.
He said whatever is easier, scrambled
probably, and unbuttoning
his suit jacket sat down,
looking at her all the while.

She stood at the sink scrambling and
when the eggs were cooked,
she sat down
opposite him and they ate.
Not much talking, mostly eating, and looking
closely at each other's eyes.
He got up to go.
"That's the best breakfast you ever made
for me," he said.

And before he left, he asked her
if she was still mad
at him from the night before.

They had yelled at each other and showed so much hate
that she ran off into the woods
beyond their yard.
"Leave me alone," she screamed,
"I need to think," and he went to bed
alone.

But this morning there was complete calm.
Her eyes clear, her face luminous,
showing none of last night's horrific pain.
She had the look that said
she had found her
peace. And, it didn't include him.

I saw that look once before
on my son's face, the night before
he took his own life.
So I knew what was coming.
It was eerie to be so certain
that this was where this story
was going.

As she said, "No, I don't hate you,"
she took his face in her hands
and smiled slightly.
She then walked him
to the door and stood there until
he drove away.
She turned and went inside.
That was the last time
he would see her alive.

Thursday Morning

When all I heard was silence
behind the locked bathroom door
that Thursday morning,
when all I saw was darkness
through the open bedroom door
when Bob went to investigate,
calling his name, Paul,
pleading with him, Paul,
open the door,
when Bob went to the garage
for a screwdriver to pick the lock,
when he opened the door
and closed it quickly from the inside
while I stood on the stairs,
waiting
as Bob found our son in the bathtub,
sitting in a pool of blood,
blue, already cold and stiff,
tongue hanging out of his mouth,
when Bob came out of the bathroom
face red, hands shaking
and told me
Paul is dead,
when all I heard were sirens
and the footsteps of the police
as they stomped though our house,
all I could do was huddle
in the corner of the couch,
my legs drawn under me,
my arms folded around me,
as I rocked back and forth,
my hands clamped into tight fists.

CHAPTER FIVE

T he night before Paul died—September 22, 1999—Bob and I had dinner with our friends, Carole and Jerry, at James Beach on Venice Boulevard just east of the Pacific Ocean. Carole brought me a belated birthday present—a red-cotton cardigan sweater, so it was a celebration of sorts. We had been through lots of celebrations with Carole and Jerry, people we got to know before we were married in 1970—baby showers, births, Bar Mitzvahs. They had two boys close in age to our two, and now one of their sons was engaged. We talked a lot about Paul that evening and not differently from what I had been saying for many weeks before.

"I'm very worried about him," I said.

Jerry tried to make me feel better. "After all," he said, "he works every day. He worked today. He can't be that bad off."

Yes, I thought. Jerry could be right. And certainly Bob wasn't showing as much concern as I. But it turned out even I didn't know how badly off he really was. He was a master at hiding what was really going on with him. That he worked every day was a miracle, but that he hardly ate, hardly talked on the phone anymore, hardly said anything to Bob and me, and went into his dark bedroom every evening when he came home from work made me very nervous. It seemed that he wasn't talking to Janet anymore either. Was this change the cause of his reclusiveness?

Still the four of us had our share of laughs, and when we got home, I was feeling somewhat better.

The next morning I lazed in bed. I didn't get up to go to the gym as usual. I don't know why. Maybe we had been out too late the night before and I just didn't feel rested enough. Bob went out to our driveway to get the *Los Angeles Times*, got back into bed, and we lay in there together and caught up on the news. After I read my favorite comic strips I read the long obituary about the death of my ex father-in-law—a renowned film editor who had twice received an Academy Award. The obit took up half a page, complete with a photo of him, and it made me sad. I loved him, and even though I hadn't seen my ex-husband since our divorce more than thirty years before, I had kept in touch with his parents. They lived in Palm Springs, where Bob, Ben, and I once visited them. Ben—very much interested in the film business even as a young boy—was indeed impressed to see two Oscar statuettes and to hold them. It was so bizarre to read that obit that day—the telling of the long, successful life of a wonderful man. Within minutes of reading that half page I found out how short and unsuccessful my oldest son's life was.

I got up about half past seven, put on my purple terry-and-chenille robe and went downstairs to the laundry room to fold laundry. I noticed the door to the bathroom was closed and didn't think much about it because it was the time Paul usually got ready for work. But after I was in the laundry room for about twenty minutes I realized that I hadn't heard anything from the bathroom. I knocked on the door and there was no answer. I went to his room and could see from his partially opened door that it was dark. I pushed the door open a little more and went inside. He wasn't there. I went out into the garage. His gold Volvo station wagon was still there. At this point I was just taking in the information—no sound from the bathroom, no one in the bedroom, the car not moved from the garage.

My heart was beating wildly, and I was shaking as I went upstairs to our room. Bob was finishing getting dressed to go to his consulting job—it must have been almost eight o'clock.

"Bob," I said, "I think there is something very wrong downstairs."

He looked up from the shoe he was tying.

I hadn't tried to open the bathroom door. I was scared. My stomach was in knots. I knew I couldn't look into that room myself.

"The bathroom door is closed and there aren't any noises coming from inside. I looked in his room too. He's not there."

Bob got up from his chair and went downstairs without a word. He barely looked at me. He pounded on the bathroom door and called out over and over, "Paul, open the door. Paul, open the door."

At first I waited on the stairs by our front door. I was afraid. Then I slowly crept down the last flight of stairs leading to the door to the garage, the long hall, our office, the laundry room, the bathroom, Paul's room, and our guest room. Bob jerked the bathroom doorknob back and forth. The door was locked. He then went out to the garage to get a tool to open the door. He knew exactly what to use—a small screwdriver—something he had used many times before when the boys were little and locked the bedroom or bathroom doors by accident.

I waited by the foot of the stairs watching and whimpering as Bob finally managed to unlock the door with a squeak. He opened the door just wide enough for him to slip through and closed the door immediately behind him. I waited, frozen, horrified, and hoping that he would find Paul all right and probably angry at the intrusion. Yet somehow I knew what he was going to find in there. From the time I noticed there was no movement downstairs, aside from my folding of towels and underwear in the laundry room, my shaking hands, my crumbling face, and my chattering teeth told me Bob wasn't going to find anything good behind that closed bathroom door. Looking back, I remember Paul always said I knew everything. He trusted my intuition. I trusted it too.

Within minutes I heard the click of the doorknob, and Bob came back out into the downstairs hall. His face was red. And not looking at me yet, he slammed the bathroom door shut behind him. He came toward me.

He took me in his arms and held me briefly. He was shaking. I could feel the cold of his hands through the thickness of my robe. His face was wet as he pressed it against my forehead. I knew what he was going to say next.

"Paul is dead," he said quietly. "Call 911."

I broke away from him. I started screaming. I didn't know which way to go. Then I made my way up the two flights of stairs to the kitchen to get the phone. I don't know why I didn't just go into the office. I kept screaming, moaning, "Paul is dead. My Paul is dead." I called 911. "My son is dead!" I screamed. "My husband just found him dead in the bathroom!" I kept screaming, "My son is dead! Paul is dead. My son is dead in the bathroom." I couldn't say anything else. The emergency dispatch lady wanted to talk to Bob. I couldn't give her the facts. I hadn't seen him. I was just the messenger. I was the screaming messenger. There was no way I could speak with her rationally. Bob came upstairs, took the phone from me, and spoke to her.

"The police will be here soon," he said.

As he walked back toward the bathroom where Paul was, I went into our bathroom to pull on some clothes. I grabbed some underpants that were lying on the floor and began to put them on inside out. I got out of them somehow and started over. I staggered on one foot. I went into the closet and put on some jeans—I still have those jeans—I'll never give them away—and found an old black long-sleeved t-shirt in my armoire drawer. Yes, I still have that shirt too.

By the time I got dressed—I had to get dressed because people would be coming to my house—I heard the sirens outside and Bob talking to the police at the door. Bob led me up into the family room and stayed with me while the police took over. I don't know how many there were. I could hear their steps going in and out of the house, up and down the stairs—just like Paul used to do while he was in the most manic state. He'd go up and down the steps. He'd go in and out the front door. Then he'd go back downstairs and shut the door of his room. Over and over. He couldn't keep still. He couldn't sleep. He kept walking. He kept prowling. This boy of mine was so troubled. He couldn't rest. He couldn't sleep. And he couldn't live—not like that.

Later I found out the police had taken off the shower door to get his body out of the bathtub. They put him on a gurney in the garage, zipped him up in a body bag, and took him away to the coroner's office. That's what they do when people are murdered or kill themselves. The coroner had to decide if Paul's death was indeed a suicide. What's the difference, I kept asking myself. He murdered himself. To me murder and suicide were the same. He committed self-murder. But the police had to make sure someone else didn't kill him. Murder. Suicide. In his case it's all the same.

All the while, I sat on the couch with my arms folded into myself, rocking, staring off into space, crying, shaking, mumbling the same words over and over, "Paul is dead, Paul is dead." I couldn't get my mind to focus on it. I didn't understand it. I didn't want to understand it.

Bob called Ben. He called Janet who answered the call while she was walking on a street in Manhattan. She had to sit down somewhere and control her crying before he could tell her the details. A friend called. Bob told him. Pretty soon other people started calling, people started coming over. The house was full of police, people from the coroner's office, a grief counselor from the police department. Our friend, Susan, came over and started fielding phone calls. Bob called work. Paul's office called asking where he was.

Bob called our cousin, Larry. Besides helping him get his troubleshooting job at the internet service provider, Larry had met with Paul several times about computerizing a new video game he was developing. Bob asked Larry to let his family know but to please ask them not to call my mother. We felt we had to tell her in person. As soon as Yael, who was Ben's special friend as well as our cousin, found out she arrived at the door.

I dreaded telling the news to my mother. She was so quick to blame. Could she blame me for his death? I never knew what to expect from her. But that day was different. I somehow knew she wouldn't be a comfort to me. No one wanted to make the thirty-minute trip to her apartment in Santa Monica. Neither Bob nor I were in any condition to drive, and I couldn't call her.

Finally, my sister Sheila and her husband Tom arrived, then Ben. I felt so sorry for Ben. He had to leave his performances of the "Three Penny Opera"—his first time on the American Conservatory Theater main stage. Then my brother Ken arrived from Denver. He was so distraught. He kept moaning. He could hardly speak, but he didn't have to. I needed him just to be with me. He held me, he sat with me, and he helped out in the kitchen and picked up people from the airport.

The rest of his family—my sister-in-law, his four children, one whose birthday was Paul's death day, his son and daughter-in-law, and his one-year-old granddaughter—came the next day. Though they all didn't stay in our house, they took over when they were there—preparing and serving food, cleaning up, and putting things away. After everyone left, I couldn't find things for weeks.

Late in the day, Tom, Larry, and Yael went to Santa Monica to tell my mother. They got her to pack a bag and brought her back with them to our home in Manhattan Beach. My sister and brother-in-law checked her into the hotel with them.

I'll never forget her first words: "It should have been me." My mother was always threatening to kill herself. Then she asked, "Why didn't he come talk to me?" Sure, I thought, what good would that have done? But it was always about her. And what could she have done or said that would have changed his mind? She never told me that she was sorry for me. She took the loss as her own. It had nothing to do with me. When I needed a mother to take me in her arms, comfort me, reassure me—just hold me—she was not there for me. When I was the most distraught I had ever been in my life—so much so that I could hardly dress myself—she failed me. I will never forgive her for that. As I write this now, years after her death, it still makes me angry. She always found ways to upset me at the most important times of my life—my first marriage, my marriage to Bob, my pregnancy with Paul. She always gave me a bad time when I, not she, was the center of attention. And the death of my son was no exception.

Well, at least she hadn't blamed me. Instead I blamed her. Indeed it was her fault. It was her whole family's fault. He was born with the family's curse—manic depression—so, he got it from her.

I don't think I ate anything the day Paul died. Just the thought of food made me sick to my stomach. It's always my stomach. My nerves affect my stomach. I can't eat. Food doesn't want to stay in my body. I lose weight. When Carole, whom we had had dinner with the night before, came over, she made scrambled eggs. I ate a few bites. Everyone took over my kitchen, and I couldn't stand it. I couldn't stand the mess.

I finally went downstairs. I didn't want to be around so many people anymore. I needed to be alone. I needed to be in a place where I could be close to Paul. A towel was lying in a heap on the floor outside the bathroom. I had just bought white bath sheets for that bathroom—soft, fluffy ones—I think they were Charisma—and new white bathmats. I went inside, practically on tiptoes. I felt cold. I couldn't breathe, like I was suffocating. I let out a breath when I could see that the room was empty. The bathmats were on the floor but the other towel was missing. I found his watch on the right side of the counter by the sink. My hands shook as I picked it up, turned it over. Blood was on the underside, the side that touched his wrist. I put it back down. I don't know who cleaned the bathroom, but it was in pretty good shape. I didn't see anymore blood in the room. I suspect whoever it was used the missing towel to wipe it up. The next day I went back to the bathroom to look for his watch. It wasn't there. I later found it in Bob's drawer. It still had the blood on it. The watch is still there now, still running, but the blood is gone. It faded away. No one wiped it away. It just faded away.

I then went into Paul's room. I made the bed, found the bedspread on a shelf in the garage, and put it on the bed. He never used the bedspread—he liked his black comforter instead—the one I bought for him years before when he went away to college. I picked up his clothes that were strewn all over the big easy chair and on his floor and threw them into his hamper in the closet. I didn't care if they were clean or dirty. I didn't move the bed away from the wall yet. I didn't want to disturb too much. A little while later, Ben joined me and we sat on the floor, our legs folded, our backs up against the side of the bed, holding hands. We just looked around at all the stuff he left behind. We still felt his presence in the room and were afraid if we touched anything it would go away.

He was such a pack rat. He kept everything. He cared about his things, and now he had left them all. I never thought he would leave his things. Even his paychecks from many weeks' work were still lying on the table by the chair—never deposited. For the first time in his life he had money—so much that he didn't need to put anymore into his checking account.

He left a letter addressed to Janet in a stamped envelope on the table by his bed. When she arrived the next day, we gave it to her, and she let us read it. In it he apologized for his behavior with her and told her how much he loved her. We later found many versions of that letter. He wrote it over and over again like a mantra—I'm sorry, I love you, I know we can be happy again—I'm sorry, I love you, I know we can be happy again—just give me another chance. Just give me another chance. But he never mailed the letter. How could she give him another chance if he never mailed it?

Here's the letter dated exactly one month before he took his life—verbatim:

August 23, 1999

Janet –

I'm looking at my collection of all of the cards, letters, and pictures that you have sent to me during our time together. These gifts paint a beautiful picture of a beautiful person who is capable of the most extraordinary depth of feelings and sensitivity. They also remind me that during all of the time that we have shared, you have continuously communicated your feelings to me. I have always felt loved by you and these gifts have reenforced what you have said in words again and again.

I feel strongly that in order for us to communicate our feelings to each other in a meaningful way, there must be a strong bond of trust between the two of us. Early this summer, when you came to Los Angeles for your birthday, our trust was challenged by my revelation to you that I had briefly stopped taking my medication earlier this year. I want you to know that I am sorry for not telling you the truth. I realize that you deserve to know all of the details of my condition and treatment. You have always been so supportive and it was foolish of me to think that you would have been anything but supportive of my decisions if you had known.

I did not consciously decide not to tell you about my decision. Around the time that I began to work full time, it became apparent that the side effects from the lithium were too much. I had to wait about a month to see my doctor—I did not want to have to take time off so early on in my new job. I continued to take my other medications and my condition remained stable. Work went well and you and I were happy. Perhaps an unconscious desire for you to look at me as a normal, healthy person led to my decision. I only wish that I had told you the truth then instead of when I did.

The rest of the summer seems to have been clouded by this issue. You were not able to trust me enough to accept my love and I was not able to see clearly enough to notice that you had not forgiven me and that it was causing a problem. I was so involved in my work and my desire to provide us with the means to live together that I didn't realize that the crisis in our relationship needed all of my attention. I am sorry for allowing my desires for the future to obscure my abilities to handle the present.

I want you to know that I love you and care for you and that our relationship is so important to me. I know that since May you may not have been able to trust me as completely as you once did. I want you to try to understand my motivations and your own and, in turn, forgive me. I want you to trust me so that you can feel my love for you again.

I have shared some of my happiest moments with you. I look at your pictures and think of your amazing sense of beauty in the natural world. Our conversations on the phone and in person have always engaged me and warmed my heart. Your face, with its beautiful pools of blue, is that of an angel. Until recently, we both looked forward to spending our lives together. I believe that this is still possible, and that if we work together, we can trust each other and enjoy a wonderful, strong, passionate relationship. You are my best friend and the love of my life. I love you.

Love,
Paul

About a month earlier he knocked on my bedroom door wanting to talk. He asked me if I thought he could get Janet back. I told him I thought so because he had done so many times before. But later on I regretted several of the things I said that night.

"I think you love not taking your medication more than you love Janet," I said.

But how could I know how horrible the medication made him feel? I also insisted he go back to his doctor. Maybe he could take something else to make him feel better.

"We could be sitting here ten years from now having this same conversation," I said.

What an idiot I was to say that. Could that thought have set him off? To think I would still be trying to get him to go to his doctor and to take his meds for another ten years. What a grim thought that was. Well, from my point of view, it was better than the alternative. I'll never know what he thought. I just know what he did. He killed himself so he wouldn't have to find out where he'd be in ten years.

As we walked out of my room that night—I on my way to pick up Bob from the airport, and he on his way to call his doctor, Paul picked up a picture of Ben and him that I had on top of a bookcase.

"I miss Ben," he said. He touched Ben's face on the photograph.

"Why don't you call him?" I said.

He never did. But he did call his doctor and later that night joined Bob and me for dinner. That was our last intimate conversation and dinner together. A month before he died. We never had another intimate conversation until the last night. How could that be? We lived in the same house, but it was like we were strangers. He wasn't talking. We weren't asking. Or if and when we did, we didn't get any answers.

Why were we so timid about confronting him? What held us back? And if we had confronted him, would it have made any difference?

I know now he didn't believe he could get Janet back, so he just stopped trying. Though he wrote the letter over and over again, he couldn't send it. He knew what I didn't know. She was really through with him this time. She already had someone else. Though she cried hysterically when she heard he was dead and she came to town for his funeral, she left quickly. She removed herself from us as she had already done from Paul.

I decided I wanted to get into his computer. Maybe I would find some clue in there, but I didn't know the password. Yael called a computer expert who said it would be virtually impossible to break into his computer without the password, but I was determined to try. I got up in the middle of the first night without him and went into his room—something I did a lot in the next few weeks. I sat in his chair and read through some of his computer and music notebooks looking for clues. And, I found one almost immediately. I tried it and it worked. His password was Albert—his brother's middle name. Unfortunately, there were no text documents at all in his computer. No journals, no clues. Just his music.

I did find a handwritten poem folded up tight and pushed way down inside a pocket in his wallet. A piece I think he wrote shortly before his death, though I'll never be sure about that. It was about how he let Janet go and how he wasn't getting any better. He knew, and he couldn't live with what he knew. He called it "Way."

Way

I was walking
I was thinking
I was running
I was sinking
You were laughing
You were loving
I was pushing
I was shoving

If you're wondering
How I'm feeling
Same old thing
I ain't healing

If you're hungry
I can feed you
Please don't think
That I don't need you

And I let you walk away . . .
Now you can go your own way.

Later on I felt cheated about not seeing Paul before they took him away, about not giving him a kiss goodbye. I kept pressing Bob to tell me every detail. Instead, he wrote them down for me in his journal. Maybe it was just too hard for him to talk about.

> I could see his stained pants and red smears on the tub wall before I even entered the room. As I stepped inside I was immediately aware of the heavy smell of blood and death in the room. I closed the door behind me, and walked into the toilet/bath area. He was half-sitting, half-lying with his head away from the faucet and drain. His head was leaning against the door of the shower, bent forward a bit, with his mouth slightly open.
>
> His right arm was stretched out on top of him, his left was more or less at his side. He wore no shoes or socks, and the skin of his lower legs and arms were stained in blood. He wore tan pants and a shirt (white, I think), and he and his clothing were covered in dark red blood. The Coroner's man told me later that he had used a box cutter to cut into his throat and wrists; I couldn't see the weapon in the tub. I later learned that it was in the tub under him. In fact, with so much blood on Paul and his clothes, I couldn't really tell where his wounds were. He had bled out in the tub, and the substance of his life had gone down the drain. There was a congealed pool of it around the mesh of the drain. I put my hand on his unshaved face with the intention of finding a pulse in his neck, but the cold temperature and stiffness of his skin told me what was obvious. I reached up and opened the bathroom window to relieve the closeness and odor. I was shaking, as I left the room, closing the door again, to tell you that Paul was dead.
>
> After I told you to call 911, I went back into the bathroom and approached Paul's body to check again. Maybe I was wrong about him. Maybe he was still alive. I touched his arm. It was cold and stiff and I could not lift it from his body, somewhat like a cooked chicken wing can't be lifted off the chicken

without breaking it away. I realized that rigor mortis was well underway; Paul had been in that bath tub for some hours, and there was no bringing him back.

Something still puzzled me. Paul shampooed and cut his hair just four days before he died. Why did he bother if he was planning to kill himself? That's what makes me believe he didn't plan it. At other times when he was most depressed he would just let everything go. Not this time. He didn't show that level of depression now. I believe the voices in his head, his hallucinations, told him to do it. He may have known during our conversation that last night—in fact he may have already bought the box cutter. He went into his room before he came back down the hall to talk to me in the office. Did he just put down his book bag or did he also put down a box cutter before he came to see me?

I'll never know the answer to that one either. I didn't find a baggie from Home Depot—I saw some box cutters at the checkout line there—they cost one dollar and nine cents. He killed himself with an implement that cost one dollar and nine cents. That's all it took. It doesn't cost much to kill yourself these days and cause your loved ones grief for the rest of their lives. One dollar and nine cents. Unbelievable.

Poor Bob. He was so angry with Paul for not talking to him, for not asking for his help. And then he left himself in that bloody bathtub for Bob to find him, smell him, touch him, and look at all that blood on him. He had to open the window of the death room to allow the smell of blood and death out—a scene that will stay with him until he dies.

Bob never had a chance to say anything to him before he died—another reason he was so angry. Bob was angry at Paul's selfishness in totally shutting him out by his suicide.

Bob tried to protect me from seeing Paul that way; so he resented my poem that expresses my guilt about not going down there to him or kissing him goodbye as he left with the coroner, but I can't help feeling I was left out of an important part of Paul's life—his death. I gave birth to him. I needed to send him off in death properly and as a mother should if a mother is unlucky enough to have a child's death precede hers.

As I was shut out of his life for twenty-four hours right after he was born, as I was shut out of his life for four hours while he was in recovery after his finger surgery, I was shut out again. I cannot repeat it enough. A mother shouldn't be shut out of any of her child's life and death events.

It's a double-edged sword. Bob is hurt that I feel that way. And I know he meant well. His first thought was to protect me. He dreaded telling me. He dreaded me seeing Paul in the bloody pool. He wanted to protect me from seeing all the gory evidence as if not seeing it could make it less real. I still wonder if my imagined images are less or worse than the real ones.

And I still believe I never should have stayed upstairs on the couch that morning. I shouldn't have opted out of the last phase of my son's life. The doctors wouldn't let me see him for twenty-four hours right after he was born, and they wouldn't let me see him for four hours after his hand surgery. But this time I had a choice, and I let him down. I shouldn't have let anyone try to hide it from me—to protect me. I needed to be brave. I needed to be with him, look at him, touch him, kiss him, and tell him goodbye. Those are my regrets. I needed to take it all in. That I didn't will be with me for the rest of my life.

Paul's Poem

You didn't even touch me, Mother.
I was only down the hall,
sitting against the shower door
in the blue bathtub.
I was cold in there.
Why didn't you touch me?
All you had to do was step inside the bathroom.
I was still there sitting on my box cutter
in just a little puddle of blood.
But I was dressed.
I still had on the clothes that I wore to work—
my white long-sleeved shirt and khakis.
It would have been okay if you came in.
You didn't have to keep the door closed.
I was lonely in there.
You could have come in.

Why didn't you come down to the garage to kiss me goodbye
before I left home?
Strangers from the coroner's office put me on a gurney,
stuffed me in a plastic bag, and took me away.
I didn't want to go,
but they had to make sure I was my murderer
not someone else.
You could have unzipped me down to my neck
and kissed me on the forehead or on my lips.
I wouldn't have minded.
Even though my tongue was sticking out a little,
I didn't look too bad.

I know you weren't allowed to visit
during my four days at the coroner's office,
but I don't understand why you didn't come
with Dad and Uncle Ken to the mortuary.
That was your last chance,
That was your last chance to see me whole
and you stayed home.
Why did you stay home, Mother?
Oh, sure, Dad probably told you to.
But you could have come anyway
How come, Mother?

I wanted you there with me
before they took me away for good,
before they turned me into a bag of ashes.
Were you mad at me, Mother?
Were you mad that I did it?
Were you mad that I killed myself?
Were you frightened to see me dead?
What was it?
You know I had to.
You know I couldn't help myself.
You know the voices made me do it.
I didn't want to.
I didn't want to hurt you,
But I just had to do it.
I just couldn't live anymore in all that pain
And now I'm okay.
And I know you'll be okay too.
You will someday, Mother.
Mother, someday you will.

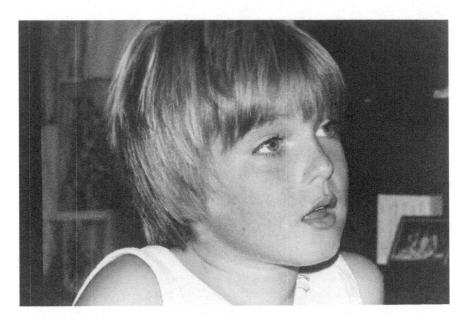

July 1978, at Ben's birthday party on Kwajalein, Marshall Island

Fall 1978, at home in Manhattan Beach at our first computer

July 1981, in the old tree in front of our house

Fall 1985

Summer 1986, happy in Maui

Fall 1989, college freshman

July 1999, while on last trip to New York City

CHAPTER SIX

....SUICIDE

M artin Amis wrote an article called "The Last Day of
Muhammad Atta," which appeared in *The New Yorker* on
April 24, 2006. He wrote, *"The Prophet said, 'Whoever kills
himself with a blade will be tormented with that blade in the fires of hell.
He who throws himself off a mountain and kills himself will throw himself
downward into the fires of Hell forever and ever.... Whoever kills himself
in any way in this world will be tormented in that way in Hell.' "*

I've heard other words for suicide as well; and in my mind, "self-
felony" and "murder of self" are the worst. Unfortunately, the culprit
cannot be punished by any court of law. Or, as the Prophet says, that
person will be punished in hell for all eternity.

People still talk about suicide in a whisper. They can barely get the
word out because they think it is such a horrific act. While suicide is
no longer a sin in the eyes of most religions—we didn't have to bury
Paul away from the rest of the dead community at our cemetery—sui-

cide begets stigma. Most of us are still not educated enough to understand how much pain would cause one to finally commit that act. I certainly didn't know what I, as a survivor after Paul's suicide, was up against.

Even my mother wouldn't use the suicide word although she talked about killing herself for years. When up against the real thing—that her grandson had killed himself—and she was asked what happened, she screeched with a look of terror on her face, "Something terrible!" She refused to give out any details. She refused to tell her friends at the retirement home where she lived what had happened, and she didn't like it when people asked personal questions. Details about serious illnesses, cancer, and how people died are too personal for others to know about.

I never understood her old-school need for secrecy or her need to keep the Pink Elephant in the closet. To her a death from a physical illness was tragic enough—a suicide from mental illness was too shameful and horrible to talk about.

Soon after Paul died, I began to write journal entries guided by a book called *Mourning & Mitzvah: A Guided Journal for Walking the Mourner's Path Through Grief to Healing*. It contains sixty exercises leading the reader through the first year of mourning in the Jewish tradition. One of the first questions has to do with asking for forgiveness. I wrote:

> *Oh why didn't you talk to me—really talk to me that last night? Instead you lied with that phony little peaceful smile on your face and then you caused me the greatest pain a mother could ever feel in life. How can I forgive you for that? So, you'll have to forgive me for not being able to forgive you for what you've done to me and your brother and your dad. You left us and I miss you so much—warts and all.*

Could our initial reactions to Paul's suicide—my inability to forgive him, Bob's anger, and Ben's refusal to address and deal with it—be the reasons why there is a prophetic admonition of suicide, why in the prophet's eye, suicide has a place in Hell forever and ever. Could the prophet have believed that suicide could never be forgiven?

Suicide

He killed himself.
He took his own life.
He ended his life.
He released his pain.
He committed suicide.

There is no gentle way to say it.
It is all the same.
What he did one night was
put himself in the bathtub and
slash his throat with a box cutter.
That's what he did.
That's the truth of it.

Calling it dying, passing away,
does not change the reality
to me and his father and his brother
who cared for him and loved him
but couldn't fix his broken mind
and keep him from his destiny—
death by suicide.

Bob often thinks that his passing was highly premeditated. After all, he bought a box cutter to tear open his throat, and he locked the bathroom door so that we would not disturb him. He thinks of his act as the ultimate "fuck you" to life, the world, and to us his parents. He left no note to explain himself. It might have helped if he had expressed remorse over what he was doing and what the consequences to us were likely to be. And he is still angry about how much damage Paul did by the act of freeing himself from a life he no longer wanted. Bob is still angry that Paul never once thought of what his action would do to us. And he is angry at his failure to recognize the path to death that Paul was on. He wrote:

> Paul's suicide was not a cry for help. He chose a time when Madeline and I would be reliably asleep. He quietly entered his bathroom and locked the door behind him. He did not put on the sink-area light that would have activated the fan and could have attracted attention. He may have used a box cutter that he specifically bought for the purpose or that he had in his own tool collection from New York. None of my tools was missing. He left no note specifically written to explain himself. He had in my view no intention of being rescued or interrupted.

> I failed to see the danger to Paul's life because his pattern was a new one. In the past, Paul would fall into mania after a time of being un-medicated. I was watching for signs of mania; I predicted to Madeline only a day before his death that he could possibly run away again. I even talked to Paul explicitly, on more than one occasion, about his apparent belief that he could act swiftly enough, if mania started, to get medical help. But in this instance, un-medicated Paul descended into a deepening depression with none of the signs that I was watching for. There were indeed signs that he was in trouble—he was reclusive, he stayed in his dark room every night by him-

self, he didn't eat with us anymore, he didn't communicate with us, and he wasn't making a lot of phone calls anymore. His mother saw those signs and worried about him. I took his growing refusal to stop and talk to me as hostility, and felt offended, but not alarmed. I was waiting for another manic break.

That was his pattern. A depression would follow mania, and then he'd be calm for a while. Then, if he wasn't taking his medications—and I was pretty sure he wasn't taking them at the time of his death—he'd become manic again. Like in the past he'd run away, spend a lot of money, make hundreds of phone calls. That was his pattern. I was expecting him to act as he had in the past. I expected to be chasing him all over the country again and trying to get him hospitalized against his will.

I am saddened that he is gone. I miss the little boy child that I remember. I miss Paul's impromptu piano performances in our family room. I miss the dream that he would get well or at least stay medicated, marry Janet, and live happily ever after. I miss Paul the computer expert, who would find the cause of various problems in our office computer systems and cure them for us. I miss the interactions that I saw between Paul and our neighbor's little girl—Paul playing piano for her or holding her in his lap and showing her how to use the computer. She asked when she was told that Paul got sick and went to heaven, "Who is going to play the piano for me?" I miss the dream that he might some day be a father to my grandchildren.

But, I do not miss the worry, the painful interactions with Paul. He could be and often was a pain in the ass. I do not miss the frequent feeling that I ought to throw him out of the house and ask that he never return. I do not miss the uncertainty regarding what will happen next. I do not miss the nights

that I went to bed with our bedroom door locked and a baseball bat under our bed to defend myself against an attack that
never came, when in reality Paul wasn't a violent person. He
just talked in a threatening way once in a while.

I do not miss meeting Paul in New York restaurants, with
him talking crazy and his eyes wild and frightening. I do not
miss the trips to various places to put Paul into or take him
out of mental hospitals. I am at peace with the end of the long
nightmare, even if it has left my heart and that of his mother
aching.

Contrary to Bob's view, I wanted desperately to believe Paul didn't
plan his suicide so carefully. I wanted to believe he would have considered and cared about what his suicide would have done to us. Early on
I thought he may have been thinking about it for a day or so, he may
have bought the box cutter for that sole purpose, but I believed he took
that fatal step because the voices in his head told him to, that he was at
the mercy of the voices. I still believe he did not have some well-
thought-out, uncaring plot. I have to believe that. I can't believe that
he cared so little about us that he thought nothing about the pain he
would cause us. He always told me he loved me. How could a son who
loved his mother choose to do such a thing to her?

Even though I worried about him and how depressed he was, I
didn't think he would take his life. Though I sometimes feared he
would, that he suicided (a new verb that people with suicide in their
lives like to use) was a complete surprise to me. I, like Bob, believed a
manic episode would be the next event in Paul's life.

But I now know he was predisposed to it. He had bipolar disorder,
he was depressed, and his love, Janet, had just left him for another man.

There was no way to save him from that. Jamison gave those three factors in her book, *Night Falls Fast,* as sure signs that suicide was in the offing. Unfortunately, I read her book after Paul died, so I didn't see those signs. Before his death I didn't even know what signs to look for. And I didn't know that Janet had left him not only because Paul refused to take care of himself but because she had another man in her life. I didn't know that until months after his death.

I developed my own theory that the voices told him to take his life to make me feel better. To excuse me from the guilt. To excuse me for not getting my head out of the sand and confronting him and getting him help—all the things that I've gone over and over in my mind. All for naught. All in hindsight. Things I could never have done anything about.

After reading Jamison's book, I know I was an ignorant fool. I failed him; I didn't take his depression seriously enough. And I failed myself. Yet, had I saved him that one time would I ultimately save him? Probably not. It was his destiny. He was on his way to suicide from the minute he had his first manic break. His intelligence also worked against him. He was smart enough to know what was in store for him for the rest of his life. He knew there was no way out of the pain and struggle. Sure he would get a little better—or seem to get a little better—or we hoped he was getting a little better, but really he wasn't. Even though he could appear to be perfectly normal—the people he worked for at the internet service provider had no idea he was sick and were in total shock at the news of his suicide—he never was totally well again after his first manic break. He could be calm one minute and agitated the next. He had trouble sitting still, he couldn't sleep, he shied away from crowds, and he never was free from the voices. Nothing—no nothing—

could make him whole again. Bipolar disorder has no cure. According to Jamison, other factors in his predisposition to suicide were his age and sex—he was a young male. All together he had all the factors of a candidate for suicide. And I, his mother, should have known all of this.

So, as Bob said, his suicide wasn't a cry for help. He knew what to do to end it all with one swipe of the knife. Yet, like my fantasy that the voices told him to do it, I believed he was too selfish, too self-confident, too much into his music and his possessions to do it. Also, he didn't talk about it. Possibly that was why he refused to talk to us. He was on his way out. Like when I decided to leave my first husband. I stopped talking to his parents and wouldn't return their calls when I knew I was going. I didn't want anything to get in my way.

So please take this information, anyone out there who is experiencing bipolar disorder in their family. Listen to me out there. **Bipolar disorder has no cure.** You can control it with drugs if you're lucky enough to have someone in your care who will stay on drugs. But if there is any slip, the result could be fatal.

Paul abused his medications—the ones he took for the mania and depression and the drugs to help him sleep, calm down the voices in his head, and to ease the shaking, rocking and agitation effects of akathisia—a common side effect of the psychotropic medications he was taking.

This is so typical of people with manic depression. Once they begin to feel better, the first thing they do is stop taking their pills. After a while, when Paul felt the beginnings of what he called "shallow mania," he would self-medicate with marijuana and alcohol and his anti-mania medication if he had any around.

He would take them in fits and starts—sometimes on them, sometimes off. And I later learned from the literature about the causes of teenage and young-adult suicide, that these drugs can cause suicide, especially when they are abused. And I have to ask, why are these warnings just for children and young adults? Why not warn anyone—no matter what age—who needs to take these drugs that suicide could very well be a side effect?

The literature about the antidepressant drug, Prozac, states:

> Antidepressants increased the risk of suicidal thinking and behavior (suicidality) in short-term studies in children and adolescents with major depressive disorder (MDD) and other psychiatric disorders... Adults with MDD or co-morbid depression in the setting of other psychiatric illness being treated with antidepressants should be observed similarly for clinical worsening and suicidality, especially during the initial few months of a course of drug therapy, or at times of dose changes, either increases or decreases. The following symptoms, anxiety, agitation, panic attacks, insomnia, irritability, hostility, aggressiveness, impulsivity, akathisia (psychomotor restlessness), hypomania, and mania *[all symptoms Paul exhibited],* have been reported in adult and pediatric patients being treated with antidepressants for major depressive disorder as well as for other indications, both psychiatric and nonpsychiatric.

Now they tell me. At the time of Paul's death, I had no idea.

That's the bittersweet part. Now there's more and more information about bipolar disorder and more and more information about the side effects of the antidepressants or selective seratonin reuptake inhibitors (SSRI), as they are now called, that they use to treat it. My son died too soon to benefit. Hopefully, others can be saved and go on to live normal lives with this disease as a result of all this new information and research.

Jamison also writes that most suicides don't leave notes. Or if they do, they are simple, non-explanatory—like "Merry Christmas' or "Do not enter, call the paramedics." We looked for a note and found none. I combed his writings, I broke into his computer, I listened to his music, and I canvassed his friends and associates and found nothing. That is until we heard from the coroner's office.

Six weeks to the day after Paul's death we received a form letter from the Los Angeles Coroner's property office that we could come and retrieve the personal effects the coroner seized from his room the morning they took his dead body away. There were only two items on the list—one was an essay written by his cousin, Yael, that I had reproduced for him the night before and I'm sure he never read. The other was a checkmark on the line item, "suicide note," and described as four yellow hand-written pages.

Suicide note? We never knew of a suicide note. No one ever told us that morning when our house was swarming with police and the people from the coroner's office and the man they sent from the victim's assistance service to try and calm us down that they found a note. For six weeks we had believed there was no note.

Questions kept running through my mind. Where did they find it? He didn't normally write on yellow paper. He used a small notebook with pale green paper. Did he have it in his pocket? Was it blood stained?

Within minutes I called the coroner's and got directions to an office east of Downtown Los Angeles, and we were on our way.

My heart was turning over. I was still asking questions. What could he have written? Did he blame me for something I had said to him the night before? I kept going over and over that last conversation in my mind. What I had said, what he had said, what I didn't say, how I had let him walk out of that room without a hug, how he walked into his dark bedroom alone, and I didn't have the sense to go after him. How I just let him go, how I believed him when he said he didn't mind not seeing Janet. Of course he minded. Obviously he minded. He proved he minded by killing himself, didn't he?

Bob also worried about what was on that note. Maybe he was too intrusive in his life, maybe he expected too much from him, maybe he shouldn't have begun to push him to move out. But, after all, he was working full time, he had some money, he could afford an apartment. We gave him everything—food, room, car, gas, telephone. Bob thought we made it too comfortable for him. I didn't think so. He was so fragile. He wasn't ready to take on the responsibility of a full-time job and an apartment and care for himself. Bob and I sometimes argued about that, but I always won. In the end, Bob agreed. Caring for our mentally ill son was our assignment—for as long as necessary.

We made the drive from our home at the beach to the coroner's office in less than half an hour—and for a change I didn't complain about Bob's lead foot. A young lady at the reception desk gave us a parking pass and told us to wait on a bench in the lobby. I fidgeted while Bob tried to look calm. We held our hands together so tightly I thought they would meld into one. Finally, it was our turn.

We were ushered into a cubical so tiny it only had room for the two chairs we were told to take. In front of us was a glass wall with a little slot for passing paper back and forth. In front of Bob's chair on my right was a door, which we surmised was for passing larger objects through. Scientist that Bob is, he stuck his hand through the slot to measure the thickness of the glass—about an inch and a half, he decided.

Finally, a short balding man with a huge belly came to the window. Bob gave him the form letter and his picture ID. The man looked down on the papers and the ID, looked at Bob's face, and checked the signatures. Then, he went to get the "property." We waited some more. We fidgeted some more. We felt the pits in our stomachs grow.

What that man pushed through that slot wasn't a suicide note after all. It wasn't even on yellow paper. It was another rough draft of the letter Paul wrote to Janet a month before his death, and it was written on the same pale green paper, obviously torn out of his notebook. All that agony for nothing. We still had no clue except our own conjectures— mine that his decision to kill himself was a totally impulsive act triggered by the voices in his head and Bob's that it was a carefully planned event. Paul couldn't help himself, but the coroners could have helped causing us so much anguish six weeks later.

I was so angry that when I got home I immediately called the volunteer who came to our house on the day Paul's body was discovered to comfort and support us. How could he have let this happen? He had been downstairs in Paul's room. He knew what the people from the coroner's office were taking away. He knew what was on the list. Didn't he know what the later repercussions would be? I was talking to him and shaking so badly I could hardly hold the phone. It was as if I was being put through this nightmare again and again. There was no way for me to escape the fact that he was dead. The reality of it was bombarding me from all sides.

Of course the volunteer was contrite. Of course he was consoling. But at that moment I was inconsolable. I thought the whole thing had been very badly handled, with Bob and me at the receiving end. Again, I hoped my complaints were heard and that no one else would have to be put through such a thing again.

Almost a year after his death, I wrote a suicide note for Paul. Of course, I wrote this, not Paul, yet in revisiting it several years later, I think it was honest and representative of his feelings about music.

Dear Mom and Dad,

Music was the most important part of my life. I lived for music and when I couldn't play anymore, I couldn't continue. So I want my legacy to be about music. I want others to have the kind of opportunity I had to pursue my dream, to go to the kinds of schools that I went to, to nurture their talent and to be given a chance to be whom they want to be. I left a huge amount of music around. I hope others will get to hear it so that they can know what I represented. With music I could be myself. I could be honest and true. As a sick person I wasn't me. I only lied as an escape from the reality of my pain and illness. It was not how I want to be remembered. I couldn't help the lies, and I don't want you to remember me as a liar. Remember me as an artist. As an artist I was my true and honest self. My art gave me all the spirituality I ever needed.

So I would like my music and my love of music to live on. Compile my music and offer it to others either as gifts or as a way of raising funds to promote jazz education. Let that be my legacy. Let that keep me alive.

Early on after Paul's death I still heard him (or imagined that I heard him). One Friday night I looked at Bob's watch at about six thirty, the time Paul usually came home from work. I then "heard" the garage door and expected him to walk upstairs and into the kitchen at any moment. He would usually go to the pantry and grab a handful of almonds and peer over the stove into the family room, chewing and staring and maybe saying a few words to us as we watched the evening news. But of course he didn't do any of those things. Later on I looked for a bag of almonds that I bought the week before he died. I couldn't find it at first. Could he have eaten them? No. There they were hidden in the basket where I keep nuts and dried fruits on the shelf in the kitchen pantry. No. He hadn't come back. It's like when I couldn't find the original copy of his poem that we read at his memorial service. I got so panicked. Had he hidden it from me? No. I had hidden it from myself maybe so I wouldn't have it as a reminder—I stuck it in the drawer of the little table in our bedroom. When I found it, I immediately memorized it—an almost unheard of feat for me. I can't even remember the words to my own poems.

I've heard that grief begins to affect our physical well-being if we don't let it out. So when I found myself crying, I figured it was a good thing. The tears were spontaneous. I cried when I looked at the wonderful family picture we took in February 1999—just months before the suicide. We all looked so well and happy, so full of hope now that Paul seemed like himself again. We could breathe a little easier, and you could see it in our smiles and the way Paul had draped his arm over his brother's shoulder.

But I couldn't let Bob see me cry because he'd get a funny look on his face, like a what's-wrong-with-you look. As if he were asking, "Should

I get you some help? Should I take you to the hospital?" He couldn't get it through his head that I needed my crying moments—that the crying helped me. So I had to hide my tears from him—steal away my real feelings from him. He kept asking me how I felt—several times a day. "How are you doing?" I assured him I was okay. I had to put on my "okay" mask because I thought he couldn't stand anything less.

At first I wanted to take that mask off and be my true self. But, I couldn't. I had learned so well that I must hide how I felt from most people. They were content to hear me say "I'm okay" when they asked. Most didn't probe any deeper, most didn't want to know anymore. Even when Bob probed, I knew he didn't want to know more either. He only wanted to make sure I was still sane, that I wasn't having a breakdown like my grandmother after her daughter died. So, I stayed sane and in control for him. Later on I realized how much putting that mask on and the playacting really helped me. I showed my okay-I'm-fine face out there, and pretty soon I began to look and feel okay and fine.

Unfortunately, my body knew differently. When my stomach hurt, when my chest burned, when the left side of my head and face ached, when I couldn't keep food in my stomach, my body was letting me know that no matter what I said, no matter how well I covered it up, my body wouldn't let me off the hook. My stomach problems started while Paul was still alive. When I first heard something was wrong with him way back in March 1993, I almost couldn't listen to all the details before I had to rush down the hall to the bathroom. After a couple of years of such reactions, I finally went to the doctor who suggested I give up dairy products. And that seems to work for me. I tell people I'm lactose intolerant, but I also have reactions after eating greasy foods as well. But, I'm lucky. My body seems to be in great health otherwise. Working out regularly to help me get through my grief has had its physical benefits too.

I found that I wasn't happy being with people, and I wasn't happy alone. I just wasn't happy, period. I also feared that my unhappiness would eventually drive Bob away. He was so loving and patient with me, and I'd just clam up. I was like ice. He looked deep into my eyes. He searched for clues. I gave him none because I saw the pained look on his face when I shared with him how I felt. He couldn't make me better, and he knew it. But that hurt him, so I didn't want him to know how I felt. Probably I should have sought out help—a therapist, anti-depressants, more meditation time—but I just couldn't. Instead I turned inward and to writing, working out and work as a comfort.

Soon after Paul's suicide I began to think about my own. I'd picture myself slashing my wrists with a double-edged razor blade—the old fashioned kind—the thin kind that my dad used in a double-edged razor. I can still see him standing at the mirror in his bathroom, in his boxer shorts and tank-style t-shirt, lathering up his face with a shaving brush and then blowing up one side of his cheek so he could drag the razor over it in short upward strokes. The memories of the double-edged razor and my dad—who was so much in love with Paul and Paul with him—seemed to tie things together so neatly that it made those suicide thoughts even more enticing and comforting.

I'd think about putting myself in the downstairs bathroom and doing it there. In the same tub where Paul did it. I would see myself over and over getting into that tub and settling in there for rest and relief from my pain. I couldn't shake the pain. I needed a way to release it. In those early days after Paul died, I understood him more than ever because I wanted to do the same thing.

Not even Ben's presence saved me from these thoughts. Yet, I knew they were just thoughts. I was depressed. I had no interest in anything. I had no enthusiasm. I felt like I was walking a thin line between being alive and being dead—like the double edge on that razor I kept thinking about. I was numb, tired—sick to my stomach—and my heart hurt.

I knew in those first months that I didn't want to get better. Getting better meant that I was accepting that Paul was dead. I just couldn't bring myself to accept that. So, I kept wallowing in it some more. I wasn't ready to give up my grieving and the pain.

It took me about six months to get over my suicidal thoughts. Maybe it was the passage of time. Maybe I was like my mother. I couldn't do it anymore than she could. For years she said she didn't want to live anymore. But while she was still healthy, she wanted to know what the next day would bring. And so did I.

So I started coming back from the darkness little by little. I started working out again, I started to get more involved in work, I became more interested in my writing. All these things kept bringing me out.

But most important, I could never hurt Bob and Ben like that. It would be devastating to them. One suicide in the family is enough. Just the thought of Bob finding my body in the same room and same tub where he found Paul was enough to put the brakes on my suicidal thoughts. Besides, I am not manic-depressive. I am not predisposed to suicide. I was only a distraught mother trying to cope with the death of her beloved first-born son. Suicide is not my destiny. Even though the literature says that family members are very likely to commit suicide after the suicide of someone close to them, it truly wasn't—isn't—for me.

Once when I thought Bob was reading my journal about wanting to take my life, I left him a note: "I am not mentally ill like Paul—not to worry."

Another thing that saved me is my vanity. No matter what, I still cared how I looked. I still looked at myself in the mirror a million times a day. I still fussed over my make up, my hair. On the one hand I thought about death, on the other I worried that I looked old and ugly and that I must primp to keep looking good. I was a total paradox.

Today I wear a turquoise bracelet on my right wrist. It says "Stop Suicide" with the telephone number for the local Suicide Prevention Hotline. I wear it for my own comfort and not because I believe the five dollars I paid for three of these bands will stop suicide. In all the time that I've worn it, very few people have asked what it says. Yet I must wear it. It keeps Paul close to me. I carry him and the suicide-word with me every day and night of my life.

Years, Months, and a Day

Joplin, Hendrix
and Morrison all died
at twenty-eight the year
before you were born.

Only one more day and
it will be ten years
since we found you,
three months shy
of twenty-eight,

that day when
we knew we would never
hug you, kiss you
or have to worry about you
ever again.

CHAPTER SEVEN

T wo months before Paul died, Bob, Paul, Ben, and I went out
to dinner to celebrate Ben's birthday at a local restaurant in
downtown Manhattan Beach—one of our old standbys that's
been around for years and years. We know the owner and the hostess
who always greet us with a kiss on each cheek.

After dinner the boys walked together ahead of us as we went to retrieve our car. It was such a pleasure to see them talking and palling
around again. They hadn't seen each other for a while since Ben was in
summer school at A.C.T. He had just come down for the weekend.

When we got home, we all sat down in the family room, and Ben
began to play Bob's guitar. He and Paul sat together on the couch—
Bob and I sat at the dining table. As Ben played Paul got up and looked
closely at Ben's fingers to see what chords he was playing, and then he
went over to the piano and began to play along, easily picking out the
tune.

My Jazzman

My jazzman
beat it out
on the mighty eighty-eights,
played those riffs,
tapped his feet
bent his head
down to the keys,
felt those sounds
on his fingertips.
Yeah, he was a hot man
on those eighty-eights.

But all too soon
his bag grew dark.
He went down,
deep down.
My jazzman
played the blues,
lost that spark,
closed the lid.
And, yeah, you got it right,
quit the scene,
laid himself down
in that bone yard
for the big sleep.
Yeah, for the really big sleep.

Bob and I watched and listened with pleasure. It was such a happy scene. We were all together, the boys were warm and friendly to one another, and Paul seemingly so healthy and creative again. I kept thinking during that evening that maybe we were over the hump at last. Maybe the old Paul had come back at last. He was playing music again and he was interacting again. The music was beautiful. It was Paul's jazz.

Paul and Ben, Thanksgiving 1996

My jazzman. That he was. Very early, from the time he could sit up on his own, I'd perch him up on the piano bench and he'd tinkle on the keyboard. He loved it, he listened, he sang along. He knew the words; he could pick out the tunes. He was a natural. Nothing was too hard, nothing out of reach. All he needed was the piano—and wow, could he play.

I can still see his fingers on the keyboard—curved, moving up and down quickly, lightly, easily negotiating difficult runs back and forth. We were in such a hurry to have his fingers separated. It's as though we knew how important that would be to him and his chosen profession.

I remember how his hands looked—a bit deformed—his ring fingers were the same length as his middle fingers, and he had scars that looked like cross-hatching between his fingers. But I can't remember how his hands felt. I can't remember if they were smooth or rough. I don't remember how his hands felt in mine.

Formal music lessons started when he was seven, but didn't last long. He had no interest in practicing, so we didn't push it. Instead he went to Karate class, played chess, and after learning a few magic tricks entertained us with his new skill. He loved to perform. Having an audience never bothered him so he was elated when he got the lead in a school play in second or third grade. In fourth grade he took up the saxophone at school. The instrument was rented, the lessons were free, and he played a bit and not well—his bumpy performances at home made Bob and me wince—but it sure whet his appetite to play music.

He showed an enormous interest in music even when he was very little. He'd say, "I want to watch a record" when he lay down on our old red-and-black plaid sofa for his naps, still so young that he confused watching television and listening to a vinyl record on the turntable. "More Cat Stevens, Mommy," he'd demand from the back seat of our Chrysler fake-woody station wagon, singing along as early as two years old with Cat while he clutched his stuffed green turtle next to his cheek.

He could carry a tune and sing all the nursery rhymes at that age too. He respected music. As soon as he first discovered the piano and tried to figure out how to make it work, he made sensitive and melodic sounds by touching each of the keys individually rather than slapping and banging his hands down on the keyboard.

After a year of sax he asked for a synthesizer. He was ten years old at the time, and Bob asked, "A synthesizer is a keyboard instrument, isn't it?"

"Yes," Paul said.

"It has the same keyboard as our piano, right?" Bob asked.

"Yes," Paul said.

"Okay, learn the piano and we'll get you a synthesizer for your Bar Mitzvah when you're thirteen," said Bob.

And from that point on we didn't have to worry about him practicing again. He was so motivated that he practiced without any prodding at all, and he made such great progress in his first year of lessons he blew his little-old-lady piano teacher away. He and I both decided to learn how to play "Chariots of Fire," and by the time of his first recital after just one year of lessons, Paul was able to play it by heart without a hitch—something I was never able to master. He also got into Bach, the Beatles, and started to become interested in jazz.

Of course the synthesizer materialized in time for his Bar Mitzvah and he was off and running. Then came the amps, the drum machines, computer—aided composition, the recorders, the stereo chorus, the mike stands, the power strips, the assorted audio and MIDI cables and adapters, the headphones—one thing after another. He knew electronics and music as if they were ingrained at birth.

His synthesizer and computer skills were a perfect match. He loved to come into my office to "play" with my first personal computer. He became our personal technician. He knew how to put our equipment together or troubleshoot if something didn't work properly.

1981 in fourth grade—in our family room performing on the saxophone

Cat Stevens Then and Now

As I walked up the stairs I heard Cat Stevens singing
the familiar words of his song, "Morning has Broken,"
and there I was back in 1973
in our old gray Chrysler station wagon
with the fake wood trim, red-leather seats,
and Paul was sitting in the back,
belting out the words with him. He was only two then,
still clutching his green stuffed turtle for dear life
as we drove along.
His fat cheeks were rosy red, his blonde hair
cut like an upside-down cereal bowl around his face.
Then I return to this day and my table at the
westside mall where the lunch crowd
is beginning to gather not knowing or caring how I grieve
for the chubby little boy sitting in his car seat
when so little made him happy.

The turning point came when he was ready to start high school. We decided he wasn't a good candidate for our local, public high school, and we began to investigate private schools in our area. The only one we had heard of was the Chadwick School, south of us in Palos Verdes. But at our interview there we found out about another option, Crossroads School in Santa Monica, about the same distance north of us. Crossroads had great academic credentials. It was like the "Fame" school in New York, described to Paul's delight by the television show of the same name. Old converted factory buildings contained the classrooms with the play yard/meeting area/parking lot located in the alley behind the school buildings. It fostered musicians and actors in its arts program. Paul interviewed there as well and fell in love with it.

Paul had always been an underachiever at school, but he tested well, so it wasn't surprising that both schools accepted him. He chose Crossroads—a perfect match for him. He fit in right away whereas he never had been accepted socially at the public schools he attended in Manhattan Beach. He was an intellectual, not in the beach volleyball playing set, not the blonde surfer, not the soccer champ—even though he tried all of those sports when he was younger. He also tried tennis and running with his brother, but found Karate, break dancing, and later on watching "The Rocky Horror Picture Show" on Saturday nights more his speed. He was gentle, non-competitive, and very sensitive. And he didn't care that he was not a jock because he was so confident of the skills he had. The boys in Manhattan Beach bullied him and beat him up because of it. From his first days at Crossroads he knew he had found his place. He had found a group of artistic and talented people like him. I don't think he was ever more content than during those high school years.

It turned out, Crossroads School planned to inaugurate a jazz ensemble during his freshman year. And from the day of his piano audition to get admitted into the jazz program, the head of the music department was in love with him. Though the rest of the faculty was still wary of his lack of motivation academically, she became his mentor and protector. Not surprisingly, his prowess in music jump-started positive academic achievements for him. By the time he graduated high school, he excelled in both music and academics. He got the school's jazz music award in both his junior and senior years, and he was accepted to every college he applied to.

Paul was a one-friend-at-a-time kind of guy, and he was loyal to each of them. In his grade school years it was Scott whom he knew from Hebrew School. They played chess and Dungeons and Dragons together. During middle school it was Shawn. They started a disc jockey business together and entertained at several parties. In high school his best friend was Martin. Martin came from Newport Beach and lived on his own as a freshman at age fourteen in an apartment in Santa Monica. As a result Martin spent a lot of time at our house. I was immediately amazed at his sophistication and ability to be so self-sufficient at such a young age. That his parents allowed and encouraged it amazed me. And Martin knew a lot about music. Early on I thought he was a better musician than Paul. He played more flamboyantly, but Paul had better skills and was more intent, more sensitive, and more adept at the intricacies of it. Martin played a role. He was for show, but at first that show very much impressed Paul and me.

Martin would spend most Friday nights at our house. He and Paul would stay up all night playing music and composing. The next morning while they were still asleep, we would find a tape waiting for us in the entry hall of our house. It was their night's work. A new composition in one night!

Martin also was in the jazz ensemble during their first year at Crossroads, but he never was too serious about it. He didn't like to practice.

Nor was he too serious about school. Even so, he and Paul remained friends for the rest of Paul's life. I think Martin thought he had failed Paul and us because Paul wouldn't listen to him or allow him to help him when Paul was the sickest. Martin and the rest of Paul's good friends, as much as they tried, couldn't get him to save himself.

Martin came to his funeral and to our house afterward and he knelt down in front of me as we spoke. I stroked his cheek and said, "You're a beautiful boy." He's tall and dark haired, and he has full cheeks and large dark eyes. His two little girls look like him. He came to our house many times after Paul died. He copied every one of his tapes and recorded them onto CDs for us. He also documented his musical instruments that we later donated to the Crossroads school.

Eric, the head of the newly-formed jazz ensemble at Crossroads, was a professional saxophonist. Paul worshipped him and was always ready to take his advice—about music and life. Eric, a big guy with ruddy skin and short blonde hair, was a freshman teacher when Paul was a freshman student. He played along with the ensemble and performed his solos in turn with the rest of the band. He took a liking to Paul, always featuring one of his original songs. He asked Paul to sit in at his gigs once in a while—Paul at the piano, Eric on sax. We knew him and liked the music opportunities he had offered Paul. Paul had really blossomed not only as a musician but also as a person under Eric's tutelage.

Except Paul met his first lover at a Christmas party at Eric's house. And that's where it all began to go downhill—at least in my mind.

At first Paul described his love interest as someone a bit older, but two weeks after they began going out he asked that we meet after dinner, that he had something to tell Bob and me. He had always told us the truth about what was going on with his life—that is, before he got sick—and this time was no exception.

We met in the downstairs den while Ben did the dishes. He sat on the bentwood-and-cane chair at the desk. Bob and I sat on the little mustard-colored, upholstered sofa bed. The darkness of the room added to the mysteriousness of the meeting. I kept staring at the deep brown wallpaper with a pattern of scrolls in shades of beiges and orangey rusts that kept repeating itself in stripes around the room. It was kind of cozy but busy at the same time. The dark room mirrored my anxiety about what he was about to tell us. I was nervous. I kept thinking: had he gotten his new girlfriend pregnant already, was he planning to drop out of school. It could have been any number of things typical of a seventeen-year-old high-school senior—drinking, drugs, car accidents—any catastrophe imaginable.

He turned his chair to face us, crossed one leg over the other and swung his foot.

"I wasn't exactly telling the truth about this woman I'm seeing," he said. "She is older, much older."

"How old?" I asked. Bob kept quiet.

"Thirty-two," he said.

My stomach turned over. This was not something typical. This was not even close to what I had imagined. I never would have conjured this up if I were writing a novel.

She belongs in jail, I thought. Paul is only seventeen years old. He's jailbait. Bob still didn't say anything, but I could only imagine what he was thinking. I knew that his brother had had an affair with a teacher while he was in high school and Bob had always envied that. I couldn't look at either of them. I looked over to the glass and wood bookcases in front of me, then to our reflections in the mirrored closet doors to my right. I turned back to Paul.

"She's not a student at UCLA?"

He looked straight into my eyes with those big blue eyes of his and grinned. He looked so proud of himself. He even giggled a little bit as he did when he was enjoying one of his own jokes.

"No."

"Then what does she do?" Bob asked.

Finally he's taking an interest, I thought.

"She has her own business. She's a graphic artist and photographer."

"What else?" I asked. "Is she married?"

He looked down, pulled his leg higher over his knee.

"Not now. She's divorced."

"What about her ex?" Bob asked.

Paul looked away, and then said quietly, "I haven't met him yet. But, she says he gets pretty jealous when other guys come around."

My stomach turned over again. I had to also worry about whether this ex-husband of hers would find my son with her and what he might do to him.

"Any children?" I asked.

He bent down and picked a piece of white thread off the carpet. He twirled the thread around his right thumb and index finger and then dropped it on the desk.

"She has a little boy four years old. He's a great kid. I like him a lot."

Paul always had liked little children. When he was little he was very loving to Ben, and he liked to play with his younger cousins. I have so many photos of him with a huge smile on his face while he's holding them.

"The full catastrophe," Bob chimed in, quoting Zorba. "No wonder her ex doesn't want other men over there." Then he asked, "How did you meet?"

Paul smiled again, the little smile that didn't show his teeth.

"At Eric's house. At his Christmas party."

"Eric introduced you? Where does he get off introducing a kid your age to a thirty-two-year-old woman?" I said.

I looked at Bob wanting reinforcements from him, but Bob was much calmer than I was. It pissed me off to think he was probably living out his own sexual fantasies through his young son.

"Well, he didn't exactly introduce us. She was just there. We starting talking, and we hit it off. Then Eric thought it was a good idea if we got together," he stopped for a second, looked down at the floor, then continued, "for my first time, you know."

Bob was smiling. I was stunned. A teacher pimping for my son. A teacher inviting a kid to an adult party. What was he thinking?

"Mom, Dad," Paul said. "I love her. I want you to meet her. I'd like you to have her over for dinner. Could we ask her over on Friday night?"

Love her? He barely knew her. And he was barely old enough to know the definition of love. How could he know he loved her? My insides were screaming.

At that point I could have said over my dead body would I invite her over. I could have called the police and had her charged with child molestation. And I could have turned Eric into the school headmaster. But I didn't call the police. I didn't go to the school. Bob was totally against doing any of that. His only concern was her ex-husband and how he would react to another man in his wife's bed.

So we went along with Paul and had his woman friend, Susan, over for dinner later that week. We thought making a legal fuss over their relationship was a sure way to lose our son. And, besides we were curious about her.

However, I did confront Eric, and he denied having anything to do with my son's romantic situation. He claimed he had invited them both to his party, and they got together on their own. I still regret not discussing the matter with the school's headmaster—another time I stuck my head in the sand. This woman not only introduced my son to sex and marijuana, she broke his heart right before he entered his third year of college. Their affair had been bumpy. With him across the country in college and her with a business and a young son, how could it have been anything else? Though they lived together briefly the summer after his freshman year, he left her because he just wasn't ready to play house, and he lived at home until he went back to school in the fall. Then they got back together the next summer until she broke it off. I really don't know why except that maybe she was tired of the hassle and my nasty looks every time I saw her with him. I was glad and very concerned about how heartbroken he was. Right after their final breakup he went with us to visit family in Chicago and Green Lake, Wisconsin, and he cried throughout the weekend. It broke my heart to see him get on the plane from there to go to New York. Although he met Janet very soon afterward, he was fragile when it came to love from that time until his death.

Even so, his music career pressed on. Besides his professional gigs with Eric, Paul began to have a regular night at our country club, playing piano in the bar. That gig continued during his summer breaks until he got sick and couldn't be relied on to show up.

Paul knew early on just where he wanted to go. When we suggested he have a fall-back major listed on his college applications, he said at the mature age of seventeen, "From my experience if you take something as a fall-back position, then you are going to fall back." He had his heart set on being a jazz musician, and we had no choice but to go along with him.

I was working out in our garden when the mail arrived. Paul retrieved it and came outside to find me, holding a large envelope in his hand. I had never seen him so excited. He was age seventeen and had just received notification that his application to the New School jazz program in New York City—a new program—was accepted. "Can I go?" he asked. And of course I said yes without a moment's hesitation even though he had already begun the process of matriculating as a freshman at California State University at Northridge, where his mentor Eric had graduated. Though I was worried that he would start college so far from home at such a young age, I had two motives: one—satisfy his desire to further develop his music ability, and two—get him away from this older woman he was so in love with. That love was tearing us all apart. It gave him a false sense of maturity and independence. He had begun to come and go as he pleased, take the screen off his bedroom window and climb out into the yard to sneak away, stay out all night against our orders, and act like no one—not even his parents—had any hold on him or control.

I thought this could be a natural breaking point. Little did I know that we still had a long way to go before that affair would be over. Little did I know that a lot of damage was yet to be done. Little did I know that Paul was not ready to take on New York that early in his life. He talked a good game, tried to act like an adult, but he was nowhere near being one. I let his mature talk and his show of independence sway me, and I also let my need to get him away from this thirty-two-year-old woman motivate me as well. Well he got back at me later. He blamed us for letting him go so early in his life. I blamed myself. I still blame myself.

For a while life in New York City was good for him. He kept up the pace. In fact, he walked so fast, he set the pace. And all he wanted to do was play his music. School, well, that was another story. He didn't want to stay in school. Every summer he'd argue, "Just give me a piano and an apartment, and I'll practice there. I don't need to go to school."

We would counter, "We won't support you unless you stay in school." And he stayed in school until he got sick. New York and The New School were where he honed his skills and became our jazzman.

CHAPTER EIGHT

Even after more than forty years of marriage I sometimes wake up in the morning and see Bob looking down at me with a look in his eyes that is so loving it makes me tear up. It seems like yesterday we first fell in love. He was focused, driven, so sure of himself. And his optimistic personality really attracted me. He was always up and out there—a direct contrast to my quiet, low-keyed, and shy frame of mind. Bob acted as if he could take on the world, and in those early years he did.

His wardrobe was another story. He wore crisp white shirts, wild-print ties, and well-worn brown or black shoes—those were the only shoes he owned. He had neatly buzzed blond hair and passionate blue eyes kept well hidden behind black-rimmed glasses. Now he doesn't look a lot different from those days in the spring of 1967. Of course there are a few lines on his face, and his waist that has grown an inch or two. He still has the buzz—though now his hair is mostly white.

Bob is a true Renaissance man. Although he was educated in science and mathematics, he can recite a Shakespearean sonnet at the drop of a hat, quote Goethe's couplets to a room filled with a hundred engineers, play guitar while belting out "Honky Tonk Woman" or "The House of the Rising Sun," and spend his leisure time playing racket ball, golf, Sudoku, solitaire, and his daily and two Sunday crossword puzzles. Nothing happens in the morning until he completes the crossword puzzle.

Those who know him notice he can be a tad impatient especially behind the wheel. He would rather drive through a maze of side streets than wait for a traffic light. Every chance he gets he'll wield his lead foot like a weapon of mass destruction, ignoring my protests and cries of whiplash. He just speeds on, taking great glee in pointing out other lawbreakers getting tickets along the way.

He was a hard guy to reel in, but once I did, he was truly committed to me, his sons, and even his mother-in-law. Throughout the bumpy E-ticket ride of our years together, he has been my rock, my anchor, my strength.

He has always taken on the hard jobs. He went to the hospital the morning of my father's cancer surgery. He was the first to see my father dead in his hospital bed. He argued with my mother to protect me from her. He didn't have an emotional tie to her as I, so he would take her on and challenge her whenever she treated me badly. He didn't care if he hurt her feelings. He just wanted to protect me from her accusations that I didn't call enough or invite her to dinner enough or include her in one or another of our family activities. He could take on any of the faces she wanted to present. The problem was: he'd get in a fight with her and not care if he pissed her off, and then she would blame me for it. She referred to him as "my husband" when she was angry with him. But in the end, she relied on him. She called him her financial advisor. He did her taxes. She loved him.

Forty Years

He folds her in his arms
and looks down at her
with his deep blue eyes
and a small, closed-mouth smile
that shows just the hint of dimples
in his ruddy cheeks—
the way he looked
as he stood at her apartment door
on Mentone Avenue
that first night,
his hair
straw-blond, cut short,
stuck straight up,
his beige raincoat
damp from the March drizzle,
carrying a bottle of champagne
under his arm.

He remembers how
after drinking champagne
after dancing so slow they hardly moved,
after she invited him
into her bed,
they were up all night
exploring, tasting as they got to know
and feel every inch of each other,
stroking faces, necks, thighs, feet,

kissing, mouths open,
almost swallowing each other,
coupling, coming, resting,

one on top, then the other,
spooned, joined
over and over again
until dawn and hunger
drove them out into the rain
to find a place to eat.

And though he admits nothing,
no nothing,
has ever come close
to that first night,
his memory of it
and the girl standing in the doorway,
with short dark hair,
a tight-fitting yellow dress,
black patent-leather stiletto pumps,
keep them joined together
now.

May 1970, Madeline and Bob's wedding day

When he and I finally decided to get married, getting pregnant as quickly as possible was my agenda. I was already thirty, and I was concerned about being too old to have a child. I was in a hurry and it wasn't that easy. I had a miscarriage a couple of months before Paul was conceived. That made two. I also had had a miscarriage during my first marriage.

And because Bob never seemed as interested as I in having children, I never expected him to be an attentive and devoted father. But he fell in love with Paul the moment he was born. He never missed a chance to hold him. He carried him swaddled in his receiving blanket over to the pictures on the wall, the pottery on the shelf, the books in the library, talking about every item in detail. He loved to teach, and Paul, even as an infant, wasn't too young to become his student. Bob also would pick him up when he cried at night, walk him about, and feed him a bottle of water to stave off his appetite for my breast if I was sleeping.

As Paul grew older, they had mini foot races, they played Legos, they played chess—Bob taught him the game at age four. Bob read Paul's nightly bedtime story—sometimes from a children's book, a parable from the Zen masters, or whatever subject Bob was studying at the time, be it astronomy, rocket science, or a historical event. You name it, Bob knew about it, and he imparted that knowledge to his boy with glee. When I could no longer cope with a three-year old who pooped in his pants, Bob, to his great credit, kicked me and Ben out of the house for the day and finally toilet-trained Paul, following the instructions in, *Toilet Training in Less Than A Day.*

He made many trips to New York to be with Paul while he was in college. They went to dinner at their favorite Italian or Indian restaurant, shopped for books or music, listened to late-night jazz. When Bob came to town, Paul led the way, walking as fast as a native, and never stopping for a light if he could avoid it. He was definitely Bob's son in

Ben and Paul, November 1975

that way. Bob loved to visit Paul in the town where Bob was born, in the town that Paul had adopted as his own.

Then came Bob's hardest job of all—trying to interact with Paul once he got sick. Paul stopped communicating with him. He didn't want to tell Bob how he was feeling. Paul refused to be honest with him. Paul later admitted he lied—especially about hearing voices—because he did not want to be hospitalized. He shut Bob out. He angered Bob. He made Bob feel like a failure. The job of fathering Paul became just too hard.

Here are his feelings in his own words:

> Soon after I learned in 1993 that Paul's doctors thought that he was bipolar, I began to read about this disorder. What emerged from this reading was a realization that he was at considerable risk of suicide. The statistics were horrendous and scary. However, the day-to-day experience of living through Paul's behaviors tended to drown out the fear and replace it with frustration and anger. Whether he was living in New York City and we conversed on the phone or he lived with us in Manhattan Beach, he was a difficult person to get along with. He was always a taker, selfish and nasty when pressured.

> He never did agree to adopt a long-term course of medication, and he most often chose to self-medicate with marijuana and perhaps other substances. At bottom, the fear was never really gone for me. I would ask him at times of relative rationality, "Do I have to worry about you?" His response was always the same, "Leave me alone."

> When I discovered Paul's body in the tub of our downstairs bathroom, my main feeling was a mixture of several powerful elements:

> First, I feared what this event would do to Madeline and our marriage. I watched with great sadness how my wife took

on the appearance of someone who had been deeply injured, and I knew I was powerless to help her feel better. It took years for her to begin to have something of the lightheartedness of our earlier days.

Second, I was angry with Paul. He left his body in our home for us to clean up or rather clear away. The stigma of that event was so deep that even today I think of it as the death room. And this is after Madeline magically renovated the room so that it retains nothing of its former appearance. He left no note to explain himself. It might have helped if he had expressed remorse over what he was doing and what the consequences to us were likely to be. But, of course, selfish Paul left no such thoughts. I think of his act as the ultimate fuck you to life, the world, and to us his parents. Madeline likes to say that he was a sick man and could not really help doing what he did. But I still am angry that he did so much damage by the act of freeing himself from a life he no longer wanted. I often think that his passing was highly premeditated. He bought a box cutter to tear open his throat, and he locked the bathroom door so that we would not disturb him. Did he ever once think of what he would do to his mother or me? I remember I had to open the window of the death room to allow the smell of blood and death out, and I realized immediately that this scene would stay with me until I die.

Third, I felt defensive about my behavior toward Paul. I remember feeling that I was not at fault for his death. I had worked hard to keep him moving on the road to health. For example, when he lived at home with us, I tried to monitor his consumption of meds and suggest that he needed to see his doctors when it seemed appropriate. I talked to him about the world, his work on computers, etc. He and I did not have a really good father-son connection. I tried to help him as best I could, but I failed to save him in the end and that will be with me always.

Just after Paul died, I felt the need to say goodbye to him. I spoke at his memorial service of my memory of him as a small boy playing gently with the piano and how that memory was connected to the adult, jazz piano player he became. I was aware that he was a wonderful little boy and that I loved him deeply. The man he grew to be was not so lovable, and I now realize that I lost the lovable Paul somewhere after he turned fifteen or sixteen. I think that had he not died so early he might have grown to be a continuing heartache especially for his mother.

So, it is no wonder that Bob felt relieved when Paul was finally gone. He had been such a drag on our lives. And most of all Bob didn't have to feel like a failure about Paul anymore.

Six years after Paul died, Bob had another hard job to do. Eric, Bob's son from his first marriage had been born in 1967 severely disabled by Down syndrome (Trisomy 21). Despite his disability and his appearance typical of people with Down syndrome, Eric was a beautiful child. He was also very happy and loving. Mentally he didn't develop past the first-grade level at school. Though his verbal skills were almost nonexistent, he learned to speak in sign language, and he was a good athlete winning many prizes at the Special Olympics as a runner. However, he could not care for himself. He went to a special school, had a sign language tutor, and later on as he turned into an adult he worked feeding farm animals. He especially loved music and knew exactly which songs he wanted to hear. He never lived with either of his parents, either together before their divorce or after each remarried.

Bob and I saw him often at the home of his foster parents, who kept him until he was twenty-one years old, and then at his community home in California's San Fernando Valley, run by the Valley Village non-profit organization. He loved to eat at McDonald's. He made the hand sign for hamburger as soon as we arrived to take him for lunch. He had a tendency to gobble down his food when he ate.

One afternoon in Spring 2005, Eric's caregiver called Bob to tell him that Eric had choked on a peanut butter sandwich while on a picnic at Cabrillo Beach in San Pedro and was near death at a San Pedro hospital. The Heimlich maneuver and trying to reach in his mouth to retrieve the food failed, and by the time he got to the hospital he had had no vital signs—no heartbeat, no pulse, no breathing—for about fifteen minutes. The doctors revived him and put him on a ventilator, but he was otherwise non-responsive.

Eric was still alive the next morning and underwent an electroencephalogram that showed some activity. "Maybe enough so that he could breathe on his own," the neurologist said. Yet the doctor gave us no hope that he would ever return to the normal life such as he had before the accident. Should he breathe on his own, he would be in a vegetative state. Then it became Bob's decision to keep the ventilator going or remove it. He chose, after consulting with his ex-wife—their first communication in over twenty years—to have it removed. "But wait," the doctor said, "the nurse needs to talk to you." She presented Bob with the idea of harvesting Eric's organs should he die when the ventilator was removed. That afternoon Bob returned to the hospital to see Eric for the last time and sign papers to donate his organs. Another hard job.

The next morning Eric was brought to surgery, and the doctors removed the ventilator. He took three breaths and died. Then the surgeons removed his liver and kidneys. By the end of the day his organs were keeping others alive.

Throughout Bob continued to power through and worked as though nothing had happened. Even after receiving a phone call with the news that Eric had died within minutes of the removal of the ventilator, Bob conducted a meeting with about one-hundred people in the room, never letting on what was going on in his life.

Bob says:

Eric's death by choking on a peanut-butter sandwich was an accident. More careful monitoring might have helped, but he was a severely handicapped thirty-seven-year-old man, and he was in the company of people who had his best interests at heart. My involvement in his death, if any, might be said to have started in the year of his birth when his mother and I decided that others would raise him, primarily because of his profound handicap. Of course, I might not have been able to save him had he spent his life with me, but there is that slight doubt. Comparing the deaths of Paul (a brilliant musician and computer whiz) and Eric (a Down's-syndrome child) seems a bit fruitless. They had me as their father in common, for whatever that is worth. I look at Eric's passing much as I see Paul's death: the bad luck of the genetic process. Even so, it hurts that I've lost two sons in the course of my life.

Twelve Hundred Head Shots

I scroll through them
one by one.
Each a full-face shot
in black and white.
His clothes change—t-shirt,
dress shirt, tie, suit jacket,
a sweater slung over his shoulders,
a shirt with open collar and loose hanging tie.
But the poses repeat again and again.

First his face is serious, eyes slightly squinting,
looking dark and foreboding,
his hair slicked back
not one out of place.
This guy means business or he's got a gun.
Next he shows a little half smile,
long dimples on the sides of his mouth
but no teeth.
Full, dark brows, deep,
friendly eyes
reflect the light of day.
Finally he smiles wide
showing teeth, dimples,
and crow's feet
around the eyes. His jaw is long,
square, honest.
This is a guy
you can trust to be your friend
for life.

When this young son of mine
played tournament tennis as a boy,
I sat on the sidelines at every match
with all my fingers crossed and my legs
and arms crossed
as if my body language and my wishing
could win him the point.

Now I click through the head shots
and wonder which look, which outfit
will get him a part on a TV series
as a smart-aleck lawyer or sinister gangster
or a part in a movie as the leading man's sidekick
or better yet, the role perfect for the Tyrone Power,
Laurence Harvey, or Montgomery Clift type
he's been told he is—
the role that will find us both sitting together
at the Kodak Theater
on Academy Awards night.
He in his Hugo Boss tux,
I in my long Armani gown,
waiting, holding hands,
squeezing them together until they hurt,
until his name is called,
and he goes up on stage to accept his prize.

It's all about Ben now. He was my younger son. Now he's my only son. Although I still think of him as my little boy, he's just shy of six-feet tall, growing to that height by the sheer will to be taller than his dad. He tends to be a thin guy and has the chiseled good looks of a leading man—strong chin, high cheekbones, wavy dark brown hair, and large hazel eyes. Ben is over thirty-six years old now and recently married to wonderful Marissa.

Compared to Paul, Ben always had lots of friends both his age and older, and he has always been very driven and competitive in sports and academics. He always had to be the best—as I described in a poem I wrote about him a few years ago:

A Birthday Poem for Ben (excerpt)

....You lived your young life in competition
reading the most books,
writing the most journal pages,
earning the most As,
running the fastest 10K,
collecting the most Garbage Pail Kids
and hitting the best
backhand down the line.

You loved the pressure
It made you nervous
(I said excited)
It was your fuel
You had to be the best....

However, when Ben was younger, he wasn't as good at taking care of his things as Paul. He lost or had two or three bikes stolen, and he let two cars get so run down they were no longer drivable. Yet he was a saver. While Paul spent every penny he ever earned—until the last few months of his life—Ben never took money out of his savings account. If he needed some spending money, he'd just earn it on top of what he had in his savings.

And Ben has always been very loving—as a little boy he would disrupt his play every once in a while and come over to hug my leg. Then he'd go back to be with his friends. Paul was that way early on, but not so much toward the end. They each went through the stage of crawling into our bed in the middle of the night. They came in on my side and I loved the cuddling.

Now Ben is the person I worry about the most—because he's now my only son. I think of all the disasters that could happen whenever he travels—by car, by plane, and even on foot. On days when I fear he is in danger, my heart and gut react more than ever. Now I try to hide my worries about him as best I can. After all, he is a grown up and has a wife to worry about him now. But still….

Some time ago I wrote that Ben is the reason I chose to live when I was most despondent after Paul died. That is still true. There is nothing I wouldn't give him or do for him. And even before Paul died that was so. He and I spent so much time together as he was growing up. I was his first tennis teacher and warm-up partner, and I took him to all the tennis tournaments he competed in from the time he was seven until he graduated from high school. I worked with him on his tennis attitude such that he had a reputation for being the "Iceman" on the courts. I helped him through his losses, his nervousness before a match, his strategizing, and his triumphs. Now I am the champion of his career. He comes to me for advice and I readily give it. He comes to me for editorial suggestions on the scripts he writes. And even though he doesn't come to me for monetary help anymore, I would still readily give that to him too. In fact, I made up my mind when I went back to a full-time job earning far more money than I ever made before that I would invest part of that money in his career. I never thought of it as a handout. It was an investment in his future.

Ramona

With ruler in hand, chalkboard at the ready
he stands on little high heels,
transformed as Mrs. Griggs,
a prissy old-maid schoolteacher,
easily portraying her haughty attitude with
clipped speech and fingers curling beneath her chin.
Next he hobbles across the stage bent over
bearing a cane,
dapper plaid pants, and a bowler hat.
As Hobart he struts, kicks his heels,
and sings "Ramona" a capella,
dancing like it's "no problemo."
What a sheer delight!

But still more,
he as the hard-hearted employer, Mr. Frost,
appears only once, but his words change
the tone of the entire play.
And, then he's there again
as the lively commercial boy
singing about hamburgers as if
he was raised on stage.

What impresses me most is his joy
expressed up there—
never a break from character,
always a wink and a smile.
I marvel at his skill and the joy he takes
from his acting performances.
Lucky him.

Ben was very worried about what had happened to Paul when he first became ill. He always had an admiration and love for his older brother, so when Paul had his first episode, Ben didn't understand that Paul's illness made him act so erratically, that bipolar disorder created mood swings in Paul such that he could be up and down many times in a single day. I hardly knew the repercussions of Paul's illness at the time, so how could I explain them to Ben?

One day I had a date to take Ben for lunch in Santa Monica. Paul horned in on it. He had missed his psychologist morning appointment and asked if I would drive him into Santa Monica so he could get to an appointment later in the day. Thinking it might be a nice outing for the three of us, I invited him to join Ben and me for lunch. Paul agreed, but something set him off during our drive, and as soon as we got to Santa Monica, he stormed out of the car and said he wouldn't go to a restaurant with us. Ben was furious and hurt. We both were. The drive to Santa Monica caused us a lot of extra time, and we truly missed a wonderful opportunity together. Even though Paul was no longer with us, our thoughts and anger about him were with us at that lunch. I tried to explain to Ben and mollify myself that Paul was sick, and on that day particularly Paul was at the height of a manic episode and couldn't help himself. But neither of us felt any better. We both loved and worried about Paul, and we were at a loss about how to take care of him.

Though these brothers were not particularly close, I knew they cared very much for each other. When Ben was born, Paul never showed any jealousy toward him. He was proud of him and liked to hold him when I would let him. Later on they always had to have equal time, equal things, and equal achievements—Paul learned to ride a two-wheel bike without training wheels, Ben had to learn too; Paul could swim and dive, Ben learned too; if Ben got a new tennis racket, Paul had to get a new book or record. Growing up they learned to take turns—doing the dishes, riding in the "really" back of the station wagon, as they both liked to call it, watching their favorite television shows, using the phone, listening to stations on the car radio. They had learned growing up to accommodate each other's separate tastes and interests, they had learned to value each other's expertise and talents, but with Paul's behavior so unpredictable, compromising didn't work anymore.

Ben had spinal meningitis when he was two years old and had to stay in the hospital for two and a half weeks. The morning the doctors released him, we took him with us to pick Paul up at nursery school. The two boys, who had not seen each other the whole time Ben was in hospital, ran into each other's arms.

I have a picture of them in my office. Paul was about five, and Ben about two and a half. They are outside the home we had in the Marshall Islands, dressed up to go to a Passover Seder. Paul, standing straight and tall, has a wide grin on his face, and Ben, with his hands folded in front of him, looks up at Paul in sheer awe. Another photo shows Ben shaking Paul's hand at the time of Paul's Bar Mitzvah with a proud brotherly smile on his face. And when Ben was Bar Mitzvah, Paul composed a special song for him and played it during the service. Unfortunately that tune is lost to us.

Ben worried about Paul when they were young. "He doesn't take care of his body," he said when he realized that Paul didn't eat vegetables.

Spring 1977 on Kwajalein, Marshall Island

Paul's idea of salad consisted of croutons, olives, and pickles. Ben cared about growing tall, Paul could care less. In fact he sabotaged his growth by making poor food choices and starting to smoke at age thirteen. Only when he was trying to find some way to cure his bipolar disorder, other than through medications, did he eat healthful foods, exercise, and quit smoking. But that regime didn't work either.

When Paul first got sick, Ben was in his second semester of his freshman year at the University of California at Berkeley. He normally was a straight-A student and very conscientious about his schoolwork. But he didn't end that semester with his usual A average. Besides the fact that he was very bothered about what had happened to Paul, he was practicing three hours of tennis every day as a member of the Cal tennis team, and he had just joined a fraternity and had to live in very riotous conditions that weren't conducive to his usual study habits.

Ben was in a very serious accident in Morocco soon after he graduated from Berkeley. He was on a tour of the Sahara Desert and the driver, who was speeding, lost control of his vehicle. The car rolled over five times and Ben ended up with head lacerations that needed ten stitches, and a broken shoulder, ring finger, and thumb. We had to arrange for his transport home when he was well enough to travel through Casablanca and New York. His traveling companion accompanied him as far as Casablanca, and we asked Paul to meet him in New York and help him to his flight to Los Angeles. Paul was relatively well at that time—in between manic episodes—but seeing Ben in such a debilitated state, unshaven and dirty, barely able to move, and with bandages on his head, his arm in a sling and his fingers taped up took its toll on Paul. Ben had always been the strong, athletic brother. Paul was shocked when he saw him. Very shortly afterward, Paul had another break, and we had to bring him back to Los Angeles—for the last time.

W hen Ben got the message that Paul was dead, he was devastated. He was performing in the "Three Penny Opera" on the main stage of the American Conservatory Theater in San Francisco where he was in the actor's MFA program, but he knew he had to come home immediately. Continuing to perform under those circumstances was out of the question. After Paul's funeral, Ben returned to A.C.T. to finish his last year, and that helped him get through the first few months. But after graduation, he was more down than I had ever seen him before. On his first night home, he called me out of bed at three in the morning and we sat and talked for the rest of the night. He had just broken up with his girlfriend, and he was very concerned about what lay ahead with his career. And his whole support system—the people he had just spent three years with in graduate school—was gone.

Plus, he was still grieving for Paul. Being back in our home and all its reminders—Paul's photo prominently on display, Paul's room very much the way he left it, and Ben's own memories of the two of them growing up in this home—were too hard to be around. There were just too many ghosts in our home, so it made sense that he had to get away.

Within days of his return to Manhattan Beach from San Francisco he decided to get out and go to New York City—a place he had hated for most of his life. But, he rationalized that New York was where he could hone his acting skills the best. And since most of his A.C.T. classmates—his support system—had moved there, he wanted to go there too. He said, "I felt being in the hustle and bustle of New York City was the best way to be proactive about my career and to get me out of my funk."

I couldn't tell him how broken-hearted I was about his decision to move; his decision had to be made independent of how I felt. I knew I couldn't keep him with me forever. Despite how much I needed him after Paul died, he had to fly on his own.

So he left for New York with just enough time to gather his things together and make some arrangements for a temporary place to stay once he got there. And at first his experience was not wonderful. He slept on people's couches until finally after three or four months, he found a roommate and an apartment to share. And since he didn't have much luck finding any acting jobs, he worked as a bartender. This was back when smoking was still allowed in restaurant's bar areas; he couldn't stand it. He did get one acting gig, playing a large part in an Off-Off Broadway, storefront-theater production of "Macbeth" for no pay and scant audiences. After being in New York for six months, he called to say he wanted to come back home—right away.

As much as I wanted to say "Come home, yes, come home right now, on the next plane," I persuaded him to stay—at least until he had a real plan in place about what he would do once he got back here. Believe me, I missed him so much, I worried about him so much, and I wanted him to come home more than anything. But my mother's intuition told me that would be an unwise decision. I didn't want him to come back to Manhattan Beach as hastily and without planning as the way he had moved to New York. And my instincts were right. Within a week of our phone conversation he was offered and accepted a good paying part in a children's theater production of "Ramona Quimby," a play about the Beverly Cleary character, Ramona Quimby. He traveled all over the east, south, and midwestern parts of the country with a team of actors and set, wardrobe, and makeup people for six months performing in front of first-through-fourth graders. He got his Actor's Equity credential as a result. When that gig was over he was ready to leave New York City and come home. And when he came back to Manhattan Beach, he came back as a success. He could be proud of his accomplishments and use his experience and the actor's credential he had earned on tour when he returned.

The Bully

Paul is a bully,
always waiting to take over my poems.
I'm writing about my mother
who starved herself last year,
hanging on for weeks in a morphine-induced coma,
using up every bit of energy I had
until she finally died.

And here he comes pushing her aside
to get to the front of the line.
He brags so the whole playground can hear.
"My suicide is bigger.
I used a box cutter; she just stopped eating."

And he's right.
Compared to his death
hers was a bump in the road.
He was my beautiful sick boy,
she, a not-so-nice shriveled old woman
who had wished for death for years.
She'd call me a bad daughter for saying this,
but I don't miss her at all.

When my mother came into our home the day of Paul's death, only thinking of herself instead of taking me in her arms and saying how sorry she was, I realized she would not help me at the time of my greatest need. In fact, as of that moment I took on yet another role. I became my mother's caretaker and comforter until she died five years later at age ninety-four. Her health steadily deteriorated and her mood pretty much matched her health. Yet, even though she was a difficult woman for as long as I can remember and treated so many people poorly, she didn't deserve to suffer. So when she was dying, I hoped that she would just fall asleep and drift peacefully into death. That's how she always wanted to die. Seeing her half-awake and alive was too much for me, and it must have been a living hell for her.

In the last days of her life, she looked like a skeleton with yellowish gray skin, sunken chest, and bony shoulders, legs, and arms. Her hands and arms had huge red-and-blue bruises like mottled granite in sporadic blotches. Her lips were dry, cracked, and peeling. Her mouth was crooked as she labored in deep rapid breaths. Her sparse hair stuck up.

She lay on her side with her eyes and mouth half open in the fetal position with her hands clutching the bars at the side of her bed. As she intertwined her fingers around the bars, we could see her nails like claws, badly needed a manicure—the silk wraps grown out. She could barely talk—her words were like moans—as she kept saying, "I can't take it anymore," or " I can't stand it." Mostly she gestured, sticking her hand through the bed railing when she wanted something. This was a vain woman. She would have hated to be seen that way.

While she was dying I kept thinking I ought to tell her to think about going to be with Dad and Paul. Maybe she could let go then and go in peace. But even though she was superstitious about observing the Jewish traditions, she didn't get a lot of comfort from her religion. I don't think she thought there was an afterlife. Maybe the thought of being with anybody somewhere after death was too foreign for her.

In the end, I just waited for the end. It was time. I had seen enough. I watched my father die a little bit every day for a year and a half. Her scene was much worse. Bob worried about what her death would do to me. I told him not to worry. I'd be fine. In fact, I'd be glad. I had no guilt about how I treated her. I was totally at peace with it. Her Camille deathbed scene had gone on for too, too long. She created a lot of this herself—not the broken heart valve—but her choice to stop eating about two months before she died. She finally decided to carry out the "I don't want to live anymore" words she repeated for the entire twenty-seven years since my dad died. In the end she was eighty-five pounds—down about twenty pounds from her normal weight. There was no going back anymore.

I think the reason I felt so little grief about Mom's death was because I compared it to Paul's. She lived a long life, and she made her own decisions about wasting it the way she did. I felt no remorse in that. It was all her choice. The only bad part was all the people she affected along the way with her miserable attitude and sharp tongue.

I think I've put Mom's death in the proper perspective. I am just not hung up about it. I was exhausted and very sad at the end, and I hated to see her suffer like that. But I got over the grief part of her death quickly. I still think about her and why not? She was in my life in a huge way. I was the only one of her children who lived near her. I saw her at least once a week until she got sick, and then it was almost every day. I called her regularly—she thought it was a daughter's duty to call a mother, not the other way around. We took her on family trips with us, gave her birthday parties, and I took her to doctors and hospitals during the last few years. And, I love having some of her beautiful things around me. Sharon Olds wrote a poem about her mother's last hours, how she lovingly got in bed with her and lay next to her. I couldn't have done that. My mother wouldn't have wanted me to do that. She would hardly take my hand even when she was in a coma in her last couple of days. She pushed me and my sister and everyone else away.

After she died, I found closure. For a while I felt like I was glossing over the details of her life and romanticizing her. But in actuality, there is no romanticizing my mother. She was one tough cookie. No, I don't feel any grief for her anymore. And I don't miss her. I don't miss the weekly visits or the daily visits when she was sick. She used me up.

Now my time is my own. I don't have to be my mother's mother. I no longer have to care for her. I no longer have to visit her. I no longer have to worry about including her in our family activities. I don't have to worry about calling her anymore or seeing her anymore or wondering how she is or how she'll treat me. I never knew what mother I would find whenever I called her or met with her. There were times when she was mean and sharp-tongued and times when she was quiet and docile. No, I won't and don't miss any of that. Mostly I fear that I won't live long enough to enjoy my freedom from her. How much time do I really have left? So, all that lost time is what I grieve for. She didn't go soon enough. Of course a good daughter shouldn't think and feel this way, but I was a damn good daughter to a damn bad mother. And she wasn't much of a mother at all. She was a taker. She wanted all the attention, and when it wasn't centered around her she lashed out and attacked the ones who were stealing the attention from her.

Like when I was pregnant with Paul. All the attention was on me and she couldn't stand it. She made my life miserable. Now, I finally get it. Now, I finally understand. She was sick. She had a milder form of the illness Paul had. And now she is gone too.

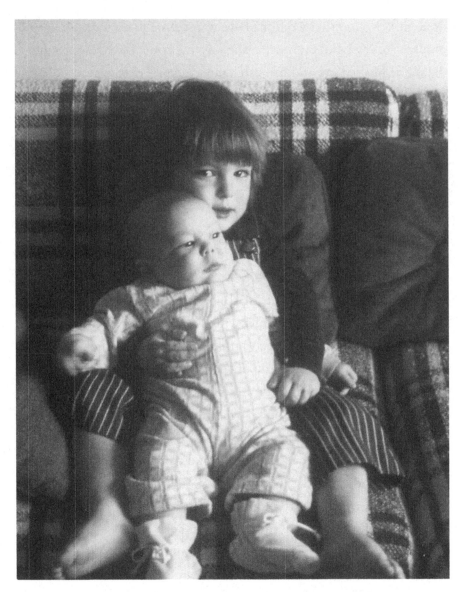

Fall 1974, Paul not quite three and Ben about three months

Fall 1979, on the deck of our new house

December 1984, at Paul's Bar Mitzvah

June 1985, Paul's eighth grade graduation

June 1987, Ben's Bar Mitzvah

Fall 1991 at Manhattan Beach (Mary Pat Dorr photo)

Ben and Paul, November 1994, Stephanie and Mike's wedding weekend

February 1997, Bob's sixtieth birthday

February 1999, Grandma's ninetieth birthday party (Mary Pat Dorr photo)

Buddha

"The dead we can imagine to be anything at all."
Ann Patchett, Bel Canto, *HarperCollins Publishers, (2001)*

He sits cross-legged in a tree
deep in concentration,
the way he would sit on the floor of his room,
learning against the bed doing homework,
composing music, talking on the phone.
His closed-mouth grin shows
he is pleased to be where he is.
No longer a skinny rail, his cheeks filled out,
his skin clear, his eyes bright.
His tree has everything—soft jazz sounds
flowing from all directions,
deep vees and pillows for sitting and reclining,
the scent of incense and flowers,
branches of books by Miller, Tolstoy, and Dostoevsky,
the music of Davis, Gould, Bach, and Lennon,
and virtual communication to those he loves.
He needs no furniture, no bedding, no clothes, no food.
Those necessities are for worldly beings.
The passing clouds give him comfort,
and the stars light his way.
Heaven takes care of him
as he imagines himself
to be anything at all.

CHAPTER NINE

Immediately after Paul died, our family dynamics changed completely. Paul didn't just die—in some ways the people we all were died a little too. Ben's role as the youngest child changed to being the role of the only child. It's all about him now. Bob and I are focused on him—not split between him and Paul. As we age, he is the one who will be there.

My role changed from being a mother of two boys to a mother of one—and the mother of a son who committed suicide. Also Bob had to deal with his grief and his new role of being a larger support emotionally to me, to help me through it. He was father and husband, and he had to become so much more of an emotional support than ever before. And later on he had to deal with the death of his son from his former marriage.

Yet through it all we stuck together as a family. We moved through our grief, supported one another, and came out the other side as a family closer than ever before.

In fact, in one of the first rejection letters I received after I began to market this book to agents, I was told my material was too quiet. I asked a publisher friend what that meant. He said it didn't have enough action in it—meaning I didn't have an affair, I didn't get a divorce, I didn't become an alcoholic or a drug addict, and I didn't have a breakdown myself. I decided to turn that thought around. I stated those facts right there up front in all my next query letters because I wanted to make the point that Bob and Ben and I are a plain, quiet, normal family that experienced a horrendous event in their lives, and we all kept moving on without anything drastic happening in our lives as a result. We are living proof that one can survive one of the worst experiences a parent and sibling can have without breaking apart in the process.

How I Survived

I remember seeing the back of my mother's head in the window as we, the last of the mourners to leave after my father's funeral, drove away from her townhouse. She was sitting like a lump in the corner of her couch, and for most of the next twenty-seven years until she died at age ninety-four she sat in that same spot. She was younger than I am now, healthy, and perfectly capable of living a happy and productive life for however long she had left. Instead she decided her life was over. No husband, therefore, no life. The day after Paul's funeral I could have opted to live out the rest of my life that way. Instead I began to pick up the pieces almost immediately.

The morning after Paul's funeral, after everyone was gone, the house cleaned up, the leftover food given to a local homeless shelter, I threw away the flowers that were all over our house. I couldn't stand the smell. Even though most of them still looked good, they smelled like death to me. Sickening sweet roses, lilies, alstromeria, tulips, sunflowers, all cut and delivered to cheer us up. I couldn't stand having them around. I took a large kitchen garbage bag, shoved them in, pulled the cord into a knot, and deposited them into the trash. I washed the vases I wanted to keep and threw the rest away. Then I opened the windows to get rid of the smell of death that permeated our house and let in some fresh air. This was the first step to moving on to a fresh start. And though I'm finally over the feeling that fresh cut flowers represent death (I buy them only occasionally today), I usually opt to buy orchid plants because the blooms last so much longer—and they are living things.

Next we had a heart-to-heart talk with Ben. The three of us sat on the couch in our family room—Bob and I with Ben in the middle. He was in his mid-twenties and in his third year of grad school. But now I had to assume a new role right away. Now I had to be the strong mother of my young son who was grieving for his brother. He had a new role too—the only child.

Ben felt uneasy about going back to school at the American Conservatory Theater so soon after Paul died. He wanted to stay home and grieve a while longer. But I couldn't let that happen. It was time for him to go back. All his classmates and fellow actors were waiting for him to come back and perform with them in a performance they had all waited almost three years for—the "Three Penny Opera" on the Main Stage with a major star in the lead role and before a paying live audience. Bob and I, a united front, told him if he didn't go back right away, he would find reasons to never go back. He was in his last year. He couldn't throw away all the work of the previous two. Plus we reminded him that we would be in San Francisco in a couple of days to see his performance, something we had planned to do before Paul died. As hard as I knew traveling anywhere at this time would be for me, we wouldn't disappoint Ben by not attending. He needed us and we needed to be there for him.

I first heard the term "walking wounded" during that visit. A father of one of the other actors had also lost a child and liked to characterize his role that way. I never liked that term. I preferred to characterize myself as a survivor, the term also used at the Didi Hirsch Mental Health Services. Bob, Ben, and I now had another role. We were the survivors of our son and brother's death, and we were survivors of a death by suicide. A double whammy.

I learned about Didi Hirsch from my friends, Ruth and Stan. Ruth said she had a friend whose son also killed himself six years before, and small world that it is, Stan and I knew each other from our hometown of Glencoe, Illinois—he was in my brother's high school class; I graduated with his brother. In fact I had heard about the death of his son on the news because he was found on the Santa Monica beach. At that time Stan was a volunteer at the suicide prevention hotline at Didi Hirsch and a facilitator in its Survivor After Suicide workshops. He encouraged us to join one soon. Besides that, he was my savior. He came to our house within an hour upon hearing of our loss, and he encouraged me to call him any time of day or night. He had been through what I was going through, and he made himself available to my family and me immediately. As a result, we see Stan and his wife regularly. Our mutual losses brought us back together.

Very soon after my first meeting with Stan, Bob and I walked to the back of the Didi Hirsch building on Sepulveda Boulevard in Culver City, California. After being buzzed through the door, we entered a small room just large enough to hold the circle of chairs that we survivors sat on. On the floor in the middle of the circle was a lonely box of Kleenex. The group had ten survivors, two facilitators, and one licensed therapist at this first meeting. Initially, I was a bit wary about the ability of the leader to help because she was not a survivor, but I was encouraged that the two facilitators were.

I came away from the second session with the same feeling I had after the first: my story, as horrible as it is, could always be worse. The only other mother of a suicide in the group told how she found her son's dead body—or rather remains—ten days after he had hung himself. I cannot begin to imagine her horror. I was spared seeing Paul dead. This poor woman had to see her son after ten days of decay. She said he wasn't even recognizable. I thought about finding Paul like that after he died. The previous spring we left him home alone while we spent two weeks in England and Germany. What if he had chosen to kill himself while we were away? What if we had found him dead and decayed when we got home? Then for sure I would have never been able to enter my house again. So it could have been worse.

Although the other mother dropped out after only a couple of sessions, while she was there I kept looking in her face wondering if what I saw in hers was how I looked to other people. She constantly cried and could barely speak. I held in my tears most of the time and spoke only occasionally. But we were both mothers who lost our sons to suicide— just one day apart. We had a special bond. She left the group before we could really get to know each other. I wanted to talk to her—not to try to help her because I knew I couldn't do that—but because I wanted to know how she was living through this horrible time in her life.

I could understand why she left. She couldn't face the reality of her son's death. She denied her son had any mental problem. She couldn't admit he had a reason to take his life. I was just like her when Bob and I went to a support group for parents of mentally ill children a few years before. It was a drop-in group and we dropped in one Tuesday night. This group was huge—there must have been more than twenty-five people in the circle. Everyone went in order telling the stories of their adult children who couldn't live on their own, couldn't hold onto a job, wouldn't take their medicine, and were, in many cases, homeless and self-medicating with alcohol and drugs. I couldn't stand to listen to these stories and never went back to that group. It wasn't for me. I didn't need it. My son wasn't as bad as all that. I, too, was in denial. What I didn't know was that he was worse. He was all of those things and more because he ended up dead. If I had stayed in that group, I might have learned how to help him, how to better care for him from others who were already caring for their mentally ill children. Instead, I thought I had it better. I thought their stories couldn't possibly have anything to do with me.

Bob's experience of the Survivors After Suicide meetings was different from mine. He remembers sitting in a circle, using the box of tissues that was available in the center of the circle, and intellectualizing the stories he heard from others about the loss by suicide of their loved ones. And when the workshop series ended it was a signal for him to let the whole experience of Paul's passing go. It was his signal to move on.

Every week at the end of our survivors' session, Carol, the therapist, told us to have a good week and to drive carefully. I always wondered why she said that. I wondered how many people from the survivors-after-suicide groups that she's led ended up wrapping their cars around a tree. I certainly could believe a few have—the groups are that depressing. So many times I wanted to high-tail it out of that little back room and feel the wind through my hair as I drove wildly away from the reality of what was going on in there. I wanted to find a place that would free me for even one second from what we discussed in that room. But I didn't. We drove carefully.

Even before Paul died, I started writing about him and his manic-depressive illness. I kept a journal to get out the frustrations of dealing with his episodes and hospitalizations and erratic behavior, and I took several classes in the University of California at Los Angeles Extension writing program. I thought about writing a memoir about Paul's illness and how he recovered from it, not as it turned out, how I've worked to survive after his death because of his illness. Nevertheless, writing became my therapy. So it was fitting that I took a writing workshop just two months after he died.

I chose an Ellen Bass' Writing About Our Lives workshop at Esalen in Big Sur on the coast of California. I had taken Ellen's workshop about a year before and had found her helpful and compassionate. No pressure—just what I needed.

Then in January, four months after Paul died, I discovered Jack Grapes, a Los Angeles-based private writing instructor and founder of the Los Angeles Poets and Writers Collective. Jack is rotund, unkempt, funny, and always ready to both cajole and encourage. He was also the perfect writing mentor for me. Jack taught me to write in a deep voice that comes from the bottom of my belly and from my heart, to write in voices other than my own, and to feel comfortable reading in front of large groups of people. He holds the last class of each workshop series at the Beyond Baroque Literary Arts Center and requires his students to prepare a piece to recite at that venue.

At first I was afraid to put my grief out there in my writing. But Jack and the rest of the class were very forgiving. When early on I apologized for writing about the same subject matter in my assigned journal entries over and over, he said, "It took Dostoyevsky five hundred pages to write *Crime and Punishment,* you have a long way to go." With that I felt empowered to write about Paul and how I felt about his death and the pain of losing him. And I still feel empowered to do it. When I told one of my cousins that I was writing a memoir about this subject, he asked if I would use a pseudonym to avoid exposure once the book came out. No way would I do that. My goal in writing this book is to tell my story in the most truthful and real terms possible. Otherwise it won't be of use to anyone—including me.

Right away I became more diligent than ever about writing daily in my journal. In the first year I finished reading *Mourning & Mitzvah* and completed its guided journal. The book's last chapter deals with the last deed of the mourning year—the dedication of the gravestone and the end of mourning. Symbolically, it all sounded like a good idea—but even though I finished the book and all the guided journal work when the time came for the dedication, I was hardly ready for it at the end of that first year. However, this material, the journal entries from Jack's class, my personal journals, and all the other writing I had done over the years since I started creative writing classes and workshops in 1995, became fodder for this book. I saved everything, always thinking I'd put it together in a book someday. And just the act of writing saved my life. My writing worked in two ways. It helped me recover and it became a way for me to keep Paul's memory alive.

In that first year after Paul's death, I took a job writing grant proposals for the South Bay Free Clinic, continuing my career in fundraising. I worked in the clinic office two full days a week—so it was a job outside my home. I thought that was a good thing, that getting up and getting out would help. But within eight months I knew that job wasn't for me. That experience was just too hard. I liked writing the clinic's grant proposals, but the people who worked there didn't give me the support I needed to adequately do my job. I couldn't squeeze the information out of anybody. I worked alone, I researched alone, I was too alone. I thought an office job would be good for me, but this one wasn't it. It was too stressful, and I didn't need anymore stress in my life than I already had. I needed the socialization of a job outside my home, but not the isolation that the job at the clinic afforded me.

I later joined a small fundraising-consulting group ostensibly to write grant proposals. However, my boss decided to train me to run capital campaigns and tossed me head-first into a role leading a campaign to raise nine million dollars for a synagogue in Irvine, California. I think he chose me for the job because I lived closer to Irvine than anyone else in his office, but it still was a lucky break. I truly loved the work and the people I worked with at the synagogue.

This job was good for me for a couple of years. Then, when my boss's son was diagnosed with a brain tumor and my boss started using me as his confidante and confessor, I realized I couldn't stay there anymore. Seeing the fear in this man's eyes every day was more than I could handle. I wanted to be there for him—and since his son died, Bob and I have become friends with him and his wife. But as the progression of his son's tumor led him toward death, I slowly moved to the door. I couldn't go through an experience like this so soon. I couldn't be an advisor for someone else yet; I could hardly take care of myself. I couldn't be there and watch this man's suffering without adding his suffering to my own. I left with regret. I just had to.

Larry's Hope

Everyday he speaks
of the tumor
growing in his son's brain.
He paces in and out of the room,
his face pale under his tan,
his eyes wide, searching,
and finding no answers.
For the last year his boy has had to withstand
the surgeon's scalpel,
the oncologist's potions
and the failure of one drug
after another to stop
his journey toward death.
He wonders if his talk is boring.
How could it be? It helps him
justify each scrap of hope.
That's all he has left.

After those two false starts—the South Bay Free clinic and the fundraising-consulting company—I decided the best solution for me was to get rehired by the company I retired from in the mid-1990s. I had already worked there a couple of times as a consultant after I retired and loved being around old friends and colleagues. So when a job opening came up in January 2003, I jumped at it and was hired. My job as a proposal manager worked for me. The work—helping my company produce proposals, a huge document or set of documents, meant to persuade the government to hire us to do their needed work instead of our competition—was challenging, meaningful, and very stressful, and I liked working with ever-changing proposal teams. I liked that each proposal project had a defined beginning, middle, and end. Also, I thrived on the socialization, the respect others had for my work, and the challenges. I never refused a high-visibility assignment. I liked to be in charge. Briefly, my job and responsibility was making sure the proposal complied with the government's requirements in the Request for Proposal—or, in tech talk, the RFP—and that it read like English and not like it was written by one hundred engineers who had trouble putting two thoughts down on paper. My job was also to make sure the documents were delivered on time, every time.

Meeting stringent deadlines made me stronger, and keeping my mind on the job stopped me from dwelling on my loss. Plus, I gained skills in setting goals, organizing work and the people I worked with, and managing to a deadline—all skills necessary to my writing career now.

What I liked most about my job was mentoring young new hires. One of my most successful mentoring experiences was with a young woman I practically begged my boss to hire. She had a degree in English (he was partial to folks with engineering or other technical degrees), lots of smarts, and proposal experience in another department at our company. When she came on board, I sat her down next to me in the proposal bay—the large work area where a proposal team works—and we worked every aspect of a proposal together until this young, shy woman could assist any author on her own and help them in any aspect of our process.

I am happy to say I've had very special relationships with the young people I got to work with at my company. A couple of my young colleagues called me "Mommy" and I loved it. Now that I've retired from that job, I have to find another way to keep the young professionals in my life.

When I first started to think about retiring, I was afraid to. I couldn't figure out what would I do with myself except stay at home in my pajamas and become a slug. I wouldn't get anything done because nothing would seem important enough to do. I wouldn't have a deadline. I knew I needed the discipline of a deadline. That's what saved me. I'd march from deadline to deadline and then complain that I was using up my life.

I kept asking myself: why was I doing my company's work—of taking men and women back to the moon? Why should I do this work instead of working on myself? I felt like I was sabotaging my creativity and healing. I was prolonging the agony and putting off the healing. I rationalized that I needed the structure, the socialization, and the money. And it was none of those. I was avoiding the pain and refusing to find out if I could live and survive without the working crutch to keep me from falling apart.

Well, I did finally give it up, but after a long, long time. I posted about retiring when I first started my blog in November 2007. And it took me until April 2010, to finally do it. When I look back at all those years of indecision, I realize I didn't make the final decision until I was good and ready. Until I felt comfortable enough with myself. Until I stopped carrying around the grief and sorrow. And the timing was perfect.

Working helped get me through the hardest of times. But a time came when I needed to be realistic about how long I could continue working such a high-pressure job full time. After my brother-in-law died in January 2010 and my friend's neck-breaking automobile accident one month before that, I was reminded yet again how temporary life is.

I also felt that I could only divert so much. Sure, it was good for me to work and have the socialization, but I also needed some space. If I were younger, I could see going on and on for many more years. But I didn't have that luxury anymore. I needed to step out of the rat race though still have the opportunity to keep my hand in a bit, possibly by consulting once in a while.

And so far, working at home as a full-time writer has produced none of the bogeymen I was afraid of. I feel comfortable in my new life. I feel so thankful that I am free to work on my writing. Now I have a good balance of business and joy that I need in my life. I can write, read, relax, and visit with the friends I've neglected while working full time, and I can experience the new stuff that's going on in my own town—the Farmer's Market that I've only visited one time in the whole year that it's been open, the shops that keep opening, the outdoor plaza surrounded by a couple of wonderful new restaurants, or just a walk down to the beach anytime I want to enjoy the open space around me. Of course I knew the risks in letting go of my full-time job. I still haven't gotten over the fear of going into the black hole again and completely falling apart. But I felt confident enough to see if I could sit and connect with sounds of birds and gurgling water in my garden—on my own terms and in my own time. So far, it's going well.

During that first year I learned how to fill up my time with diversions. And surprisingly enough these activities have become a way of life. At first Paul was with me all of the time. Everything I did, everywhere I went, I was reminded of Paul. To get relief I looked for escapes—anything to mask the real world from my brain—diversions, being busy, having a long list of to-dos every day to keep my body and mind occupied. And, now, though I'm much recovered from the need for these activities, I do them because I enjoy them. They are a habit—a good habit. Here's my list. I'm sure you can think of others that would serve you well. I know I vowed that this wouldn't be a self-help book but I feel this list might serve a purpose:

One: I read. I'm always reading something. I always have more than two books going. And no, I don't read self-help books on how to heal after the death of a child. A while ago I thought I would curl up on the big easy chair that we used to have in Paul's room, read all the books people gave me at one sitting, and be miraculously cured of my grief. I never opened a one. I donated them to my local library. Instead, I read my *New Yorker* magazines (I'm always two months behind), the fiction or nonfiction books that I select and that are selected for me by my book club, and lots of poetry and memoirs.

Two: Bob and I go to the movies. I could go every night. I almost don't care what the movie is about. It's an escape from the reality of my life. For a short time I can sit in a darkened theater and experience another's life. People used to tell me to avoid certain movies that have to do with the death of a child—seems like a slew of those came out right after Paul died or maybe I was just more aware of them then—but, I didn't listen. I still don't mind going to movies with that kind of subject matter. That means I can see how others suffer through it.

Three: We also go to the theater and opera. We have season tickets to two theater companies and subscribe to several operas a year. I find myself getting fully involved in what is happening on the stage and forget for a while who I am and what I have lost. In the past years we've gone to more movies and theater and opera than ever before. If I have my way, we'll continue to do so in the years to come.

Four: We travel. Fortunately, our very dear friends invited us to join them at a villa they rented in Tuscany for one week in the first July following Paul's death. It was truly a gift of love and understanding. We traveled on our own, first to Brussels, Bruges, and Florence. Then we met our friends at the villa, toured the small hilltop towns, drank wonderful wines, and marveled at the fields of sunflowers in full bloom during that time of the year. At the end of the week Bob and I went on to Pisa, Lucca, and Bologna before returning home. We felt very much restored, probably because we didn't take Paul with us. And since then we have made it a point not to think about him on the trips we take. When we're home, the reminders are everywhere. When we're away—and in the last several years we have traveled to Eastern Europe, Spain, France, and most recently Northern Europe—we leave those sad memories at home. We leave the photos, memorabilia, and reminders at home. I don't look for him while we're away. He is nowhere in sight. I don't think about all the wonderful places and things he chose to miss.

Five: I pamper myself—facials, botox injections, umpteen bottles of anti-aging creams for my face and body, manicures and pedicures, massages, hair straightening, makeup, Manolo Blahnik high heels. The list goes on and on. All of this stuff feels good, helps me look good, and boosts my mood. Why not? Just because I am one of the walking wounded doesn't mean I have to do it looking like a dowdy old woman. Old I am, but not dowdy.

More true confessions—I don't take drugs—no Zoloft or Prozac for me although I have been taking St. John's Wort for some time to help keep me calm. And I don't do therapy. I find support groups depressing beyond words, and after visiting a recommended therapist within days after Paul died, I made up my mind that I wouldn't seek out talk therapy unless it meant talking with someone who had experienced a loss similar to mine. Otherwise it made no sense to me. What could a person without that experience tell me?

And no, I didn't return to smoking. I quit smoking over forty years ago, and I never thought about starting again. Sure, at first I drank a little too much wine, though lately I've even cut back my wine consumption to a glass a day—better for me, my doctor says. I also manage to go without any alcohol in the months of January and July like I've been doing for the last ten years or so. Even the first January after Paul's death I went on my usual one-month alcohol fast. Why? It feels good. I like the break. January is the perfect month for an alcohol break because it is right after the winter holiday indulgences, and July is six months later. I like the idea of an alcohol detox every six months. It's another way I know I'm in control.

One last subject. Sex. Sex has always been an important part of my marriage. Bob and I still have sex about as regularly as we did before Paul died. I'll never forget when we were living in a hotel in New York after Paul's first manic break and my sister-in-law called to see how we were doing. She also asked what we were doing and we were honest— we told her we had just finished having sex. She was surprised at our answer, probably wondering how we could act like a normal married couple at a time like that. Being in a hotel makes Bob want to have sex more than usual though he could have sex any time any place if I were up for it. I give him huge kudos for keeping at me on that subject, because if it were up to me I would have let my grief leave me sexless a long time ago. He is very patient with me and has the wonderful ability to give me some of the best orgasms I have ever had even at the height of my grief.

What I Quit

Besides the problems I had with my first jobs after Paul died, I also quit some of my other activities. Not like me at all. I've always taken great pride in being responsible and keeping my agreements. But I wasn't the same person anymore. Even though I looked the same and said I was okay, I wasn't. I was grieving. And the things that had been important in my life before Paul died no longer meant very much to me.

First, I left the Cancer Support Community (formerly The Wellness Community) Board of Directors. Wellness is a cancer support group I've worked with and still support financially since the late 1980s. In those first few months after Paul died, I felt I didn't have enough sense of purpose to do what was required—to raise money. I couldn't even sit through a meeting without getting antsy. I just didn't care anymore. I couldn't concentrate. I had no energy. I didn't have the will to follow through. After I left, I missed the people but not enough to go back and do the work.

Second, we sold our membership at the Manhattan Country Club—our local tennis club—after being members for over fifteen years. One day after having our membership up for sale for a few months, we had an opportunity to sell and we did—that very day. It was over just like that. I exercise at another gym now, but it's not the same. I miss my support group—people I exercised with every weekday morning at the club who always had a funny comment, a snide remark, or racy innuendo that made exercising fun as well as good for my body and soul.

Third, another indication that my tennis days were numbered, I dropped out of a weekly tennis class with an instructor outside of the club. I just couldn't focus on that little yellow ball anymore. Paul's face got in the way. Now that was a big deal. For years I lived for my daily tennis game. In the 1970s and 1980s I competed on a cut-throat women's doubles team at our tennis club, and I was the major inspiration for Ben's interest in the sport. I warmed him up for his junior matches and rooted him on to many championships. It was a source of our close bond. Though I still miss the instructor with whom I worked for more than twenty years, even he couldn't light a fire under my racket and get me going again. Ben gives me a tennis lesson once in a while just so I can keep up my skills. But I have to admit that tennis isn't very much a part of my life anymore.

WHAT I COULDN'T DO

And with all the diversions and the things I was able to move through in the first year, some things were just impossible to do right away.

Soon after Paul died, we had friends over for dinner—yes, I still could cook—and they brought a beautiful picture frame as a hostess gift. The frame's flower print in shades of reds and pink gave off cheerful vibes and well-being. And, with the gift came the suggestion that sounded more like a "should"—as in "you should use it for your first photo of your now family of three." I won't go into how that made me feel. Suffice it to say, all those good vibes vanished. There was no way that I was ready to take a photo of just the three of us—Bob, Ben, and me—and put it in that frame. It took me another three years to even pose for one at a little gathering we had to celebrate Bob's sixty-fifth birthday in 2002. There was no choice then. It was a situation I couldn't run away from. And you know, I couldn't put that photo in that frame. One of our last photos of Paul sits in there. Was I being stubborn, obstinate? Perhaps. I just knew that it was too hard for me to adjust to our family of three that soon.

I also had difficulty signing our names on greeting cards. I had always signed us as a family—"Love, Madeline, Bob, Paul, and Ben." And, with no Paul I had to sign with just the three names or none of our names at all. We could just be "The Sharples." Just "The Sharples" worked for a while. Now I happily sign "Love, Madeline, Bob, Ben and Marissa." We are a family of four again. Marissa is Ben's new wife and our loving daughter-in-law—though I prefer to call her our daughter.

One more thing I confronted was what to do with Paul's entry on my telephone and address list. Well, I never solved that issue. His name is still in there. And, in the address spot I've entered Heaven. Not that I believe in a heaven, it's just a placeholder in my mind. I haven't deleted his name from that list, and I don't expect I ever will.

How Bob Survived

Bob says he doesn't have a clear answer to what he did to deal with Paul's death though it took quite a while for his anger and regret over the damage to our lives to calm down. For a short time he returned to meditation to quell these feelings, but that did not last long.

On two occasions he tried to get photos of Paul's body in the tub from the Manhattan Beach police, but he was told that they would not release pictures. He eventually lost interest in that subject. He also spent a lot of time listening to Paul's recorded music (listening to Paul's music and any jazz for that matter was hard for me), marveling at how good he was even though he was badly disturbed by his illness. Bob organized Paul's records, books, and tapes, watched videotapes Paul made, and cleared out Paul's large collection of electronics and associated musical instruments—and found interesting artifacts among his possessions. For example, he discovered a small amount of pot, photos of Janet, and videotapes of Paul and Janet on a last vacation to the desert. And though he tried to return much of this to Janet, she refused to take them. Although we in no way blame Janet, who was in an impossible situation with Paul, we both feel that the collapse of Paul's relationship with her may have been what precipitated his death (as corroborated by Jamison in *Night Falls Fast* that a young man with bipolar disorder could resort to suicide after the loss of a love).

As he read more about bipolar illness over the next couple of years, Bob was struck by the notion that he had failed to take stronger action to save his boy, given the likelihood that his depression might have led to his death. But right behind those thoughts came a realization that even then he could not really have made a coherent plan to save an adult male from himself, other than have him placed in a psychiatric hospital. We had tried that at various times from 1993 to 1999, and sometimes we were successful in getting him admitted, but he was very good at talking his way out of confinement.

So Bob's grieving process mostly consisted of allowing time to go by so that the sharp edges of fear, pain, and regret would begin to lose their effectiveness. He simply accepted that his lovable, little Paul grew to be a troubled, mentally ill, young man who took his own life.

For several years he kept a small jar of quarters that Paul left behind, probably because Paul had touched each of the quarters one at a time. Eventually, Bob gave himself permission to spend them, perhaps marking the end of his grief. Even so Bob was subject to sudden episodes of sadness that were separated by long intervals of normal life. But he never came close to feeling the same level of grief over Paul as I.

HOW BEN SURVIVED

When Ben looks back at the decisions he made just after Paul's death and right after graduating from A.C.T, he feels they were a big help in his survival. Perhaps they even saved him. He kept busy doing what he loved, he had a group of people in his class and in New York City who knew and loved and supported him, and he expressed his feelings and grief in his work. Even when things got to be too much in such an intensive graduate school program, Ben had friends and a girlfriend who were very helpful in getting him through his grieving.

Ben didn't initially want to go to New York career-wise because he wanted to be in the Los Angeles area to pursue film and television, so it seemed that his decision to go to New York City might have been hasty and precipitous. However, it helped him escape from the unhappy memories about his brother in Manhattan Beach, it helped him get a real start to his career, and he would be with a lot of his classmates from grad school. He says, "Going to New York gave me just the kick-start I needed because living there forced me into survival mode and also forced me to really get going on my career. There couldn't have been a better decision."

Although the first year was tough for all of us, we got through it. It, of course, didn't mark the end of our grief and mourning for Paul, but the events of that year helped us to live through the immediate impact of his death. I even made an effort to go out to lunch once in a while, hard as it was.

Lunch

I sit by the window at a corner table in a macrobiotic restaurant on Santa Monica Boulevard. The room, filled with small wooden tables and straight-back chairs, is almost empty. A couple of people are eating at the counter at the far side. Plates of breads and muffins are on a ledge above the counter. A sign above the counter says no dairy and white flour are used in any of the bakery products. I smell the herbs and the heavy aroma of Indian spices in the soup pot heating behind the take-out counter.

I look toward the window and see Linda crossing the street. I check my watch: 11:50. I've only had to wait five minutes—not bad for her. I haven't seen her in at least eight months—not since before Paul died.

I'm apprehensive. This is one of my first lunch dates in such a long time. It is still hard for me to venture far from home and socialize. I'm not even sure I can still carry on a decent conversation. Crowds really bother me, though the vibes here, the sound of quiet instrumental music are soothing. Maybe today will be okay. Maybe this healthy place will be good for me. And I've looked forward to seeing Linda for so long.

She enters the restaurant, spots me immediately, and rushes over to our table. I get up and we hug, giving each other an air kiss. "I'm sorry to keep you waiting," she says as she sits down across from me.

I fold the menu and set it down on the table in front of me. "That's okay," I say. "It's great to see you finally. I know how hard you've worked at getting us together."

"Yeah, you're a hard one to pin down." She puts on her reading glasses and picks up the menu. "Do you see anything here that you like?"

She's right. I have been hard to pin down. I want to avoid these social things where I have to sit and talk and make an attempt to eat.

I pick up the menu again and pretend. I'm good at pretending. "Oh, yes. You chose a great place. I'm not a total vegetarian like you, but I love this kind of food." I look back down and study the menu a bit more. There are lots of salads and soups to choose from, but I'm drawn to the bowls. "I think I'll have the brown rice and veggies with tahini sauce," I say. Maybe that will stick. I've had a very hard time keeping food in me—especial dairy products—I hope this food might work for me.

She looks up, takes off her glasses, and closes her menu. "That's my favorite thing here. I'll have that too."

I look out the window at a car swerving to get out of the way of a jaywalker.

"I used to go to Hi De Ho Comics across the street to buy my son Ben his Garbage Pail Kid cards," I tell her, making every effort to keep the conversation light. After all, this is a girl's lunch—with lots of chit-chat and gossip expected. "They were his passion when he was twelve, and like a good Mommy I would drive all the way up here to find him the ones he couldn't find in the South Bay."

She looks at me like I'm talking in Chinese. "Garbage Pail Kids? Are those anything like the Pokémon cards that are so popular now?"

"How do you know about those?" One of Paul's last social inter-actions was with a young boy who came over to visit us with his parents. Paul had never seen Pokemon cards before, and the boy gave him a couple. I found them in his wallet when I went through his things after he died.

"The kid next door collects them. He showed me his album and gave me one of his extras."

"Well, the Garbage Pail cards were really sick. Definitely not my type of humor. Cartoons of chubby kids sitting in garbage cans dressed in all kinds of regalia. Now there are boxes of them on a shelf in his old

room at home. I can't imagine they'll ever be worth anything. And I can't imagine why I spent so much money on them. Twelve dollars for one card. I must have been nuts."

The waiter arrives. We order the same thing with a mixed salad to share.

"I'll have chai," she says.

"Just water for me—without ice." Ice-cold liquids going through my system gives me headaches.

The waiter takes our menus, turns, and leaves.

The small room is beginning to fill up with the lunch crowd. All the counter seats are full. I'm glad I arrived early and snagged this table in its little corner alcove away from the flow of traffic. Two waiters are hurrying back and forth across the wood floor.

I can feel Linda looking me over. I wonder how much I've changed in the last eight months. I wonder how much damage eight months of grief can do to a person. I look out the window again, gaze at the comic-book store, and yearn for the days when Ben was little and Paul was free from his manic-depressive illness, still alive, just the pain-in-the-neck teenager who used to drive me up the wall.

Linda's question brings me back. "Are you working?" Good, more chit-chat. I'm still safe.

I put my elbows on the table and hold my chin in my hands, looking straight at her.

"Yes, I still write grant proposals for the homeless shelter down-town. I went back to work almost immediately. I have to keep busy or I'll go nuts. The problem is working at home alone. It's so hard to con-centrate sometimes. Too many memories of Paul's death there."

She nods and takes off her sweater, sweeping her thick red hair up off her neck as she moves the sweater across her shoulders. The sun pours through the window, laying a bright light on our table. "I know what you mean," she says. "Luckily for me I have a lot of client meetings that take me away from my office. I miss the face-to-face people interactions when I work at home alone."

I sit up straight, push back my chair, and cross my legs at the knees. "Are you still trying to help retirees transition into their next lives?" I ask, still trying to avoid the real reason for this lunch date. Linda is a real people person. She's a great facilitator and motivator. I've always envied how comfortable she is in front of a room full of people.

"Well, you should know how hard that is. You haven't been a very successful retiree yourself," she says.

Linda and I first met at college. She was in another sorority, but her hair got my attention—carrot orange, large, curly, gorgeous. It overwhelmed her thin face and body. "You look great," I say. "I love that color green on you. It matches your eyes. And, your hair is still gorgeous."

She gives me an impish smile while combing her fingers through her mane. "It comes out of a bottle now. I tone it down from my natural shade—a little more geared to my age."

I continue with the girl talk. "Yeah, I won't give up the bottle either. My stylist weaves low lights through my hair so some of the gray shows. I think going totally dark would really age me too."

"Low lights? I never heard of that before."

"Oh, sorry. I thought you knew. Those are like high lights in reverse."

I look up and spot the waiter coming toward us from behind the counter. I spread out the fork, the knife and put my napkin on my lap. I take a sip of water. He sets down our bowls of rice and vegetables and puts the salad in the center of the table. I take a bite, chew, and barely swallow it. It tastes delicious, but I have no appetite. I haven't had one for months.

Linda looks like she doesn't eat much either, but that's no different from always. She's always been thin and never had to watch her weight. Without her sweater on I can see her prominent collarbones and flat chest underneath her pale green t-shirt. She never wears a bra. "Have you seen Alice and Richard lately?" I ask.

I've known Alice since I moved to Los Angeles in 1961. After I graduated from University of California at Los Angeles, we took art lessons together for years, every Thursday night, until I stopped painting. Now she has a couple of paintings at the Smithsonian and one of Chelsea Clinton that she personally presented to Hillary. She also painted a wonderful portrait of Bob and me that gets rave reviews from our visitors.

I reconnected with Linda a few years ago when Alice and Richard renewed their marriage vows in the backyard of their home in Ojai. I kept looking at her across the yard as we all stood in a circle during the ceremony, telling my husband Bob that I knew her from somewhere. Once we started talking and asking each other where we were from and where we went to college and how long we'd been in Los Angeles, we discovered that we first met at the University of Wisconsin. We clicked immediately and though we were never very friendly at college, we've been good friends since that Ojai party. We even tried to figure out how we could work together, but never came up with anything common to both our skills and interests.

She looks up from her bowl and sets her fork down. I take a bite of salad. I gulp it down.

"I was out there last weekend," she says. "They're great. Alice is doing a new project—a series of paintings of naked old ladies."

"I know. That project is amazing. She wanted to paint my mother, but she refused. I offered, but she said I'm not old enough."

I try another bite of the rice while Linda digs into the salad. The waiter comes by to see if we need anything else. We don't. "And what's Richard doing?"

Linda puts down her fork, picks up her napkin, and wipes her mouth. Her once fine, clear skin now has deep lines—in her forehead, around her mouth, in her chin. Yet I don't find her less beautiful than when I first met her over forty years ago.

"Oh, you know Richard," she says. "He putters in the garden, leads that men's group in LA once a week, and does those wonderful sculptures of old men. Sort of companions to Alice's old ladies."

"I love their creations," I say. "Alice and Richard are amazing. They live simply on that idyllic piece of property and are so mellow and happy together. They are like the love children of the 60s. Like they never grew up."

Linda takes another bite of salad and a sip of tea. She squints. The sun is coming straight at her now. "I know. I've always called them the oldest hippies around. Did you know they are planning to write a book someday about the art of aging with images of their work?"

I take another bite and chew for a long time. Then I put my fork down. I can't eat anymore. "Yes," I say. "They are in the perfect spot to inspire their creative juices."

"Madeline, are you all right?" Linda asks. "You're not eating anything."

"Sure, but I can't seem to get much down. It's called the stress diet. Whenever I'm stressed, I lose weight."

"Well, some would think that's lucky," she says. "I have a hard time keeping weight on myself." She takes her fork again and tries to pick some carrot sticks off the salad. They fall off so she picks them up with her fingers and munches, picks up one or two more, turns them around in her fingers, and drops them into the bowl. They are so fresh looking—almost the color her hair used to be. "You know, we haven't talked about Paul," she says. "Would that be all right for you?"

I look up. "What do you want to know?" I ask. I uncross my legs and re-cross them with the right leg on top. The time has finally come to get down to the real stuff.

"Well, I know he killed himself. Alice told me that. But she didn't know how he did it," she says.

I look out the window again and see a woman with two young boys enter the comic-book store. I stare at them for a few seconds. I want to scream at her and all women to take care of those little boys and cherish every minute they have with them. Then I turn back and reach around to the back of my chair and into my purse for a tissue. I wipe my eyes and look back at Linda. "He put himself in the bathtub and slit his throat," I say.

She clamps her hand over her mouth and chin and opens her eyes so wide they seem to take over her face.

The waiter comes by to take away our plates. He asks if we want any dessert.

"Why don't we share the apple crisp?" I ask. "Maybe we can manage to eat that."

Still holding her chin in her hands, she nods up and down, and the waiter leaves.

"I'm sorry to shock you, but you wanted to know." I take her hand and she squeezes mine. But, that's all the comforting I have in me right now.

"Oh my God," she says. "How horrible for you." She lets go of my hand, wipes her eyes with her napkin, and straightens up in her chair.

The waiter comes back with our dessert and two spoons, and we each have a few bites as I watch a fly on the other side of the window trying to get inside. In the bright light its body looks like electric blue velvet.

"This is delicious, isn't it?" I ask.

"No," she says, "I can't eat anything more."

Finally, we pay our bill and get up. She puts her sweater back on, and I take my purse from where it's hanging on the back of my chair. She puts her arm around me as we walk out the restaurant door. I put my head on her shoulder. Linda has never married or had children. At this moment I think she is lucky. She didn't have the worries, the sleepless night, the fears. Right now that's all I think about. Right now it's hard to remember the good parts.

February 2002, Bob's sixty-fifth birthday

CHAPTER TEN

S o many people have asked if I found comfort in God after Paul's death. And the answer is a flat "no." Paul's death has not brought me closer to God. For me, there is no God. I can't relate to a God that would take away my son. I look for a spiritual connection but can't seem to find one. I've tried praying. But to whom and for what? Paul's death has brought me closer to myself. I've become more in touch with my feelings and ways to cope by myself. These are the things that comfort me. Going to Esalen Institute and Big Sur helps, but that is not turning to God. That is getting away from my regular life and giving myself space to reflect and write and be with people who have the same writing interests as mine. My writing has become my therapy and the way I get in touch with my feelings and myself. I've found my own way.

So I've turned further away from God. And it's not only about Paul. It's about the disasters in the world and in our nation. I never really believed in God—even before Paul died. I've always been an agnostic with a strong leaning toward atheism.

September 23, 2002

The phone rang once
startling me awake from a deep sleep.
I jumped out of bed to answer it,
knocking over the Waterford
crystal perfume bottle
on the way.
And all for naught—
no one was on the line.
I looked over at the clock—
only 5 A.M. but I was up for
this day, September 23, 2002,
the third anniversary of Paul's death,
a day that I dreaded for so long.
And all I could think was
Paul was calling to check in,
letting us know he was still around
somewhere. And somehow
that one ring was a comfort rather
than a wake up call.

The scare tactics of religion turned me off as a teenager. Live a good life and you'll have a good afterlife. To me, once you're dead, you're dead. You're gone. That's it. There's nothing after that. There's no God, no heaven, no nothing. No matter how much magical thinking comforted me, I knew leaving the hall light on for him wouldn't bring Paul back.

Even with these feelings, I joined a religious synagogue after Paul died because the rabbi who came to our house almost immediately and then officiated at his memorial service was so helpful and compassionate. I wanted to support him. I also thought at first that it might help me. But, no, belonging to the synagogue hasn't helped. Having the rabbi as a good friend does.

I also still show up in synagogue for Jewish high holidays—the New Year and Day of Atonement. I've always enjoyed the Jewish traditions—family Passover dinners and break-the-fasts, the socialization of being in the synagogue with my family. I use the time to sit quietly, think, meditate, but not to pray. I wouldn't know how to pray. I've never done it. But I like the music, the feeling of belonging, and having my family surrounding me.

I also don't believe that Paul is with God. Even though I wrote a poem about my vision of him in a heaven of some sort—I called it Buddha because he was a Buddha kind of character—I don't really picture him in heaven. I don't picture him anywhere but back here with us on earth among the living. That's where a young guy like him should be.

Although it may be completely nuts, I do believe that if I dream about him he is close by or with me. It's interesting that when September rolls around, I dream about him more. That's the month he died. One year—on his death day—the phone rang very early in the morning. As I reached for the phone, I knocked over a crystal perfume bottle off my dresser, and picked up after one ring. No one was on the line, but I couldn't help but think it was Paul checking in. I even mentioned it to a friend who also lost a son to suicide, and he said he had experienced the same kind of thing, that that kind of magical thinking is not unusual.

Over the years I've been told that I needed to go into therapy. Even my husband has suggested it more than a time or two. But I've steadfastly refused. I just didn't think a therapist could help me if he/she hadn't been through my kind of loss.

And of course, the most truthful reason why I didn't seek help early on was because I didn't want to stop feeling the pain. I didn't want to heal. I didn't want to forget. I couldn't take a chance that a therapist would help me. I refused to face the fact that I could possibly get over this death. I refused to believe that would even be possible. In my mind it wasn't. So I wouldn't read the self-help books, I wouldn't see a therapist, I wouldn't do anymore "how to deal with the grief" workshops. I refused to give up on the grief because I didn't want to stop grieving for him. I didn't want to ever forget the pain. I didn't want to ever even come close to forgetting him or anything about him. I was afraid of forgetting him because if I forgot him who else is there to remember all the things I know about him?

It was obvious that Bob and I both needed help. We had a hard time just being together because our coping mechanisms were so different. He would keep saying that only I needed therapy. To spite him, I wouldn't go. That is the truth of it. He was afraid I was having a breakdown; I was afraid he was drowning his pain and anger in alcohol.

In the end, I've found that it just takes time. I'm glad I did it my way. I came out of it alive, happy, and thriving. Sure, I have bad days, but nothing I can't get through.

Prickly

"You're prickly," my husband said,
hard to get along with,
and snappish."
I just stood there, surprised.
"I'm sorry for being prickly,"
was all I could think of to say.

I am never so blunt
when critical of him.
He would retort as he's done
so many times before,
"I guess I'm just not good enough.
You should just find someone else,"
he'd say. And, of course,
I would quickly shut up,

I wonder what prickly means.
Do I hurt to the touch
like little pin pricks?
Do cacti envy my prowess?
Do the cats that roam the streets
and sleep under cars hiss
and scatter when they see me coming?
Do the few stars
that burn through the haze
look down at me in wonder?

222 ~ MADELINE SHARPLES

What keeps me in balance and helps me feel better and experience joy is my spiritual regime of writing, working out, going to Esalen at Big Sur for workshops, meditating, and experiencing some far-out cathartic work like visiting a sweat lodge and getting a tattoo. I've also found ways to assuage and comfort my anger, sorrow, and fears that arose from Paul's death.

Though writing has been a part of my life for a long time and a huge help during the height of my worries and grief about Paul, poems just started coming out during one of the first Writing About Our Lives workshops I took with Ellen Bass at Esalen. Poetry seemed to be the only way I could really express my emotions. For a while my poems were all about Paul. Now I find poems going on everywhere, any time. I like to say: "now there's a poem," and off I go to write. Poetry is still a great part of my writing life. I've produced four chapbooks, and I've co-edited two volumes of the poetry anthology, *The Great American Poetry Show*. I've also written the poems for a book of photographs, *The Emerging Goddess*—one of the first projects that helped get me out of my writing dark hole. I was thrilled when the photographer asked me to write the poems, giving me another subject to write about instead of the dark, death-related work about grief and Paul I had been doing. I've also had many poems published both on-line and in print magazines. Now I challenge myself to write a poem every day while I travel. I enter April and November poem-a-day challenges, and I've recently challenged myself to write a poem a week about people I see and have imaginings about, but whom I don't know. I look outward, not inward, for a change. And, I've branched out and started a novel.

But it doesn't matter. Poetry, journaling, creative non-fiction, fiction, painting, singing, acting. And all of them are great outlets. I recommend some kind of creative outlet for anyone who's been through a loss like mine or any other grief experience. Do anything that will take you away from what's going on inside. My friend, Kitty, writes and paints and sometimes combines the two.

Esalen continues to be my healing and writing place. I'm not daunted by the six-hour drive to get there. Once I pass Santa Barbara I feel like I'm on my way to heaven. The smell of pine and sulfur—Esalen has natural hot springs baths—the organic fresh food, the view of the ocean's waves hitting the rocks, the conversations, and the quality of the writing workshops I've attended provide the right amount of healing balm and writing inspiration I need. I try to go there at least twice a year. And once I've made my reservation, I'll let nothing stop me from showing up. I write there. I share there. I let it all hang out there which includes participating in the clothing-optional hot-springs tubs. Esalen is a place where I don't hide. The people I know there won't let me hide. I know because I've tried.

In my late twenties and early thirties, I began exercising regularly. At first three to four times a week, and then after Paul died, I upped my workouts to every day of the week. I couldn't get through a day without exercising. When I don't exercise, I'm sluggish, less energized, and more apt to be tearful. I just don't feel like myself. I have my own little routine. I use an elliptical cross trainer and treadmill for my cardio workout and weight machines or free weights for my upper and lower body areas on most days. Once in a while Bob and I will go for a long walk on the Strand near our beach. So I didn't give up this part of my life after Paul died. I actually got more compulsive about it.

I also exercise to keep my body in shape, ward off osteoporosis, and keep my weight down. There I've admitted it! No matter what I've gone through, I'm still a very vain person—maybe because taking care of my body and my hair and face is one of the ways I am able stay in control. I hold on to this control like a vise. If I let go, I feel everything about me will fall apart. Even on the day of Paul's funeral I had to have my hair and makeup just so.

Making It Hard

The bright room is almost full.
All four walls of mirrors reflect women and men
in baggy shorts and sleek black tights.
The music is so loud
the woman in front of me stuffs earplugs in her ears.
Lisa G says, "work from the core;
your workout relates to your real life."
I want to get on with it.
I don't come here at 6 A.M. to listen to a lecture.
The neon sign on the wall says "sweat,"
and that's what I want to do.
The woman behind me complains.
I don't know her name, but here she is every week
always in the same spot, always complaining, always in black.
Black tights, black sports bra, black thong leotard,
black headband on her head of black hair.
Even her lipstick looks black.
A drill sergeant in baseball cap and high-top aerobic shoes,
Lisa begins her litany.
"If it were easy, everyone would be fit," she shouts,
"Don't come here and expect it to be easy."
She doesn't know my name. I like it that way.
I like the feeling of being anonymous here.
I don't know anyone and no one knows me.
No one knows about Paul, that he died
or any other thing about me either.
Being anonymous is a benefit.
It keeps me in shape, calms my mind,
gives me the space to be myself.
It's a mini-vacation from the horrors of my life.
So I thank Lisa G

for getting me moving,
for making it hard,
for making it hurt,
for showing me how to
trade one pain for another.

A few times a week I add a yoga or Pilates class. I've found yoga and Pilates are wonderful ways to unwind and stay focused. I first started doing yoga when I was pregnant with Paul. I had no formal lessons and didn't attend any classes then—we were unable to afford them in those days, but I learned enough on my own to help in my recovery after his birth. I continued with yoga for a few years after that—especially during my pregnancy with Ben. Afterward I got into tennis and running, and yoga fell by the wayside for over twenty years. I picked it up again after Paul died, and I've found it incredibly hard. In my young days my body could twist like a pretzel. Now I'm like a stiff wooden board. Yet, yoga helps with all kinds of things. It calms my heart, it makes me concentrate on nothing else but the yoga position I'm trying to make my body do, it evens out my breathing, and it helps me work out the knots I get in my neck and shoulders from all the work I do at the computer. I'm perfectly comfortable holding the hardest poses. They soothe me, they stretch me, and they take me away from the inner conversations I have within myself. Pilates is more forgiving for me. It's less strenuous. And it helps me stay flexible. It just doesn't have yoga's calming effect.

I've found working out is also a great way to quell my anger.

One morning soon after Paul's death I attended a circuit-training exercise class where the instructor has different kinds of equipment at stations all around the room and the students go around and spend forty-five seconds doing the moves required at each station. I got to the punching bag, put on the big red gloves that were still sweaty from the hands of the last person who wore them, and began punching. Normally, I hate boxing. I always destroy my inner arms when I attempt it. But I began and I didn't want to stop. Instead of the target I clearly saw Paul's face on the bag, and I began punching that face as hard as I could. I didn't know I was so angry with him. I thought it was only Bob who was angry with him. But, I found my anger at that class, and I knew I could go back to the gym and punch him in the face whenever I wanted. And it helped.

I first dabbled in meditation at the Shambhala Center when it was in West Hollywood. I also meditate at home where I've set up a little shrine that I sit before —though not as regularly as I should. Also many of my Buddhas sit with me in my office with their calming faces at my beck and call. Just the practice of Tonglen—the deep breathing in of pain and the breathing out of healing and compassion toward others— that I learned about from Pema Chodron's *When Things Fall Apart* makes me feel wonderful. If I could help create a world where no other mother would have to feel the pain I have felt in my life, then I would be wildly happy. I know this is impossible, yet Tonglen is a step in that direction.

I know meditation is good for me. It works. Just recently when I was stressing about an upcoming reading, I meditated several times and it calmed down my thoughts and heartbeat. And all my diversions— the work, the writing, the exercise, the yoga, the Pilates—are all like forms of meditation for me. Sometimes I meditate amidst crowds of people. I sit quietly, keep my hands on my lap, and concentrate. I don't fidget, I don't tap my foot. I didn't get the reputation for being a serene, calming influence at work and among my friends for nothing.

Meditation Practice

I face the shrine,
place my palms together as in prayer,
bow, and walk into the room.
I choose a spot in the second row
and sit in the middle of a brilliant red cushion,
cross my legs, straighten my spine,
and take a quick look around
before I gaze ahead,
lowering my eyelids until
my eyes focus on the gold-leaf mandala
adorning the lacquered altar before me.
Soon the tang of incense sends
a trail of smoke, like a fine silk thread,
up toward the ceiling.
It disappears above my head.

I begin to settle down and listen to
my breath moving in and moving out.
It sounds like I'm in an echo chamber.
This is not my breath.
It's the sound of something far away.
I keep listening. The echo gets louder and louder,
enveloping me, swaddling me in its raspy arms.
I'm lost in this warmth until I startle.
My head lurches forward,
my eyes pop open, my body arches.
I lose concentration and barely catch myself
from keeling over, disrupting the meditative mood
pervading this room.

I fold my legs again.
I straighten my spine again.
I fix my gaze again.
Yeah, I'm ready this time.
I can do this
if only my right ankle will stop
distracting me, aching, giving me fits.
I count my breaths,
I cleanse my mind.
I must let my ankle hurt, let my nose itch
I must watch my breath move in and out
I must push invading thoughts aside.
Okay, take it easy,
Stay calm.
How hard is that?

The leader, sitting slightly elevated in front,
strikes the copper gong once, twice,
and then produces several more short bursts of sound,
letting the prolonged vibrations permeate the air.
It's time for walking meditation,
and am I ready for that.
I know I can do that.
My legs feel like a couple of stiff rails.
But wait a minute.
Is this supposed to be a walk in the park?
No way. Of course not.
If it were easy, everyone would do it.

I enter the circle of my fellow-meditators
and walk the perimeter of the room.
I tuck my left thumb into my left fist
and cover it with my right hand,

holding my spooned hands close to my belly.
I become aware of my feet
as I take slow step after slow step
around the room.
As I walk, my arches rise
my toes curl like a ballerina's,
my feet are like wings made to propel me,
elevate me into a perfect pirouette. And,
I am there, walking, breathing, getting it,
one step, one in breath, one out breath at a time.

I also had a cleansing and inspiring experience at a sweat lodge out in the Los Angeles San Fernando Valley. All I was asked to bring was a robe and some food to share. About twenty women attended. First we sat in a circle in the leader's living room and ate and shared our reasons for being there. My sharing, of course, was about Paul's death. That was my only reason for being there. After we took off all our clothes and put on our robes, we filed out into the leader's back yard to the sweat lodge. It was dark and cold out there. Only a small light on at the back of the house guided our steps.

We must have been in the lodge for almost two hours—though I had no idea so much time had passed. We went through four rounds of heat, with each round getting progressively hotter as we kept adding more and more hot coals to the pile in the center of the lodge. In between rounds we opened the door, drank some water, and walked outside. We sat or lay naked against the walls of the lodge while inside.

During the second round we were asked to pray for others. As I don't believe in prayer, I wished that no other mother would experience the pain I went through during the years of Paul's mental illness and the horribleness of his death. I also wished that we would someday find a cure for mental illness so the many people who had the disease could live a long good life. This was the first time I had ever articulated my hopes for others.

The leader asked us to throw something away into the fire during the third round. I threw away my worry, fear, and guilt. Then my vanity, then my tears. The fourth round was the shortest and the hottest. Instead of being asked to pray, we chanted and sang. We acknowledged our seven chakras with a different sound for each—ee, ah, oh ... going up and down the chakra scale a few times. We ended by singing "Amazing Grace." By then I was ready to stop. The hut was so steamy from the wet heat that I couldn't even see my way out.

Afterward, we dried off, dressed, and sat in our original circle again. Our leader asked us to share again. Then she asked me to do a special wish with a pipe full of tobacco. She asked me to go out into her well-lit front yard and give the tobacco to any tree outside and make my wish. I wished for peace for Paul and that I would someday, somehow see him again. I don't really believe I will, but I wished for that all the same. I cried. The experience was cleansing. But because the twenty-five-mile drive from Manhattan Beach to the San Fernando Valley in traffic at night is too daunting, I never went back.

I sat spread-eagled facing the back of the narrow black leather chair-like contraption, wondering what the hell I was doing there. My bra strap was pulled down and I had one arm out of my white t-shirt to expose my right shoulder. Dan-O, the tattoo artist, had already checked the size and shape of the design he had prepared for me. "A little smaller," I kept telling him until the five-pointed star was the size of a nickel, and he and I agreed exactly where he would place the tattoo on my shoulder. We had also picked the color. I looked over at his right arm covered with flowers and leaves in bright colors like out of a Disney cartoon, and I pointed to an electric blue. "That color," I said, just because I liked it.

I had put myself into that seat because two years before, I had announced to my long-time friends Wendy and Carole that I wanted to get a tattoo for my sixtieth birthday. They were both discussing theirs. Wendy has a little butterfly on her ankle and Carole wears a tiny red heart high on her right shoulder. Because I've always been a me-too kind of person, I didn't want to be left out.

But two years is a long time. If I had never mentioned it again, they wouldn't have held me to my spontaneous proclamation. Only I—the mom who had spent many hours dissuading both of my sons from doing something to their bodies that they could be sorry for once they grew up—needed to follow through with it.

When I reminded Carole just before my sixtieth birthday—mind you this was my first birthday after Paul's death and who knew if I was in my right mind—she decided to take over. Natural-born producer that she is, she found the tattoo parlor, the Black Wave on La Brea Avenue in Los Angeles, and the artist. And she arranged the afternoon.

On the Wednesday just after my birthday, she first took me to the eyebrow lady who plucked my eyebrows so thin I looked like I belonged in a silent movie. Then we had one of our usual calorie-conscious lunches at a favorite Italian restaurant a few doors away from the tattoo parlor. Leaving our cars parked in the restaurant's parking lot, we walked to the Black Wave, carefully stepping around an old man sleeping so peacefully on the sidewalk he could have been in a bed at the Waldorf Astoria.

A young girl greeted us. Her smile emphasized her tongue, chin, and eyebrow jewelry. Her white skin perfectly offset the tattoos around her upper arms and ankles and on her lower back. Dan-O, a thirty-something blonde guy appeared. His bare arms were covered with tattooed drawings—his left arm not yet colored in. He said it would take about another year to finish the work on his body—or "canvas" as he liked to call it.

He was patient, gentle—like he had been through this kind of scene before.

"Have you ever tattooed a sixty-year-old woman before?" I had to ask.

"That's about half my business," he said.

I was amazed to hear this, but I pressed on.

"Does it hurt?"

"Not a lot," he assured me.

"More than a bikini wax?"

He gazed at me and put his hand on his hip, "Well, I've never had one, but not from what I hear," he said.

So, there I sat with my eyes tightly shut, clutching the chair back, and clenching my teeth together, and waited for the first jolt from his tattoo needle so I could finally find out for myself. Guess what? It hurt. It hurt a lot—like the rat-tat-tat of needles being shot from a Tommy gun. Fortunately, the hurt didn't last very long.

When all is said and done I can say I got the tattoo because I wanted to prove I still had some life and adventure in me in the first few months after Paul died. I wanted to prove that I wasn't dead, that Paul hadn't killed every last drop of life left in me.

Most days I don't remember that the tattoo is there. But I show it off proudly when I get a chance.

"Awesome," a friend said when he saw it and found out I did it to celebrate my sixtieth.

Yeah! That's right. It is awesome. Getting a tattoo, despite the pain, brought me joy. And when Bob comes up behind me and kisses the blue star on my right shoulder, I know it was worth it.

I still have my fears. The greatest is that something bad will happen to Ben and Bob, and I'll be left alone. Bob has had health issues, which he keeps pretty much in check with medication, diet, and now with exercise. Yet, when he starts talking about getting his affairs in order and stopping to smell the flowers more, I worry about him. So it's a good thing that he's now working a little less, playing some golf once in a while, and ready to travel more.

My fears for Ben have always been irrational. I worry about losing him for any and every reason—driving on the freeway, flying, getting sick. He's my only son now—my only child. And I know if anything were to happen to him, it would be the end of me. That's a place I don't want to go. It's a place I mustn't go. And I don't know how to let go of that fear.

Even so, I've figured out a way to move on. I realize that I have a lot of giving left in me. I've worked in non-profit organizations for a long time—writing grant proposals, managing special events and capital campaigns, running development programs, and sitting on boards. That is extremely value-added work. And it helps my mental attitude. It feels good to volunteer. I get so much more from doing that than what I put in. I look forward to volunteering again possibly at Didi Hirsch. Working to overcome the stigma of mental illness and suicide is how I want to use my volunteer hours. I think I have a lot of experience along those lines. And I think that turning all my anger, sorrow, and fear into good works, is just what I need to stay healthy myself.

Aftermath

They came in droves at first,
out of concern, out of curiosity.
They sent flowers, cards
and sweet notes saying
call anytime,
anytime at all.

Now it is quiet.
A few friends
invite us out
or come by.
The rest have moved on,
glad to have done their duty.
They now have nothing left to say.

Don't they know I'm not contagious?
My son's death will not rub off on them.
I'm the same person I was before.
A sadder person, perhaps,
but needing my friends
just the same.

CHAPTER ELEVEN

....PEOPLE IN MY LIFE—IN OR OUT?

Almost immediately after Paul's funeral, people began to disappear. Perhaps they were threatened or couldn't face the realities of my life. Maybe my loss and grief brought too many reminders of the losses and grief in their own lives.

Sometimes when I run into people I haven't seen in a long time, I ask myself if I'm contagious. When I saw Laurie, a woman I've known for over thirty-five years, at Ralph's market one evening about six months after Paul died, she had a shocked look on her face when she saw me. It was as if she was surprised to see me up and about and doing a normal thing like grocery shopping. Clearly, she was seeing someone she didn't want to talk to, and there I was in her face.

"Hello," I said. I brought my basket right up close to hers, and she had to respond. She couldn't just ignore me. She sashayed up to me— she always walks that way—with her basket full of carrots and lettuce and packages of chicken and bread, and she trilled in her high-pitched singer's voice.

"Madeline, it's great to see you," she said without looking me in the eye. She never looked me in the eye. I could see from the way she kept looking from side to side and over my head that she was actually looking for a way away from me, a way to get me out of her sight.

"How's your fam…." I started to ask, and in mid-sentence she took her basket, turned it around one hundred and eighty degrees and was gone. No goodbye, no nothing. Gone.

Did she think Paul's death would rub off on her children? Was she unable to say something about Paul's death? Didn't she even have the words, "I'm sorry about Paul," in her?

I turned down another aisle and caught a glimpse of her reaching into the frozen food locker for a pint of ice cream. And then I remembered her daughter used to walk to school with Paul in second grade. Well, all right then. It all began to make sense to me. By all means. She needs to protect her daughter from him, from his memory, from his fate. Not talking to me is her self-protection.

Bob and I ran into her and her husband several years later at the movies, and we got the same brush off. She said a quick hello with a surprised look on her face as if she couldn't understand what we were doing here; how can we be normal enough to be able to go out to the movies together on a Saturday night? Of course those are just my projections. I've never had a chance to talk to her long enough to know how she really felt. And really, right now, I don't care if I ever do.

Before Paul died, I was working on a book about fitness for women over fifty. My book partner was a woman who trained fitness trainers at University of California at Los Angeles, someone I met several years before when she was teaching step aerobics at the gym where I worked out. We had a lot in common—mainly that we were old broads who took care of our bodies. Early on she told me of her desire to write a book for women our age, and I offered to work on it with her. We put together a book proposal, wrote the first couple of chapters, and took photos of each other demonstrating various exercises that we intended to use as illustrations. We wanted this book to be user-friendly with normal-looking, older women as role models, not skinny models the readers couldn't relate to. Even so, we were having trouble marketing the book and took a little break from it.

Judy was out of town when Paul died. She called when she got back in town, and I told her the news about Paul. With that, she told me of her father's suicide. Why did she wait until then to tell me? I had known her for years. She knew about Paul's bipolar illness. Maybe her sharing about her father could have forewarned me. Or maybe she just didn't want to face it like so many survivors I've met. I certainly know the feeling. I didn't want to face it—or even believe it at first—because it was so painful. She also told me she didn't want to continue working on the book. "I'm through with it," she said with no explanation. After all our work, she decided to drop it just like that. And as it happened, she was through with me too. That's the last I heard from her. Probably being with me brought up too many old memories—ones she had successfully buried for so many years.

Carrie is another story. We were both at Esalen Institute for a poetry workshop and roomed together by chance. We had never met before but discovered we had some mutual acquaintances. We hit it off instantly and were inseparable for the week—so much so that people thought we had known each other for years. We ate together, sat next to each other during the workshop sessions, shared our poems before we shared them with our group, and felt comfortable giving each other notes. When it was time to leave, we exchanged phone numbers and promised to be in touch once we were home. Because she also lives in the Los Angeles area, I thought it would be easy to keep in contact and continue our friendship and writing conversation. But that wasn't to be. We exchanged phone calls once or twice. The last time I called, she said she had to take another call and would call right back. I'm still waiting.

I couldn't understand why she so quickly dropped out except for a remark she made during our week together, "Your life is too much about death." Of course I have no rebuttal to that. It was the truth. I spent the whole week writing about Paul and a friend who was in hospice dying of lung cancer. It wasn't a secret. Death was on my mind. Death was my subject matter. If it offended her, she didn't have to befriend me or exchange phone numbers with me. She could have dropped out at the time we said goodbye at Esalen, and that would have been that. I would have understood. Even though she was right that my life was about death, it also was about living through it. Now I look on that loss as perfectly all right. I'm getting up there in years, so it's best that I spend whatever time I have left with people who really want to be with me.

We've lived next door to Sherry and her husband, Dave, for over twenty years, and she was always a person I avoided. Bob sometimes played racquetball with Dave, but I have never wanted to get socially involved with her. Even at Bob's hint that they were wine lovers like us, I wasn't interested.

I had always found her too loud—I could hear her yelling at Dave, her stepson, or their son, Steve, through both our exterior walls; too nosy—she always seemed to poke her nose outside whenever I was out in the garden; too domineering, and much too pushy. I couldn't believe her chutzpah when she appeared at our door with her oldest daughter and a six-pack of beer as soon as she found out we had two young, handsome, male houseguests—my nephew and his friend—staying with us for a few weeks. That was the end of my patience.

But it all changed the day Paul died. She offered to put up out-of-town relatives, she brought over bagels and cream cheese in the morning, and she supplied the coffee for the open house after the funeral. She was just there with calls and flowers and kind words, and then the basket. The word "suicide" didn't make her back off.

One night right before the first Thanksgiving after Paul's death, Sherry left a basket on my doorstep. Her note said that she dreaded the holidays after her mother died, so she gathered—"harvested" was the word she used—a few things to ease the holiday season for me. As I read her note and looked through the basket, I cried, not only out of the dread of being without Paul on Thanksgiving, Hanukah, and his New Year's Eve birthday, but for the generosity and caring of a person I hardly knew. In such a quiet and unassuming way, she showed me real human compassion and understanding. She never needed to ask me a lot of questions, and she didn't intrude on my privacy. She just let me know she was there for me if I needed her.

Among the items inside—each one separately wrapped—was a book about coping with the loss of a love—unlike most others. This one was in poetry—she knew I wrote poetry—and the first book I was able to concentrate on enough to read through after Paul died. She also included a journal, a sweet smelling candle, a box of absolutely delicious chocolate covered graham crackers, and a smooth gray stone.

This stone became my biggest comfort. Just large enough to fit in the palm of my hand, it feels the perfect size when I close my hand around it. One edge is round and the other is triangular. One side is plain; the other has the word "son" carved into it. Right after Sherry left the basket on my doorstep, my little stone became my night-time friend.

I soon got into the habit of going to bed with it. Once settled, I held it on my chest just between my breasts. I liked its coldness on my aching heart. It helped me relax. Holding it in my hand and reading the word with my thumb also helped. I carried it around in my pocket for a while. I wanted to feel that it was there for me. Then, I began to wonder about my own sanity. Was I trying to exchange my son for a stone?

When I got more together and began to feel better, I let go of it and let it rest on another item from that basket—a little, silk-covered, sachet pillow that smells like lavender. It has hand-painted butterflies and the word "heal" printed on the silk. They are still there on my bedside table after all these years.

A Stone Called Son

I sleep with a stone.
It's gray and small enough
to fit in the palm of my hand.
One side is smooth, the other
has the word "son" cut into it.
And when I put the stone
in the crook of my index finger,
I can read the word with my thumb.
I like to place it between my breasts
and feel its coolness on my chest.
It quiets the pain in my heart
and slows down my heartbeats
so I can rest.
Sometimes I hold it all night
and find it in my fist when I wake.
When I'm not sleeping, it sits next to my bed
on a tiny silk pillow imprinted on one side
with the word "heal."
Well, it takes time.
A healing pillow and a stone called son
can't do all the work.

Though I could have so easily have closed myself off, I soon began to open up to new friends. At first I seemed to gravitate toward people who were also immersed in the grieving process.

Kitty and I met at an Esalen writing workshop in December 2002, and now we share writing, attend workshops together, and room together when we're there at the same time. Her husband had died eighteen months before I first met her, when I was about two years into grieving for Paul. We had a lot to share and talk about. That she is a psychiatrist made it even more juicy, since she is so easy to talk to and so questioning. Early in our friendship she just came right out with it in an email, "When did you choose to live after Paul's death?" I hadn't even told her—or anyone—about my thoughts of suicide, yet she seemed to know they were there. What I wrote back was:

> *Okay. Here's the answer to your question about choosing to continue my life. That question comes up for me almost every day. And every day the answer is "Yes, I choose to continue." I know what suicide does to a family, and I couldn't do that to my husband or son again. And, I want to be there especially for Ben—he is young, has so much to look forward to in life. I want to be there for him and share in his life adventures. I know the statistics show that people who have had a family member or loved one commit suicide are more inclined to commit suicide themselves. But, I'm determined not to be one of the statistics. Unfortunately, the attraction was very great, especially right after he died. Then I literally saw myself getting into the same bathtub and slitting my throat as he did. Fortunately, we've totally redone that bathroom—demolished it totally—and there is no way I'd want to contaminate the new, pristine, sterile room or waste the money I spent redoing it. And like you, my work and my writing and my working out help. Also, my husband—also named Bob—is so loving. I am really very blessed to have Bob and Ben in my life.*

Recently I visited Kitty in her home outside of Portland, Oregon—on a little tree farm. She has an art barn with huge views from all sides where she can look out to the forest while she creates her paintings and poems. Death and thoughts of death have no business in that room.

At the first Esalen writing workshop I attended after Paul's death—when I was very raw—I found a soul mate in Eleanor. I wrote honestly about what was going on in my life and what had happened to my son—something I never hesitate to do—and Eleanor was attracted to my story and the way I wrote about it. We shared our experiences of losing a first-born child at such a young age even though the cause of their deaths was very different. That Eleanor, who experienced her loss several years before, was just getting started on her book, inspired and encouraged me. At the same time it gave me permission to take my time. I had wanted to write a memoir about Paul even while he was alive, but the months right after his death were too soon to get started. I think it takes about a year at least to let emotions settle down before embarking on this kind of writing project. I could do small pieces and poems, but a project of this size would have been too daunting right away. Eleanor was writing about the aftermath and how she had survived. There was no way I could do that in less than a year after Paul died. She understood.

Eleanor's daughter was killed in a horseback-riding accident, and she wrote a memoir, *Swimming with Maya*, that focused on that loss and about her decision to donate her daughter's organs. She has been on the circuit promoting her book. She also works through the non-profit organization The Compassionate Friends that supports parents who've lost children, and she's a keen advocate of organ donation. She has met the man who received her daughter's heart. What a blessing and affirmation that there is a way to live on after death.

Carrol and I both attended an all-day suicide-survivors' workshop early in the year 2000. She had lost her son to suicide a couple of years earlier and she was helping folks get over their grief. We literally looked at each other from across the room and bonded. She was so warm and sympathetic to me. I needed her friendship during my first year of grief. She and I both had lost our sons to suicide, so she was easy to talk to and cry with. She also inspired me to want to help other survivors—something I'm pursuing now. Unfortunately we don't see each other often because of our separate interests and projects, but we both feel very supportive and warm toward each other.

Ursula is another new friend. We met when our mutual friend, Adele, was living her last days in a hospice. Ursula, Adele's executor, is an artist. Because I had studied art for many years after I graduated from college and always visit art galleries and museums when I travel, knowing a fellow artist was very attractive to me. Ursula is outspoken, and accepting and caring of my poems and me. I had given Adele my chapbooks long before I knew she was sick, and she shared them with Ursula. One day Ursula sent me a beautiful leather book with her art collages illustrating some of my poems. This was an unbelievable gift. She also shared my poem about Adele with Adele's family.

Though our time together is limited, when we do see each other we usually go to an art exhibit—one that's a little quirky or out of the way. We recently drove to the Pepperdine University art gallery in Malibu on a beautiful sunny day when the ocean was like blue glass to see an art exhibit by someone named Zelda. Until we got there I didn't realize that this Zelda might be Zelda Fitzgerald, the wife of F. Scott Fitzgerald, but sure enough it was. We saw Zelda's hand-painted and drawn cut-out dolls and her representative paintings of nursery rhymes and fairy tales. Without Ursula I wouldn't have known such a treat existed. Who knew that Zelda Fitzgerald was an artist? My take on her had always been that she was a manic-depressive lady who sometimes considered herself a dancer.

Now don't think that all my relationships revolve around the loss of a loved one. Those experiences were just the catalysts. Now we hardly discuss death. Our other common interests—writing and art—keep us together.

And I'm happy to say I've moved beyond those few people. In the last few years I've discovered how easy it is to reconnect with old friends and make new friends on Facebook. I love that aspect of social networking. Five years ago, when Bob gave me a sixty-fifth birthday party, I reveled in being with so many loved ones. My whole family, many friends from work, many from all the years we've lived in Manhattan Beach and the Los Angeles area, and even friends from my high school days. I felt so blessed to have so many people I love in the same room. These are the people who came to my rescue with their love and support after Paul died. These are the people who made me believe that life, no matter what, is still worth living. And I told them so that night. I told them that when Paul died I didn't think I could get to the next day. Nor did I feel that I wanted to. So because of them I was able to get to my sixty-fifth birthday and feel comfortable enough to celebrate it. I consider that a miracle.

About four months after Paul died we saw his ex-girlfriend Janet. She was in Los Angeles on a business trip and had about two hours to spend with us. I was thankful to get even that. We spent the first hour dancing around the subject of Paul. She told us about her job, her boss, her life in New York, and we shared about our work, Ben, and what was going on with us. She complimented us on how well we looked, seeming surprised that we had managed to keep ourselves together.

246 ~ MADELINE SHARPLES

I brought it up. I wanted to know about her new boyfriend. I wanted her to know I was happy that she'd found someone who was normal, who wasn't needy, who could care for her, and whom she could bring home to her parents without their cringing. She never could do that with my son. Her parents didn't like or trust Paul because of his manic behavior and how it affected their daughter. So Paul didn't want to spend much time around them even when he was invited over.

I was angry that morning. Just being with her made me feel so cheated. I felt that this beautiful young woman was lost to me. She was moving on. She had another life that didn't include us and her memories of Paul.

I didn't blame her. It was just a fantasy, a pipe dream that Paul and Janet could ever have had a normal life together. I was kidding myself to think he could live with her in an apartment and take care of her. He couldn't even take care of himself.

But, Janet knew. As much as she loved my son, she had to protect herself from him. Even when I thought he was doing well, one night during one of her last times with him in Los Angeles, he got drunk at her hotel, got in the bathtub, fell asleep, and left the water running until it dripped into the room downstairs. He could have drowned himself that night—that would have been an accidental suicide. Neither Paul nor Janet ever told me about that night. Paul wouldn't have. He lied whenever I asked how he was. "I'm fine," he'd say. "How are you?" He never admitted he was sick or in trouble. Why didn't Janet tell me about that or her growing feelings of uneasiness about him? I guess she was slowly backing away from him and me even then.

I totally understood intellectually even though I felt so sad and disappointed about the way things turned out.

Janet also decided to get rid of all memories of Paul, including that unmailed last letter he wrote to her. She packed them up and brought them to us—all her memories packed in a large manila envelope. In it were a couple of pieces of his creative writing, a dress, a green glass vase, a book, the tapes he made for her, the Christmas CD he created for her, a drawing, and all the photos (she was a professional photographer and photography editor) she took of the two of them over their seven years together—with the negatives. That was it. I was astonished at how little there was in her memory collection, but I am not astonished at her need to get them out of her life. She said she wanted us to keep them for her, but I knew she would never want them back. What would she want with a bunch of tapes and pictures from her life with a crazy man who killed himself? How could she explain him to her children ten or fifteen years later?

Janet looked beautiful as we sat in the restaurant in the Mondrian Hotel. The all-white décor of that room set off her flowing red-brown hair perfectly. She wore lipstick, a ring, and little diamond earrings. I had never seen her in makeup or jewelry before. When I first met her, she didn't even shave under her arms. Paul liked that. I wondered how her new beau felt.

She was changed. She was obviously happy—so happy that I think she was afraid to admit how much to us. I was happy for her and so, so sad for me—that she was not my daughter. I wanted her to be my daughter so much.

During that lunch I sensed that she didn't want the memories and reminders that Bob and I represented anymore either. Unfortunately, she couldn't put us in that manila envelope and give us away as well. Still I knew that day that I would never see her or hear from her again. I was right.

Ben was one of three in his class at grade school who lost a brother. Dean's brother, Darren, was the first. He was killed in a car crash. I went to his funeral with Ben at the Manhattan Beach Community Church. We had to sit with the overflow outside listening to the proceedings through the loudspeakers. Afterward we went to the Manhattan Beach Badminton club and made our condolences. I felt so sad for the boy's parents. I knew them, but not well. Since Ben and Dean had gone through all eight grades together in the Manhattan Beach schools I would see them at school functions and around town.

A few days after the funeral I bought a box of cookies and brought it over to their house. I didn't know what to stay. I just stood at the door. I didn't know how they could deal with their son's death. Little did I know that I was in for the same kind of loss.

Like us they've lived in the same house over thirty years, just around the corner. I usually pass it on my walks to the beach, and every time I go by, I can't help thinking about the grief that must have gone on in there.

Paul's death was the second. Then Geoffrey, Rory's brother. Ben and Rory had been good buddies since second grade, and we spent a lot of times in the early days with his parents. Geoffrey's funeral took place where we held Paul's—the Hillside Mortuary. The room was full, and many of his friends from high school were there. I know how hard it was for me to start losing my friends before I turned forty; I can't imagine the way high school age children feel when one of their contemporaries die.

In the week after Geoffrey died we went to his family's house several times at sundown to recite the mourner's prayer—a Jewish tradition. One evening as I was approaching the house I saw Ben talking with Dean and Rory. The three of them were sitting on a low wall south of the walkway to the house. What was so moving about the scene was their mutual experience of each losing a brother. Dean and Rory lost theirs to automobile accidents, not to suicide like Ben's brother, Paul.

I don't know what these guys spoke about that day. We were all very sad about Geoffrey's death, but I suspect that Dean and Ben were also thinking about and mourning their own brothers' deaths.

When I got the call about Geoffrey I thought Bob and I might be of help to his parents, people we had known for several years. Even our rabbi thought so and asked us to go there right away. And at first they seemed to respond to our concern and show of love. We hadn't socialized for a long time, and I thought maybe our common losses could bring us back together.

That was not to be. Once the mourning period was over, his mother told me in no uncertain terms that she wasn't about to resume old friendships or take on any new friends now. That was and has been fine for me. I didn't want to push myself on anyone who didn't want me around. I had enough problems of my own. I certainly didn't need hers. Plus who knows if I would have been any help to her? It was too soon after my own son's death. However, I wasn't the only friend she turned away. I found out later from a mutual friend that she had un-friended her too.

Another family in our town also lost a son several years later. I see the mother often, mostly walking on the Strand along the beach. We played tennis together at our public courts when our children were small. We've spoken a couple of times after her son died—once at a local restaurant and once at our gym. She is friendly and always says she wants to get together and talk to me, but it never happens. I suspect she feels it will dredge up too much. I would be very willing to talk, but I'm not willing to be rejected. I sometimes say, "Hi," when I pass by her, but that's as far as I go.

So, I haven't spent a lot of time talking or comforting people I've known who have also had children who died. I have been the recipient of a lot of comfort from my dear high school friends, Stan and his former wife Bonnie, whose son shot himself six years before Paul died. Bonnie was in my class in high school and through the years we would see each other at reunions. She now lives in New York, and we get together when I visit there. She was so caring when Paul died I felt I could go to her at any time, as I did with her former husband, Stan.

During the 1970s we lived on Kwajalein, a Marshall Island, for nineteen months. With only three thousand people living there, we became quite close with the people Bob worked with (I was a stay-at-home mom during our time there) and many of the families from other companies. The island is a military base, and Bob was managing a military-funded program there. We had a slow and easy life on the island, filled with all kinds of beach and water activities. I remember getting up early, and while the boys were still sleeping, I began to write in a journal. That writing resulted in my first published piece—an article about our life on the island for my company magazine.

But sadly, six of the children we knew in those days have died, including our son. It seems so strange to me this could happen to such a small group of people. After we heard about the sixth death, Bob asked if there could have been something in the water, something in the air, something about that lifestyle. Who knows? None of them died very soon after leaving the island—each was well on his or her way in adulthood. Perhaps the deaths of Mark, Paul, and Danielle were the most curious. I believe Mark's death was drug-related, and Danielle's was a suicide of sorts—she was a homeless alcoholic. Do their deaths as well as Paul's suicide stem from the carefree time they had while living on an island in the middle of the South Pacific? I doubt it. They all swam, played t-ball, partied on the beach, snorkeled, fished, picked up shells

Fall 1978, just back from Kwajalein

and beach glass on the sand around the island lagoon, went to free movies on Saturday afternoons, and rode their two-wheel bikes without having to look where they were going. They all went to an excellent American school. After all, we lived on a military base, and the United States Government provided the children with the best.

I do know how much Paul missed the island once we returned home. Since Ben has no memories of his years or of his friends there, he never complained. Maybe had we stayed there Paul wouldn't have had such difficulties and the stresses that trigged his bipolar disorder, but I'll never know about that either.

Michael's death happened while he was serving in the military, and then in the last six months two more of our Kwaj kids died. Mitch died suddenly of cancer, and Stephanie died five months later during a gall-bladder surgery. Both were in their late thirties. Mitch and Stephanie had reconnected after thirty years and were engaged to be married. Her dad described them as star-crossed lovers.

Bob and Stephanie, Mitch, Michael and Mark's dads all worked on the same project while we were on the island. Danielle's dad was one of the island doctors. He and his wife were our good friends.

Remembering

Danielle

I remember a wiry blonde girl,
about five years old
with big eyes wiser than her years.
She took my son, Ben,
by the hand and led him
to the rock-lined cliffs
at the lagoon's edge
or to the park where
wasps hiding in trees
swarmed around them.
Screeching they ran to catch up
to their older brothers
all tan and freckled from the constant sun.
With them they stood
on the rocky cliff
lowering their baited hooks into
the warm Pacific,
and brought out little iridescent fish
in shades of blue and gold.

She left us this spring
like Ben's older brother
many years before.
Both lost their souls
in that deep lagoon.
They never found such magic
anywhere else.

Stephanie

I never got to know her
as an adult.
Only as a child years ago
on a tiny island
in the South Pacific.
She went to school with my boys
and played with them
at the beach
and at patio parties
given by our colleagues and friends.
She was adorable then
and I'm told brilliant, talented
and sensitive
before her untimely death
this past July.
She was way too young
to leave us. Only thirty-eight.
I needed time to get
to know her all grown up.

CHAPTER TWELVE

....CHILDREN IN MY LIFE

I always answer the dreaded question, "How many children do you have?" this way, "I had two sons. My oldest son died."

After the initial gasp, I hear the second most dreaded question, "How did he die?" Then we get into it.

"He had bipolar disorder," I say. "He killed himself."

It's as simple and as hard as that. I feel the rush of heat on my cheeks, I sense my heart breaking just a notch or two as it begins to beat faster, and I hear the familiar rumblings in my gut. Even if I look nonchalant and calm, my body tells me how I really feel.

I wait for the next dreaded question and sometimes it comes and sometimes not. "How did he kill himself?"

If you have a thought to ask this question, don't.

I try to avoid specifics; not to protect myself, I already know all the gory details. No, I want to protect the asker, especially if he or she has children. I want to protect imaginations from going to a place where they have no reason or need to be. People can't help asking these questions. They feel their interest is comforting to me, but I find it more of a burden. The tables get turned, and I feel the need to comfort them. It's happened over and over. When they say they just can't imagine losing a child, let alone losing one the way I lost mine, I say, "Don't go there. You don't need to imagine it."

When I got pregnant just less than two years after Paul was born, I stewed over having a second child. I had Paul and was so in love with him, and I had just settled in back at work. Another child would disrupt all that. I actually thought about having an abortion. But those were just thoughts. I remember sitting on a high stool at the bar between my family room and the kitchen and talking to my sister on the phone about it. She said, "I don't believe in abortion as a means of birth control." And I agreed with her. I used birth control for a year after Paul was born—an inter-uterine device, the Dalkin Shield, the one that damaged millions of women—and I never felt comfortable with it. I had a constant draggy feeling in my lower gut. When I finally told my doctor I wanted it out, he took it out so quickly I barely felt a thing, and from that instant I felt like a new person. After that I decided not to worry about birth control. I also didn't think it would be easy for me to get pregnant. When I did, I churned about it—so much so that it alarmed Bob. One of the reasons I wanted us to marry sooner rather than later was my desire to have children, and here I was waffling after having one. But, work wasn't the only reason. I feared having another Caesarian section delivery. The recovery was so hard and painful. I also feared having another deformed child. Paul had his funny fingers, and I was concerned about how another child would turn out. My age was another factor. In those days being over thirty was considered old to have children, and when I had Paul I was over thirty-one. With the next one, I would be thirty-four.

Thankfully, I gave up on those abortion thoughts and began to welcome the idea of a second child. In fact, I turned down a management position offer at work—a rare offer for a woman at my company in the early 1970s—because I was pregnant and didn't want to commit to working full-time when my children were small.

After I had Paul, I worked part-time and was still working part-time when I became pregnant with Ben. I tried the nanny route until Ben was about a year old, and then I decided to quit my corporate job entirely because the hours were too confining, the work was too regimented, and I was very uncomfortable having a nanny raise my children. I gave up a corporate career for my children and went into the real estate business so that I could dictate my own schedule and come and go as I pleased, most of the time. Real estate let me do a lot of paperwork from home during the week or host open houses and show property on the weekends when Bob was available to care for the boys. When I got back into the corporate world ten years later, I was not sorry to see that the time to become a corporate leader had passed me by. I got off the corporate ladder early on in my life and never looked back.

The Dreaded Question

It happens again like so many times before.
I'm at my sister's house,
talking to her neighbor,
someone I've just met,
and she asks me the dreaded question,
one that I'm avoiding
by talking about what a great day
this has been in Portland
and isn't my sister's garden just beautiful
and what do you do for a living
and where are you from.
And there it is,
after I've tossed the salad greens
put the tomatoes in the bowl
and sliced in the avocado
"How many children do you have?" she asks.
And never missing a beat
I say, I had two
but now, only one.
My oldest son died.
Then I leave to get myself together
and wonder what she and my sister are saying
while I am lying down in my room.

I also made up my mind that win, lose or draw, I would have my tubes tied when I gave birth to this second child. I decided I never wanted to go through a third or even fourth Caesarian.

Only after Paul died, did I realize how stupid that decision was. I traded one day of excruciating pain and a couple weeks of discomfort for the opportunity to have a third or even fourth child—probably why I was asked over and over by the hospital attendants if I was absolutely sure I wanted to go through with the tube-tying procedure that meant never having another child.

Nowadays, thirty is almost the normal childbearing age. Some think nothing of having children well into their forties, and even their fifties. I've read about a few women successfully giving birth in their sixties. Ah, the miracle of science—not an option during my childbearing years.

Once Ben was born, it was as if he and I belonged together. He was a cranky baby and I held him against my heart and upper abdomen and nursed him almost constantly to keep him calm. With that we bonded. Paul was always Bob's pride and joy—his little pal. Ben and I were joined at the hip—or more literally, at the abdomen—from the beginning.

Later on I thought about adopting another child. Ben always wanted to have a sister. When we lived in the South Pacific I was so taken with the many Marshallese children who were impoverished that I thought I could help by adopting one. I didn't act on that thought either. I guess it wasn't even a serious or well thought-out idea and looking back that also was a huge mistake. So, I encouraged a friend to go ahead when she considered adoption after having bad pregnancy experiences with her two natural-born children. "A pair and a spare is the way to go," I said. Now Ben is left with all the burdens of being an only child. If only I had listened to him and adopted a daughter. It's as though he had a premonition of Paul's fate.

At a time in life when many women friends have grandchildren and I do not, I've still managed to have a life full of children—other people's children and other people's grandchildren. Starting with my brother's five grandchildren—two named after Paul—children are very much a part of my life. I love them, I spoil them with gifts, I pay attention to them as if they were my family, and I'm with them as much as time allows. I feel very blessed for that, but it's not the same as if they were my own grandchildren. I see my brother's wife with her grandchildren. She is like a mother to them, she's the one they run to. I'm not there. Not yet, but hopefully soon now that Ben and Marissa are married. It's always good to hope.

CHAPTER THIRTEEN

....DEMOLITION

At first I felt I had to keep Paul's things in plain sight just the way he left them. And though I didn't want to make his room into a shrine, I felt I couldn't give his things away yet. Then four months after he died, I took the first step in that direction and packed away his clothes.

He left his room with clothes strewn all over the floor and on his big easy chair. I didn't know what was clean or dirty, so I washed everything except his wool shirts. He loved those plaid shirts. They were old—from a second-hand store—soft and with rips and buttons missing. He didn't care. He wore them around the house over a tee shirt like a jacket. As I folded them one by one, I put them close to my face to smell them. They still had his smell—a sweat and smoke mix. I couldn't send them to the cleaners. I didn't want the smell to go away. I laid each flat on his bed, carefully did the buttons, and smoothed out the wrinkles before turning it over and folding in the sleeves and sides. After the last

262 ~ MADELINE SHARPLES

fold, I straightened the collar. A collar of one of the shirts kept curling up. It didn't want to stay flat. I piled the other shirts on top of it.

I kept folding—his sweaters, his tee shirts, his khakis, his jeans— even the ones so shredded at the knees they could be rags—his boxers and his socks until I had neat piles of his clothes on his bed.

Before placing them in the boxes, I made a list just in case we finally could give them away, and so Ben would know what was inside. He wanted some of Paul's things, mostly his records and CDs—Paul's clothes wouldn't fit Ben. Paul was small-boned like me, and several inches shorter than Ben. Paul's clothes didn't fit Ben's style either—he's not the tattered and shredded type.

Aside from his clothes, Paul was meticulous about his things. Every record in his jazz music collection was in alphabetical order on the shelf in his closet. So were his books. He saved every book, greeting card, ticket stub, concert program, school notebook—they were all there on the shelves in his room. What he didn't have on the tables in his room or shelves in his closet he packed away and put on his closet shelf. He made everything fit in boxes—little toy cars and stuffed toys, a Dungeons and Dragons painting kit, a box of pins he collected at the 1984 Olympics, a baggie full of guitar picks, his Rubik's cube, a shoehorn, a collection of pencils held together with a rubber band—like an intricate puzzle.

I felt so intrusive—as if I were invading his space. He was such a private person. He would hate having me go through his things. I kept saying, "Paul, forgive me. I just have to. I'm trying to find out what happened to you. And, being in your room with your things is the best way to find out."

I still churned about how he could have ever left his things. He was so attached not only to things, but to places and people. From early on in his life he hated change. That's why I never really believed he could or would do it. How could he have let go of his things and everything else he was familiar with?

Once during the height of one of his manic attacks, he sold some of his records and musical equipment and then when he recovered and was rational again he couldn't rest until he bought it all back. Now his things are scattered all over the place. Ben took his little Buddha figure. The tall candlesticks are on the top shelf of the bookcase in my office. The one that looks like a spiral of leaves sits on the table in front of the sofa in our family room. I never asked him where these worn, old iron candlesticks came from. Now, I'll never know. Like him, there are so many things I won't ever know about. It's finished but still unfinished. A mystery that will stay unsolved forever.

I used to wear his sunglasses every day. They're black-rimmed and hug my face like goggles. I didn't carry a purse when I went to his funeral. I held on to those glasses. I kept clenching and unclenching my hand over them all through the service.

Sometimes I used to see him sitting outside the Starbucks in downtown Manhattan Beach in those glasses and his black bomber jacket. He would sit all folded up with his legs and arms crossed, and his body all hunched over like Rodin's "The Thinker" tapping his foot in time to the music in his head. He liked to stop at Starbucks before going to work. He never bothered to make coffee at home. Now I sometimes think I see him there—a thin young guy, with black-rimmed sunglasses and hair buzzed so short he looks almost bald. But that's not my son, Paul. Paul's gone. All I was left with were his things.

Now I don't even have those. After about a year I finally was able to give away his clothes and shoes. I wrote grant proposals to raise money for a homeless shelter in downtown Los Angeles. They needed men's clothes—especially shoes and his shoes were in pretty good shape, compared to his mostly worn clothes. But, I still have his records and books. They are meticulously catalogued on Excel spreadsheets and reside in neatly stacked and labeled boxes in the garage.

Just one year after his death—September 2000—we dismantled Paul's stereo system and electronic keyboard equipment and changed the configuration of his bedroom to get ready to have the carpets cleaned. As we waited for the carpet cleaners, we decided to roll the pennies and small change he had accumulated in a large decorative coffee can. The can was very heavy. We poured all the coins onto our family-room table, sifted through them, and picked out the quarters, dimes, nickels, and any foreign coins in the bunch. I took on the task of creating stacks of ten pennies each, made up of two stacks of five. I wanted to touch each of the pennies my son had touched before me. I counted out two then three pennies, then three, then two to make up little five-penny stacks. As I picked up each penny my fingers became sticky-green and dirty— evidence that I had touched every one that he had touched before he tossed it into the can. Now all the coins are gone. Bob took the little stacks of ten, put them in penny rolls, and deposited thirty-nine dollars into our bank account. Paul never liked to spend his loose change unless he was really strapped. Only when he was getting ready to leave on one of his flights of fancy, did I see him rolling his coins like we did to cash them in for paper money.

That day we also put the large chair from his room out in front of the house to be picked up by the garbage men the next morning. The cushions were off, and I dug my fingers around in the dirt, deep down around the bottom of the seat. I found two cuttings from his finger-nails—small, crescent-shaped. He always kept his nails neatly trimmed. He always carefully cut the coarse stray hairs that grew on his fingers where they had been surgically separated and grafted with skin from his groin.

While we were in the cleaning-out mode, we resurrected all the videos left out in the garage and found a home video taken on a family vacation to the western states in 1987. We watched it almost immediately.

Ben had received a camera for his Bar Mitzvah. He was a squeaky-voiced little boy still shorter than I, and Paul was not quite sixteen. Paul was a student driver and excited because we promised to let him do a lot of the driving on what would turn out to be our last real family vacation. The video shows him easily climbing the rocks at the national parks in Utah and a marvelous close-up of his beautiful eyes taken while we were eating lunch in Taos, New Mexico.

By the end of the day of cleaning I had had enough reminders. I couldn't bear to hear Paul's music on the CD that Bob wanted to play while we were on our way to dinner. Paul was even in my dreams that night—agreeing to go on vacation with us if he could have some beer. Just like Paul—always ready to take the bribe, never willingly doing something unless there was something in it for him. And no, he didn't get the beer.

So his fingernail cuttings went out with the garbage, his electronic equipment donated to Crossroads School, his pennies back in circulation to be touched by many others, and his other cherished possessions scattered to the winds. He left us slowly but surely—except from my heart and gut. After we finished the counting and dismantling, I went to the gym but could hardly work out my gut hurt so much. Not a heartburn hurt, but a real stomachache. As if Paul was punching me out, punching me for disrupting his presence here. But I had to. I couldn't let his room become a filthy shrine. I had to move on no matter how much it hurt.

Instead of following Paul into that tub, I obliterated it. I had the tub, the sinks, the toilet, the floor removed. I had the walls totally removed down to the studs so that no trace of that bathroom or what had happened in there was left. That was the next step—transformation. Even though I never saw him dead in there, every time I went in there I imagined I saw him dead in there. I couldn't comfortably use that bathroom anymore and neither could Ben when he was home. Bob, until this day, no matter what I did to transform the room, thinks of it as the Death Room.

I designed the new bathroom. I picked out the tiles for the floor, the walls and the shower area. I picked out the sinks, tub, toilet, mirrors, faucets, lights, and towel racks while our contractor hired the laborers and oversaw the work. After four long months of dry wall and plasterers, tile and grout guys, painters, and electricians in my downstairs, the bathroom turned out perfectly. A long photo of the Manhattan Beach pier hangs on one wall and reflects in the mirrors on the opposite wall. Fluffy towels in shades of green and blue, matching the ocean in the photo, hang on the racks.

It took us almost six years from the time he left his room for the last time to do something substantial to it. Once in a while we used it as a guest room. But the closet still had his books and records in it—first on the shelves and then in neatly packed and labeled boxes—and the dust that had accumulated since Paul last played his keyboards on the floor in there. Ben took his bed for his own apartment, and he stacked those boxes of books and records out in our garage, leaving the closet with the layers of six-year-old dust empty and ready to be transformed with file drawers and bookshelves and a place to store my out-of-season clothes.

Demolition

Bathroom

We don't have to look into that room anymore
and wonder if spots of blood still remain
on the floors and walls.
We've demolished the scene of the crime.
We will no longer step into that tub and see Paul
in his white, long-sleeved, work shirt
and khaki pants sitting against the shower door
in a bloody puddle.
They've taken it all away.
The old aqua-blue tub,
the toilet, the sinks,
and the faux marble counter
with burn stains from the tiny firecrackers
he set off as a teenager.
The god-awful blue and yellow vinyl flooring is gone.
Sterile white tiles and fixtures
take their place
in a room with no memories
either of life or death.

Bedroom

Six years later
instead of the dark room
he walked out of for the last time,
leaving the door slightly ajar,
his bed never slept in,
his dirty laundry
slung over his over-stuffed chair,
his paychecks left on the side table
uncashed for weeks,
his pictures and posters meticulously thumb tacked
in perfect rows on the walls,
his books and records all lined up
in alphabetical order in his closet
along with his shoes and plaid shirts from second-hand stores,
his keyboard, electronic drums, amplifier,
and his music, each tape labeled and packed
in a canvas bag,
so we could easily choose
a piece to play at his funeral.
Instead, the room now totally bare
except for a new bay window
that looks over the garden
and new shiny hardwood floors.
A writing table and a comfortable sofa
will go in there
with space in the closet
for shelves of poetry books,
and files of poems
hoping to be published.

Garage

Boxes labeled Paul's fiction A–Z,
Paul's jazz records K–O,
Paul's rock and roll A–F,
stacked where I can see them
as I open the door
and park my car every evening
after a long day at work.
On top of the boxes
are a pile of Dungeons and Dragon games
one tarnished, brass-duck bookend
he got for his Bar Mitzvah,
the purple treasure chest
where he kept his pot, and
a cigar box filled with medals and belt buckles
his uncle brought him from Russia.
Against the wall
leans a roll of drawings
he made in Bellevue's psych ward,
each declaring his love for Janet,
now married with two children.
A photo of her
with high-pointing breasts,
slim waist, flat stomach, and round, firm buttocks
shows her proud and so ready
though Paul was not.
He let her go.
He let it all go
with one swipe of the knife.

Did this transformation mean that I had finally given up hope that he would return? Did I not have to leave the hall light on for him anymore? And, if needed, could I ever move out of this house without having to worry that he wouldn't have a place to come back to—the house in which he grew up and died? Of course, the answer to all those questions is yes. But it doesn't mean that I want to or ever will.

When I decided to transform his bedroom, I declared it would be my room—my writing room and office. With Ben out of the house and on his own, Bob and I had enough room for each of us to have our office.

Paul had been my muse for so many years; so I decided he could continue to be my muse in my new room. It's where I decided to finish telling his story—about his illness and how the medicines didn't work for him and how hard he fought against taking them (because he realized he couldn't live a creative life with them) and how he just couldn't live without them. I don't want him to be forgotten. I want the world to know a beautiful person named Paul Ian Sharples once lived there. So it is fitting to write his story in the place that once was his room.

I transformed the room slowly and methodically. My original thought was to push out the room a foot or two into the yard, but we found that to be too costly. We settled on installing a huge bay window, side-opening windows, and a long window seat, creating a room that had so much more light than when Paul had lived in it. We then replaced the carpet with wood flooring and had the walls painted medium taupe. The ceiling, the newly installed crown molding, the window trim, the floor moldings and the doors are a stark white. The sound of the wall of dusty orange bookshelves being demolished in the closet added to my excitement, and soon the closet was ready for installation of file drawers and shelves. I couldn't wait to move in my books, writing files, and office supplies. I also store a collection of Paul's writing in those file drawers. I found them in a box when we finally cleaned out his things from the closet. We next ordered my huge desk/draftsman's table, desk chair, sofa, lamps, and a tall, narrow shelf unit—all the furniture I had room for. The shelf stands to the left of my desk and holds memorabilia, photos, a few special books including the book of Matisse cutouts called *Jazz: The Text* that Paul gave me, and the first Buddha of my collection—a smiley guy with a fat belly and tiny hands and feet all in the prayer position.

I write in there alone. I sit at my large black draftsman table opposite the bay picture window. I look out to the garden, at the three palm trees, the small cement pond, and the ginger plants behind it, all designed to create a calming influence on my writing work. I can hear the gurgle of the fountain when the windows are open. Once in a while a bird comes to take a seed from the birdfeeder or a dip in the pond. If I'm not sitting at my table, I can sit on the window seat or on the orange sofa.

Before I moved anything into the room, I performed a cleansing ritual. I placed little glass containers of salt in each of the four corners of the room to suck out the bad toxins. Later I smudged it with a bouquet of sage I brought home with me from Esalen. Afterward, I felt so good about the room. I knew I had done the right thing in making it my own. It took me a long time to get to that place, but it was worth the wait.

And, I absolutely love being in there. I wish Paul could see it. I think he'd like it. The sofa is like a futon—he once slept on a futon in this room—only richer and more elegant. A lava lamp in shades of orange like the one Paul wanted me to buy him the day we spent walking on Melrose right before his birthday, in December 1995, stands on my desk. I had just bought him a pair of black wing-tip shoes, and he saw a lava lamp in a shop window and immediately asked for it. But I wasn't feeling generous enough to buy it that day. Now I know a lava lamp gyrates in time to music. I didn't realize that Paul didn't just want a lava

Madeline's office, November 2010 (Paul Blieden photo)

lamp. He needed one. He needed the lamp to calm him down and to help him deal with the pain from of his illness. And he needed it to keep time with his music whether it was the music he played on his keyboard or in his head. So I needed one too.

At first I worried about how it would feel taking over his space, how it would feel to make it mine. And now I know. It's a feeling of cleansing, healing, and of being in a safe and comforting space. I feel calm in there, and that calm helps my writing. Maybe the little reminders of Paul in there help too. His candlesticks are on the top shelf of the bookcase, his photo is on the next shelf and a portrait of me when I was pregnant with him hangs on the wall. I posed for my drawing class a few weeks before he was born and had it in my art portfolio all these years. I decided that it must go into this room. I also have a photo of a sunset taken on September 22, 1999—his last night alive. I met a photographer at an art fair who had photographed every sunset in the year 1999, and I ordered the photo of Paul's last sunset. It's a beautiful reflection of an orange sun in a deep blue ocean—and so peaceful. I even have a new piece—also a reminder of Paul. My friend Ursula made an assemblage called "Backbone" out of felt-covered wooden mallets originally used to strike the strings of a piano. It was another thing I had to have. Another thing to remind me of him.

I've also added many other Buddha statues to my collection in my office—besides the ones in other parts of the house and garden. They are on my desk and on the end table next to the sofa. No, I haven't erased Paul. He's there with me, inside me. I'll never be able to erase him.

Garden, November 2010 (Paul Blieden photo)

CHAPTER FOURTEEN

Very close to the first anniversary of Paul's death we had a ceremony to dedicate his gravestone. My sister came into town from Portland and the morning before the ceremony we went to Bristol Farms to buy food for the little gathering we would have at our house afterward.

Bob left early to pick up my mom who no longer could get around on her own, and my sister and I promised to come soon afterward. I wanted to speak with the rabbi about the ceremony and get directions from him because this would be the first time I would drive to that cemetery on my own. He said we could follow him, but he wasn't leaving for quite a while since his schedule wouldn't allow him to be there much before the half past noon ceremony start time. That was fine for me. I definitely wasn't in a hurry to get there. I was nervous about going through this event and still trying to decide if I should read one of my poems or say anything at all during the ceremony.

Officially this dedication ceremony marks the end of the Jewish year of mourning, but mourning wasn't over for me. And even though I made much progress in that first year toward surviving his loss, official or not, I was not through mourning for Paul.

Three Cemeteries

On a cool, sunny day in Normandy
the breeze does not disturb
the graves at the American Cemetery.
No matter where you stand,
looking diagonally, horizontally,
or straight back and forth,
each alabaster–white grave marker,
each chiseled engraving
is in perfect precision
and symmetry
as far as the eye can see.
The grass covering the graves
mowed just the right height,
a shade of green
from a Technicolor garden.
A rectangular reflection pool,
the curved wall inscribed with the names
of 1,557 Americans missing in action,
the center bronze statue commemorating
the spirit of American youth,
and the Omaha Beach below
create a restful setting
for the 10,000 allied soldiers
killed in 1943 or '44
during World War II.

On a gray, rainy day
in Prague,
hordes of tourists stroll
through the Jewish cemetery.
Their feet crunch
the brown and yellow leaves
covering the ground.
Housing 800,000 graves—
some over twelve layers deep—
this cemetery, not functional since 1787,
verges on collapse.
The packed gravestones lean
every which way
in a hodgepodge of rectangular, square,
and triangular shapes
so old, so worn and broken
the Hebrew or Yiddish markings
are hardly readable.
Just like the Jews
who were forced to live
crammed together in
the Prague ghetto,
these gravestones want
to escape the barriers
that keep the visitors and vandals out.

On a stormy day
in Los Angeles
we drive through the gates
of Hillside Cemetery
and curve around the drive
to the back wall
and a small plot
of miniature, flat, rectangular,
gray and black marble gravestones
lying flush
with the closely cropped grass,
marking the cremated remains
of fathers, mothers, aunts, uncles,
and grandparents.

Full sun interrupts the downpour
just long enough
for us to kneel
at our son's grave
on his December 31st birthday,
wipe away the raindrops,
leave a smooth black stone
and four yellow roses
and allow our tears to fall.

Even now my whole being reacts to the thought that Paul is really dead and that I'll never see him again. I feel an emptiness in my gut, I feel my heart racing, I feel my neck and shoulders tightening up, I feel my face quivering, I feel my throat constricting, I feel my eyes flooding.

When we finally arrived at the cemetery for the dedication ceremony, the first greeting was from my mother. Not a hug and kiss, not caring words like, "I've been thinking about how you must feel today." Instead, in her usual shriek-y voice she shouted, "What took you so long? We were so worried." It was the same tone she always used when her children did something she didn't like. "How could you do this to me?" she would shout. She always judged our actions by how they affected her.

So I was annoyed immediately. Couldn't she have understood how I was feeling that day? I had to be at this cemetery to dedicate my son's gravestone in a plot surrounded by old, old dead people. I kept thinking he shouldn't be here, thinking he doesn't belong here with all those old people, thinking he has too many things to do and places to go yet, thinking he can't do any of them because he is here.

He was too close to the freeway. I could hear the noise of the cars and I worried that the noise would disturb him. He was so sensitive to noise and the music and voices that played around in his head, and I had chosen to lay him at rest in a noisy place where he couldn't concentrate on his music.

I had more guilt about cremating him and placing him in this cramped plot of miniature graves at the back of the cemetery. I was brought up in the conservative Jewish tradition that didn't allow cremation. And even though our rabbi told us it would be okay and that the Jewish cemetery where we chose to bury Paul allowed it, it made me feel uncomfortable. What would my Jewish relatives think? Would people think I didn't care enough about him to spend the money on a regular gravesite? So I wasn't in a hurry to face my family that day. I couldn't help wondering what they thought of where he was. But I had been so rushed, so pressured about what to do when he died. The decision was excruciating. It was exhausting. It was hasty. Of course we weren't prepared. What parent is ever prepared for the details and aftermath of a child's death? I wasn't supposed to make those kinds of choices for my son. He was supposed to make those choices for me.

Bob and I decided to have Paul cremated as a compromise. Bob wanted cremation and just a simple ceremony to scatter his ashes— that's what he wants for himself. I agreed to the cremation if we could bury his ashes and have a memorial service. I wanted him in a tangible spot where I could go visit whenever I wanted. I didn't want to look out to the Pacific Ocean and think with uncertainty, "Oh, he's out there somewhere."

I was nervous as I walked toward the gravesite. Unlike the sunny and hot day of his memorial service one year before, this afternoon was chilly. The sky was dark like my sad, brooding mood.

The others waiting for my arrival—my aunt, cousins, a few dear friends, and one couple who very much empathized with us because they had buried two of their children—greeted me with hugs and kisses.

Bob was at my side and held my hand as we gathered in a circle on the grass next to Paul's grave—very much squeezed next to the other surrounding graves. The Rabbi spoke, said some prayers in both Hebrew and English, and recited a beautiful poem. Then we all recited the Lord's Prayer and the Mourner's Kaddish—a prayer that affirms life rather than rants about death. That was enough for me. I didn't need to speak myself. The rabbi then took off the red cloth that covered Paul's black granite stone and the dedication was over. Just like that. One year of mourning officially over with the swift removal of a red cloth—like the curtain rising at the start of a play. Well, I wasn't ready for the play to start. I had more mourning, grieving, wallowing to do. The first year was over. I had made a lot of progress in that first year, but I still had a long way to go.

Most of the gravestones at that cemetery had a Jewish star or Menorah on them—usually between the date of birth and the date of death. Since Paul was a piano player and he wasn't religious even though he had gone to Sunday school, Hebrew school and was Bar Mitzvah, we requested that a tiny grand piano be etched on his stone. It is indeed fitting. Otherwise the stone is simple. It has his full name, Paul Ian Sharples, and the words, "Beloved Son and Brother," underneath. The last row has 1971 (his birth year), the piano and 1999 (his death year). There is no more room for more words on that tiny, flat, rectangular stone.

Since Paul's death it has been our tradition to visit this site on his birthday and death day every year. Nothing, even though he was born on New Year's Eve day, gets in the way of that visit unless those days are on the Sabbath or holiday when the cemetery is closed.

Each year I dread the anniversary of his death day—especially the going to the cemetery part. I know he isn't there—just his ashes are there in that tiny plot in the urn area underneath a black granite headstone with the piano on it. But I have to go there. I have to touch the headstone, smooth away the dust, brush off the dead grass, lay down a sweet smelling gardenia. We also put a stone on his gravestone next to the flower—another Jewish tradition that shows someone has visited. I cry. It's so easy for me to cry there.

We don't stay long. All I need is a few minutes to reconnect, to stop what I'm doing in my busy life to just be with Paul. I dread going, yet when it is over I feel like I want to go back more often. And I wonder why I don't. Maybe it's because he's with me everywhere—all around our home, in my office, in the car, wherever we are when we travel, in my words, in my mind, in my soul, in my heart. I don't need to look for him in the cemetery. Being there only affirms his death. The other places keep him alive for me.

Protective Cover

The rabbi sets the baggie of ashes
into the tiny grave
and we, shovel by shovel,
cover it with dirt.
After a year we lay a gravestone
on top of the bare earth
as an added protective cover.
I return to that gravesite
two times a year—
my son's birthday and death day,
always wishing I could
lift off that granite stone,
dig away the dirt,
and take that bag
out of its resting place.
If only I could reach inside that baggie,
place those ashes into the palms of my hands
and transform them
back into the son
I once had
many years ago.

I made a memory list. I wrote down all the things I could think of that were unique to Paul. I kept adding to the list, going back to it, rereading it so I didn't duplicate what was already on it. It was as if I was racing with time. I didn't want the passage of time to fade his memory from my mind. So, I kept grabbing, scratching at the surface of my brain to remember, to rediscover, to reconnect with how he looked, what he said, what he did. I continually searched for little mannerisms that were so Paul, such as how he walked so fast I had to almost run to keep up with him. He got that way from living in New York. My dad walked fast too. My dad was so in love with Paul. I can still see them: Paul perched on my dad's lap, both gazing into each other's eyes with proud grandpa and grandson grins on their faces. Maybe they are somewhere taking long fast walks together. I'd sure like to believe that. But I don't.

♪ *I'll always remember he slept without closing his eyes all the way*

♪ *I'll always remember he walked fast and way ahead of us*

♪ *I'll always remember he had long, thick, black eyelashes surrounding clear-blue eyes*

♪ *I'll always remember he played the piano, legs crossed at the knees, leaning way down over the keyboard*

♪ *I'll always remember he liked to wear second-hand clothes and didn't mind if they were ripped*

♪ *I'll always remember the way he stood at the pantry door munching almonds*

♪ *I'll always remember he liked to climb—trees, rocks, up the highest diving boards*

♪ *I'll always remember he was meticulous about his things*

♪ *I'll always remember he could play almost any tune by ear*

♪ *And that he was always a loner*

♪ *And how much he loved Janet*

♪ And wasn't hugged enough after she left him

♪ I'll always remember he was sensitive

♪ I'll always remember he drove too fast and erratically

♪ I'll always remember he got lots of parking tickets

♪ I'll always remember he was in love with John Lennon

♪ I'll always remember he liked Doc Marten shoes

♪ I'll always remember he tapped his foot when he sat down

♪ I'll always remember seeing him on the stone stoop drinking coffee at Starbucks

♪ I won't ever forget the feel of his cool pale skin the last night I saw him

♪ Or the sound of his voice

♪ I'll always remember his hair was thick

♪ I can't forget he knew all the nursery rhymes by the time he was two

♪ I'll always remember that he and his brother called the back of the station wagon, "the really back"

♪ I'll always remember he loved to fish.

I don't try to hide the fact that he existed. His pictures are all over the house though now some are irreparably faded. Even though I know it's uncomfortable for others to hear me talking about him, I do. I tell about my experience with him. What a calm baby he was. How easy it was to care for him. I talk about his finger surgery and what an impact it had on his life.

I kept his piano (now refinished). His sheet music, thumb drum, and traveling guitar are upstairs in the family room. I like having his things around me. I feel that having his things around respects his memory. I don't try to hide him or anything about him because I know how quickly people forget.

That hurts. That's what I'm scared of the most. That after I'm dead no one will remember him. That's why I find ways to memorialize him—every year around the time of his death day,

So many people suggested we sell our home after Paul died that I almost started to agree with them. We contacted our favorite realtor and actually looked at a few properties. But, when I found out about the realtor's code that a death in a house must be reported if it occurs within three years of selling that house, we decided to wait. We thought that three-year rule would lower our home's value. And that turned out to be a blessing. We put our property search on hold, and we've never resumed it. I knew I couldn't really sell this house. And at first I was a little cuckoo about it. I didn't want him to think we had forgotten about him—why I had to leave the hall light on for him.

I wanted him to know we were still here waiting for him when he decided to come back. I waited and waited for that familiar sound of the Volvo screeching into place in the garage, the sound of the door from the garage opening and closing, and his long strides as he went down the hall to his room.

Now those sounds and thoughts in my imagination are gone.

For years I couldn't move any of his books and records out of his closet. They were all lined up in there in alphabetical order, and I knew they had to be documented before they could be packed away. I finally got Ben to do that job. He created Excel spreadsheets listing each record and book, and he packed everything away in boxes that are now piled up in the garage. Because these things were so important to Paul, I can't bear to let any of them go. We moved his tapes and CDs into our family room. At first I tried to keep them segregated from our collection, but that proved to be impossible. Now Paul's collection has become part of the family's.

Paul left us about thirty cassette tapes of his original music, now copied on CDs thanks to his high school friend Martin—truly a gift of love. Martin also created an MP3 web page for Paul with his picture and samples of his music. When I visited his site, I found out many hundreds of people also had experienced his music. Unfortunately, the web page is no longer available. It went by the way of all free music on the Internet.

The day Paul died, the director of development at Crossroads School, where Paul and Ben had attended high school, called. She was sympathetic, soothing, and selling as is the way with development directors for non-profits. I know. I used to be one. What she suggested was an endowment fund in his memory that would benefit the high school's jazz music program. How smart she was. She knew exactly how to hit home. Paul had greatly benefited from that program, so I was sold on the idea of giving back to it immediately. By the time of his funeral four days later we had it set up. When Bob spoke he said, "Many of you have asked for ways you can help. One way is a donation in his name to the Paul Sharples Endowment Fund at the Crossroads School." He also suggested donations to the research needed to quell once and for all this killer called bipolar disorder. Right after Paul died a lot of friends and family contributed to the endowment. My sister and her husband still do. Bob and I are the major donors—through our personal checks every year on his birthday. I also donated through deductions from my work paycheck before I retired.

I consider Didi Hirsch Mental Health Services the organization where we attended the Survivors After Suicide group, a charity near and dear to my heart. We donate to Didi Hirsch at the end of each year. We also walk in its yearly suicide prevention run/walk. A banner with the names and faces of others who have committed suicide is displayed at this event, so we donate to have Paul's face on that banner. And we attend the Didi Hirsch Erasing the Stigma luncheon every year.

I truly believe Paul felt this stigma and shame, and that is what kept him from seeking help and talking about his illness. The work Didi Hirsch does to erase that stigma and to prevent through its suicide support groups and suicide-prevention hot-line would have been so useful to us while Paul was alive if only we had known that a place like Didi Hirsch existed.

We also donated a plaque at the Jazz Bakery. Paul played there the last time he played in public for the Crossroads Jazz Ensemble reunion concert in the December before he died. I think he only played one tune, and it was hard for him to even focus on that. The rest of the time he walked around the facility and in and out the door. After Paul died the director of the Crossroads music department sent us a photo of Paul playing that night. Paul was one of her favorite students, and she was deeply upset by his death.

During the first year after Paul's death we made a donation of the Micronesian handicrafts we had collected while we lived in the South Pacific. We had redecorated our house—completed just before he died—and decided we had lived with these wonderful wooden and palm-frond artifacts long enough. It was time for others to see them and learn from them. We made the donation in Paul's memory because the time he spent in the South Pacific—living on Kwajalein in the Marshall Islands and visiting Ponape, Yap, Palau, and Guam—were some of his happiest times. The collection of over eighty pieces is housed in the Pacific Asia Museum in Pasadena, California.

We planted a coral tree on our property on the first anniversary of Paul's death. It stands at the edge of our driveway like a welcoming sentry in the place where an old Monterey pine once grew. We knew we wanted a flowering tree—but not just any old one. And, after a long search we decided on a coral tree that has red-orange flowers in the spring that match our red-tile roof. I had seen them growing along the parkway across from our house, and I loved their look. Sometimes they bloom with the branches totally bare of leaves, giving the tree a very Asian feel—like a natural bonsai.

We bought the largest tree our local nursery had—one in a twenty-four-inch box—with a trunk about six inches in diameter and about six-feet-tall. We wanted the tree to grow into a climbing tree. It has a strong trunk with lots of vees for climbing and sitting and is very fast growing. We had hoped that whether we're still at this house or not, some little boy or girl will find joy in climbing that tree and sitting in those vees. How Paul loved to climb the pine tree as a boy, a daredevil from an early age. He loved diving off the high dive, he loved the rock climbing trips offered by his high school, and he loved to snow and water ski—sports where he could exercise his fearlessness were just up his alley. He certainly never had my fear of heights.

However, the joke is on us. A coral tree can never be a climbing tree. As it matures, more and more thorns appear on its trunk and branches—not very hospitable for little climbers. It is beautiful nonetheless.

At first Bob said we should plant the new tree in memory of Paul on Arbor Day, the last Friday in April that was ironically the day we cut down the old dead pine. But no. I wanted to plant it on September 23, Paul's death day.

And as planned the tree arrived full of leaves on the morning of the first anniversary of his death. Two men from the nursery dug the hole—about two-feet deep—and planted it. One of the men had just come from his daughter's first communion, so I was grateful that I could get them to come that day at all. I was determined to have the tree planted that day. Any other day would have been meaningless.

Now, more than ten years later, the tree is enormous. We have to have it trimmed every eight months otherwise it would take over what little front yard we have. Its leaves turn yellow and die off in the winter, and it is gradually showing a few beautiful coral blooms.

Just before the sixth anniversary of Paul's death I decided to donate a bench to the city of Manhattan Beach in his memory. We wanted it installed either on the parkway and jogging path across from our home or over at Live Oak Park a few blocks away where we used to bring Paul to play when he was a toddler.

This wasn't easy. We sent the form in, indicating what type of bench we wanted, where we wanted it placed, and what to put on the dedication plaque. The city is very strict about keeping memorials dignified and unobtrusive so I complied with a simple dedication. Then we heard nothing.

Finally, just a week shy of the seventh anniversary of Paul's death, the bench was installed. It sits on the parkway facing our house. Just where I wanted it. Just what I wanted to reinforce my memory of Paul sitting on a beach chair on the hill across the street with the children from next door during the Grand Prix bike races that went by our house on a Sunday in July every year. In those days there was no parkway. A railroad track was up there, and a train came by that shook our house once a month or so. The children didn't perch their chairs up as far as the tracks, but they still had a bird's eye view of the race. That's what gave me the idea for the bench—something to remind me of that smiling boy looking so proud and happy watching the racers with his friends.

Dedicated to Paul Ian Sharples 1971–1999

The bench on the parkway sits above a little hill of California ice plant with purple blooms and yellow and orange nasturtiums. It is white cement with a plaque prominently on the front that says: "Dedicated to Paul Ian Sharples 1971–1999." Walking by it and sitting on it makes me tear up. I know Paul is not there but having that bench there makes me feel closer to him. People have said it was a good thing to do for myself. I never thought of doing this as a reward, as something I did for myself. I think of it as another way to remember him.

Yet no matter what we do to honor his memory, we cannot bring him back. All the memorials assuage our hurt a bit, but they do nothing to erase it. And, really, don't you think that these memorials are just for us—to keep him alive for us and for others? He is in a place where he will never know the difference.

When our niece Stephanie was pregnant with her second child— she knew the baby would be a girl—she decided to name her Samantha Paul. I was so honored and moved that this little baby would have Paul's name—and not even a feminine derivative of it. Stephanie was adamant that she didn't want to use a Paul derivative like Paula or Paulette.

I flew into Denver that day to represent our family at the baby naming, looking forward to meeting Samantha Paul for the first time and to see my older great niece who had already captured my heart four years before.

I sat with the congregation and watched Stephanie carry her five-week old daughter, my great niece, up the few steps to the pulpit. She held the baby, all peaches and cream with a fuzz of red hair, tight to her belly with her hand on the small of the baby's bare back. Next to her walked her husband Mike holding their four-year-old daughter Alyssa's hand. They stopped just short of the podium where the rabbi met them. He had interrupted the Friday-night Sabbath service to honor and congratulate this family and officially name the baby.

They looked small up there within the three-story-tall sanctuary, against a backdrop of redwood paneling and hand-woven tapestry sliding doors that enclosed the ark—a large cabinet that holds the sacred Hebrew scrolls containing the Five Books of Moses at the center of the pulpit. The rabbi laid his hands on the baby's head and pronounced her name, Samantha Paul. Samantha for Stephanie's maternal grandfather and Paul for her cousin, our son Paul, and then led the congregation in a prayer of rejoicing, good fortune, and long life. He kissed the baby's head, and shook the hands of the other three. As he resumed the service, they left the center of the pulpit.

I thought how fitting for this newborn—with fingers so long that her mother hopes she will have Paul's ability to play the piano—to have Paul's name and to be officially named just days after the third anniversary of his death. I dreaded the start of that week and my need to visit his gravesite. Then I looked forward to the end of the week and to the joy and happiness that accompanied the birth of this child so badly wanted that her mother went through months of the medical probing and prodding necessary to become impregnated via in vitro fertilization.

In honor of the event I decided to give Samantha Paul something of his. I chose his silver baby cup and had it engraved with her name on the front and his on the back. Stephanie cried, my sister-in-law Barbara cried, and I cried when they opened and read the card that said, "I thought you ought to have something that belonged to your cousin Paul." The cup was well used and banged up, but after two polishings, it looked shiny, aged, established. I hoped Samantha would drink from it and bang it on the table and throw it on the floor as he did.

I remember buying it. We were in Bullock's. He was in a stroller and less than six-months old. We had just moved to Manhattan Beach and were in a rented house saving our pennies to buy a home of our own. But I wanted him to have a lasting keepsake, and when I saw the cup in the display case, I couldn't resist. Now, I'm glad I made the stretch to spend the twenty-five dollars the cup cost then.

Seven days before the seventh anniversary of Paul's death, a baby boy was born to my nephew Mark and his wife Lyssa. I had been told they were considering naming him Ian, Paul's middle name, but only after Lyssa called the night after he was born, did I know for sure. Lyssa said, "It's a good family name." Ian also has a remembrance of Paul—a little, silver piggy bank with a tiny curly tail.

Now I know the true meaning of the Jewish tradition of naming babies for the dead. It's to keep their memories alive. Now there are two little children named for him—Samantha Paul and Ian. I never would have thought that Paul's first cousins would have felt so strongly about Paul to honor him so. Though I still worry all the time that he will not be remembered after I die, I feel comfort in knowing others out there think of him enough to name their children after him. It is a true honor to him and to Bob and Ben and me. I like to think that he somehow lives on in these children.

Black Bomber

Swaddled in this
black bomber jacket all weekend,
I am safe from the Big Sur chill.
It's too large for me.
And that's okay. It was Paul's.
I bought it for him
years ago at American et Cie on La Brea
before he went crazy
and decided to leave us
way before his time.
I like how it snuggles me,
like he's in there too giving me a hug.
It's the only piece
of his clothing I have left.
I've given away the rest:
his favorite plaid shirts
that smelled of sweat and smoke,
the torn jeans he salvaged
from second-hand stores,
his worn brown Doc Marten oxfords
that took him miles on his manic escapades,
and the tan suede jacket
he had me repair over and over
because he couldn't let it go.
Like this jacket —
I'll never let it go.
It has stains I can't remove
and threads unraveling,
My son is gone.
But this jacket—
try and take it from me.
Just try.

CHAPTER FIFTEEN

From the moment Paul had his first manic break, our family changed as a unit and each one of us changed individually. It was like falling off a cliff. We were going along like any normal family with two sons in college, dealing with grades, what we're going to do during summer vacations, where will Paul settle after he graduates, how we're going to pay the bills, can we afford a long vacation, what work do we need to do next on our house, and all of a sudden every plan, every routine, everything we ever thought to be important, changed. As a result, I think we all functioned out of fear that if we stopped to really look at what had just happened to us, we would break apart and be unable to put the pieces back together again. We each held ourselves and the others together.

And our family dynamic continues to change as we move on— change for the better. Paul's illness, death, and the aftermath have brought us closer. That we had to immerse ourselves in our work and diversions—first my work life and now my writing life, Bob's work in the aerospace industry, and Ben's perseverance in the film and television business—was all to the good. We also benefitted from acting stronger and more together than we really felt.

If Bob were grieving, no one would have known. He was our rock. He kept everything and every one of us in order. For him grief had a beginning, middle, and end. He was able to compartmentalize the grief part of his life and live the rest of his life as if nothing had happened.

Though he still works at high capacity as a consultant in the aerospace business and earns huge respect, this seventy-plus year-old complains for the first time that his body doesn't perform the way he wants it to. So lately he's been working out regularly with a personal trainer, walking, and improving his diet. He has decided to do something about the aches and pains in his back, knees, hips—you name it, it ached. Perhaps giving up his nightly ice cream routine has helped.

Ice Cream Party for One

He opens the freezer door
every night at ten.
He muses,
what will it be tonight—
the rum raisin, the natural vanilla bean
with chocolate chunks,
the caramel swirl?
He does not discriminate.
Even the coffee in the back,
probably old and stiff, will do.

LEAVING THE HALL LIGHT ON ~ 297

He takes out two,
maybe three, containers,
sets them on the red granite counter
and takes out a bowl
from the cabinet above his head.
His fingers curl
under the rim of each container
and pull until the top gives way.
With his serving spoon at the ready
he mounds scoop after scoop
into the bowl,
licking his fingers one at a time
as he goes.
Finally, he walks to the table,
pulls out his chair,
and sits hunched over,
spooning the cold ice cream
into his mouth, finally
scraping spoon against bowl,
spoon against bowl,
over and over
until all the melted liquid is gone.
He walks back to the kitchen,
leaves the bowl and spoon
unrinsed on the counter
and comes to bed.

No More Emergencies

Our lives
are quiet now.
We don't rush,
we don't worry,
we don't fume
over things we can't control.
We let those things alone.
We've had our emergency,
nothing could ever top that.
Everything else is small,
just an irritation, an itch, a pebble in a shoe,
a little worry,
nothing we cannot shake away,
nothing we cannot brush aside
as we continue to move on.

Over the years as I became more centered and steady, my husband became more tearful, more touchy, more sensitive. I see his eyes well up so often these days—a song, something on television, a little baby—almost any kind of tenderness will set him off. He is so sweet and attentive to the little children in our lives. And, he's become more loving and understanding of me.

These days Bob doesn't think of Paul often. But, since I keep Paul's photos and things all over our house, he can't help being reminded of Paul. When he actually looks at one of the pictures and gets what the image is, he tells me his mind says GONE! The same thing happens when he looks at pictures of his mother, father, and brother. Bob doesn't think that any of these loved ones are waiting for him to join them after death. They are all gone. He has only his memory, and most of his memory of Paul is in connection with music and musical subjects. Those are the topics that bring Paul fleetingly back to Bob.

Yet, in my mind Bob is lucky. He sometimes dreams he sees Paul still alive. One night he dreamt Paul was up early in the morning, dressed and ready to go someplace with us. Paul had a big smile on his face. I don't have many dreams of Paul, at least that I can remember. I wish I did. Sometimes I wake with the feeling that he was in my dreams, but I don't remember the details. Once I heard his voice in my dreams. He said, "Hello," like the last hello on that last night. It was clear, strong and so like his voice. At first I believed that dreaming about him meant he was close by, that he was here with me somehow. But I know better. I know that he is gone.

Bob also keeps very busy with his diversions—writing our family history, reading, the family bills and records, crossword puzzles, Sudoku, golf, gym workouts, and a favorite computer game or two. Paul Simon wrote a song, "Slip Slidin' Away" in which he says:

"...a good day
Ain't got no rain...
a bad day's when I lie in bed
And think of things that might have been."

Bob's intense work over the last decade has helped him from spending a lot of time thinking of things that might have been.

Bob does not miss Paul. He says, "I do miss the wonderful little boy who was with us for maybe thirteen or so years, and I don't miss the adult Paul I knew in the 1990s."

So Bob will answer a resounding yes if asked if he has survived Paul's death. He never was in a state of mind where his own physical survival was in question. He thinks rationally—like the scientist that he is. He has to put everything in order as if he's solving a calculation or formula for it to make sense. His thought process would go like this: After all, in the early days households with ten children born would sometimes have only four or five survivors. Such experiences would have threatened the survival of mankind if they led to the death of parents from grief.

That's how Bob thinks. That's how he is constructed. He says, "I have accepted Paul's passing as unfortunate, but probably related to a genetically inherited illness common in Madeline's family. I hope that such a misfortune does not befall my son Benjamin and his children."

What he is strongly aware of now is that he will be gone one day just like Paul and all the others. This reasoning makes Bob even more anxious to enjoy what time he has left on this planet.

He also says that Paul and Eric's deaths have caused him to have an even stronger attachment to Ben. He is down to one son and hopes that Ben survives longer than he does. He was so happy at the time of Ben's wedding—that he was marrying, not burying, a son. And he so looks forward to Ben having a happy marriage and whatever comes after that—perhaps a grandchild or two for him to play with in his old age.

I think one of the greatest achievements of this period in our lives is that our marriage survived. Actually, I think the main reason we survived Paul's death at all was because of the strength of our marriage. Bob and I have been together for over forty-five years.

According to Bob, our marriage survived by a combination of my persistent drive to deal with the pain, suffering, and loss, and his willingness to wait until I got better. We realized early on that our grieving processes were different, so we were patient with each other about that. We also give each other a lot of space. We respect each other. We both are good at what we do professionally so there's no competition or jealousy there. We have no reason to put each other down. We don't get into arguments about the small stuff or let the small stuff get in our way. We've lived through too much big stuff to let that happen.

Another big factor in the survival of our marriage was that we decided to stay in our house. We could have easily listened to the many people who told us to move, but the very act of tearing our house apart—going through all the things, deciding what to keep and what to throw away—would have torn us apart as well. It would have been too much of a stressor too soon after Paul's death. So even though the house was where Paul died, we have always found a lot of comfort in it. Our relatives and friends come and go in our house as if it were their own. They call it The Family House. Plus, I couldn't find a better place to live. We're six blocks from the beach. How could we leave that? And we've continually upgraded it so that now it looks more like a new house rather than one more than thirty years old.

Bob likes to say to me, "You'll miss me when I'm gone." He's always had the unreasonable premonition that he'll die way before me. And yes, he's right. I will miss him—if he dies before me. We are still very much in love and best friends. I can see that love in his face. His eyes and whole face soften when he looks at me. He just exudes love from every pore. My greatest concern is that I haven't been as loving to him as he has to me, although my love for him is just as strong.

This love has also been the glue that has kept us together—a glue stronger than the trauma of Paul's death. It was enough to help us in the most trying of times that a couple could ever go through. Plus neither of us has any other place to go. We're together in it for the long haul—richer, poorer, sickness, health, and a son's death. Not a lot comes between us, except for maybe a few "unspoken or spoken" agreements when it comes to Paul and his death.

I suspect Bob hates all the reminders of Paul around the house. He has counted the photos—all twenty-seven of them. He doesn't even like the reminders out in the garage. He recently asked what was in one of the boxes, and when I said some of Paul's toys, he shook his head in disgust and walked away, saying sarcastically, "Oh, yes, that's sacrosanct." Most of the time he doesn't mention it, but I think he'd like all the photos and Paul memorabilia to go out with the trash.

Fading

Even as our youth and beauty fade,
even as we tread
ever more carefully
on the waning waves of life,
you must never doubt me.
I, the woman, you took in your arms
oh those forty-five years ago,
am still here for you
and still in awe of you,
now and always.

We can never know
when the clock will strike twelve for us.
So, in the meantime, my beloved,
come with me down the long hall.
Let me cook you the best meal you've ever had.
Lay down your glasses,
throw your crossword aside,
and let me nourish and feed you
until our days together are done.

Yet, Bob allows my Buddha collection. He even contributes to it. When we've had a particularly hard time of it, he brings me one. Most importantly, is our agreement to visit Paul's grave twice a year together. Bob never waivers from accompanying me there. He makes sure we have a stone to leave on his gravestone.

I am bothered when Bob doesn't acknowledge Paul's existence when asked about the number of children he has. Nowadays he says he has one son. But I won't call him on it because I understand where he's coming from. It's probably a good defense mechanism. If he said he actually had three sons and now only one, he'd have to speak about both Paul and Eric's untimely deaths. Why would he want to do that? He needs to protect himself from that.

Sometimes my love is mixed with anger and worry. I tell him he shouldn't be so hard on himself about his perceived shortcomings and the affects of aging, and he thinks I'm being critical. "It's because I love you," I say—again and again. I tell him it's because I love him, but he doesn't get that. Maybe I'm just preparing myself for the inevitable. I don't want any surprises like Joan Didion had when her husband dropped dead one night at the dinner table. So I get angry to protect myself. Can anger and love be related? Yes, I think so.

Yet even with those few disturbing things, we are definitely on the same wavelength now about Paul's death. Like Bob, I think we are a happier family without Paul. After he had his first manic break, he was impossible—so selfish, so needy, so arrogant, and so much of a taker. We don't have the worries anymore. We don't have the fears. We don't have the heartache.

It took me a long time to get to this realization and write it down on paper. But, I've finally made it. I'll never forget my beautiful Paul, but I'd like to forget what a pain in the ass of a person he was. It was my dream that he would recover and we could have some semblance of what we had before, but in reality it would still have been difficult living with him. Bob and I live happily without him now.

A Poem that Wants To Be for Ben

They are always about Paul, my dead son
the one who died of his own free will
so many years ago.
My hordes of poems go on like a mantra:
his mania, his depression, his delusions, his escapades,
his suicide. They never fail to mention
his piercing blue eyes, the little half smile
that never showed his teeth, the smoky smell,
and the way he slumped over the piano like "The Thinker"
as he played.
Paul and his death have been my muse.

Ben's living eyes brim over with love
as he looks down and folds me in his arms.
He is the son who says
I love you
every time we speak.
His smiles are wide
even when he faces disappointment
in his own life.
This son is the reason I choose to live.
Why isn't he the reason I choose to write?

Ben has finally accepted his new role as the only child. He's also moved on in the way he thinks about Paul's suicide. He couldn't understand why Paul could do such an act that resulted in hurting so many people. Ben felt—as is typical of the healthy way he lives his own life—that Paul could have found a way to stay alive and take care of himself, that Paul's illness was an excuse to be a selfish asshole. It gave him an excuse to check out. Now he's accepted that Paul was so ill he couldn't help himself. It took Ben a long time to come to terms with that. But Ben's initial reactions came out of his love for his brother and an acute sense of loss.

Ben says, "At the same time, Paul and I had a bond that I can't explain to anybody. I felt his death on a deep psychic level. It felt like losing a limb. To the outside observer it doesn't make sense that I grieved so much. We weren't that close, and I didn't like how he was in a lot of ways. But we had an inexplicable spiritual and psychic connection that's much deeper than all of that, and I felt that when he died. I feel it now, our spiritual connection. I feel his presence. When he died, I felt his presence everywhere for a long time. I still do from time to time."

Ben still misses Paul and sometimes wishes he were here so he could talk to him. But that wishful thinking is not impeding Ben's progress. He's a happy man, proactive in his life and career as a writer, producer, director and actor, currently producing a movie called "Breaking Evans" about an aging tennis star like himself. (Besides Ben's career in entertainment he also teaches tennis when he has the time.) He is more spiritual, and even more compassionate and understanding toward family and others—perhaps as a result of Paul's death. He also feels closer to his family.

Ben has had to do a lot of growing up since Paul died—he's had to grow into his role as the only son who would one day have the burden of caring for his aging parents. So he has become self-sufficient and self-reliant. Ben is a man now—even though I still think of him as my little boy.

That he has finally found the love of his life in the last five years is another reason for Ben's journey into maturity and balance. He and Marissa actually went to high school together and though they were friends at school, they never socialized outside of it. Then fourteen years after high-school graduation, Ben found an article about Marissa online. He immediately contacted her. They have been together ever since and were married in August 2010—a huge step for a guy who in the past had a tough time making the tough decisions. Is that a result of healing? I think so. Though he doesn't have a brother in his life anymore—at least not physically—he has the love of his wife, family members, and many friends to make up for it.

Today I Saw You on the Hill

Just after my morning walk on the highway
up to South Coast,
just after my relaxing soak in the big corner bath,
just as I start my trudge up the hill,
towel in hand ready to dump in the box,
I see you engrossed in a conversation.

I know you instantly,
the buzz cut,
the long sideburns,
the slight build,
the intense blue eyes,
giving full attention
to your friend
as you talk.

Today for some reason
the clothes are wrong.
Instead of your Doc Martens,
you wear bright, striped sneakers
Instead of the brown, leather, book bag
slung across your body
that I bought you for school,
you have a backpack.
Still I know it is you.

As on the other days when I see you
in your dark gray sweater
or black jacket
and levis crossing the street
or on the pier
or at the piano
or sitting outside Starbucks.
As when I see you at work,
young, brilliant, and so sure of yourself,
I have no doubts.

Please go on, my beautiful boy.
Give it a rest.
I don't want to think about you here.
I don't want to write about you anymore.
I've written about you ad nauseum
and still you won't leave me alone.
Even here among the hummingbirds
and the pines and salt air
I'm not safe.

You're dead. Your choice.
So stop bothering me already.
If you wanted to stay in my life
and bother me,
why did you choose to die?

For me it's a mixed bag. I just turned seventy years old. That should signal a time for me to slow down. But no, I'm still as driven as ever. I don't act old. I don't feel old. I'm just chronologically old. I've created a whirlwind of a life for myself. Even in retirement I'm working like I've created a new job for myself. I now have a job as a writer.

The same is true for how I take care of myself. Though I finally gave up dying my hair, I've grown it longer than I've ever had it before. Short, easy to manage, permed hair reminds me of old-lady hair. I don't want to acknowledge that I'm an old lady yet.

And you know what? All this stuff, including the playacting, works. In trying to look good, to make others believe I am okay, I actually believe it myself. It has actually turned into the reality of my life. It's the truth. I am okay. I have moved on. I live a full life. I'm not sitting on that proverbial couch and vegetating like my mother did. I've found happiness—in my marriage, my son, my new daughter-in-law, and my writing life. Just being here makes me feel good.

As a result, like Bob, I don't miss the Paul I knew during his illness and all the worry and fears that came with those horrible seven years. But, paradoxically, I do miss having him in my life. I still talk about him. I still relate stories about his birth and childhood, if it's applicable in conversations, as if he were still around. I still brag about his musical skills, and I miss his playing music in our house. He was smart, articulate, sensitive, well read, and highly skilled in computers. Paul had such a focused way about him that I began to think of him as a Buddha-like person. Like the line about eagles in the film, "A Thousand Clowns," I can never have enough Buddhas.

Obsession

In homage to Paul
I collect Buddhas.
The little statues
I have in my home and garden
remind me of the way
he sat cross-legged
on his bedroom floor,
the way he concentrated for hours
playing his music, and
the way his face and head
with closely cropped hair
radiated a quiet wiseness.

A new Buddha sits on my desk
cross-legged,
hands folded face up
cupping a lotus blossom.
This one, the Buddha of long life,
called Amitayus,
was cast in Nepal out of gold colored metal.
Amitayus also wears a shiny crown lined in crimson
instead of the neat rows
of snails chiseled
on my other Buddha heads.

Not one of my Buddhas
is exactly alike.
One stands in my garden carrying
his sack of candy to offer
children as they pass by.

He laughs as he oversees
the birds that dip into
my round cement fountain.
One cast in deep brown,
kneels on top of my bookcase
his hands together in prayer.
A healing Buddha
draped in red and orange
points his right hand
to the ground.
Another, carved in white stone,
faces his palm out
to give a blessing.

Some of my Buddhas
are cracked with age,
some overgrown with slimy moss.
No matter.
They comfort and calm
the knot in my belly
as they keep my son's memory
alive.

I also have my new writing life. When I finally decided in April 2010 that I was going to leave my day job and pursue writing full time, I worried that leaving was a huge risk. Would I revert back to the wallowing? Even so, I decided I had to do it. I wanted some time for myself and with my husband, time to travel while we're still mobile, and time to write books and poems. An almost 24/7 job managing proposals in the aerospace industry just doesn't support that. And how many years could I continue at that pace at my age?

Now I introduce myself as a writer. When asked if I work, I say, "I recently retired from my day job. I'm a full-time writer now." I explain that even though my former day job was related to writing, I now have the opportunity to concentrate on my own writing projects. I've organized my life so that I leave a good amount of time for writing every day, and I manage my writing time so that I finish the daily products that I assign myself.

My days go like this: I get up early but not as early as I did when I was working full time. I go to the gym. I come home, and have breakfast and a cup of tea, shower and get dressed. Then I go downstairs to my office and stay there until I feel my writing work for the day is finished. Included in this time is my marketing work—blogging, Facebook and Twitter posts, poetry submissions, and other online networking. My day also includes a large amount of time for reading. I'm thrilled that the book pile on my to-be-read shelf keeps getting smaller and smaller.

To stay on this routine I've decreed that I will not schedule more than one appointment/meeting/lunch date a day—excluding weekends or when we're traveling—so as not to interfere with my writing time. I have plenty of days ahead of me so why bunch up too many activities?

Some days I'm in my office for hours, first working to get this book to the publisher and now on my novel. I also write a journal entry, a poem, and/or a blog post almost every day. Writing is like an addiction; I get itchy if I don't do it. My office is like magic to me. I could spend all day in there and never feel confined. I see the outside garden and the fountain from my writing table. The fountain attracts the most beautiful orange and yellow birds. Some have red heads, some take little dips in the pool, some surf on the leaves that hang over the fountain, some just hover over the water too wary to wade in. This time in my office makes me feel so good.

I leave no time for grieving in my writing life either. And because this routine works well for me I plan to keep at it.

Though Paul's death has been a horrendous loss, he has left me many wonderful gifts. One was the gift of poetry that I've mentioned here before. Since those early days when poems just came spontaneously, I've honed my skills, participated in workshops, and have had many of my poems published.

Many of my first dark poems are in this book. The poem "Aftermath" was published early on in The Compassionate Friends Summer 2001 newsletter, "We Need Not Walk Alone." Though I write prose now more than poetry, poetry is my love. I feel that anyone, any situation, any place is poem fodder. Writing poetry never leaves me lonely. Even though most of my poems are still sad, they've been my companion and my savior—something I can turn to any time, any place. I once wrote a poem on a magazine tear-out while on an airplane without any paper or my computer. Writing is the gift that saved my life.

Another gift has been a stronger me. I became stronger because I had to be. I had to show Ben that he could go back to his school and not have to worry about me. Also I had to show Bob that I was okay—even at times when I wasn't. I didn't want him to worry about me either.

I also became physically stronger. Paul's death gave me an almost obsessive need for exercise. At first it was one of the things that kept me sane. Now it keeps me healthy both physically and mentally. I made a conscious effort to keep up my exercise program so I wouldn't end up with extreme effects of osteoporosis that my mother had—a humped back and a protruding stomach. She didn't take hormones, she didn't take calcium supplements, and she didn't do weight-bearing and stretching exercises. She started a walking program only when it was way too late.

The amount of effort I've put into exercise has paid off. My body is trim, I don't have a stomach, my back is straight except for a little protruding of my right shoulder because of scoliosis, and I don't have a lot of aches and pains—not even from my scoliosis. I can proudly tell people that I'm seventy, and I like seeing their looks of disbelief. I'm still a trim energetic person. The only thing exercise hasn't done for me is make me taller. What started out as an obsession has turned into one of my greatest gifts.

I grew stronger from a combination of things: meeting and interacting with people who had been through similar experiences; writing classes and workshops; going back to work outside my home and my desire to compete on the job and to excel in my work; receiving my company's Women of Achievement award for my accomplishments both inside and outside of work, and my persistence, as Bob says, to deal with my grief and become a productive person again. Thankfully Bob stuck with me through it all. Probably what gave me the most strength was finally finding a balance between keeping Paul's memory alive and moving on with the rest of my life.

I now have a terrific bond with Ben—another gift Paul's death has given me. Once Ben settled down and found his way in Los Angeles and once he was happy with a woman in his life, our relationship began to thrive. I no longer had Paul to worry about. I can be completely de-

316 ~ MADELINE SHARPLES

voted to Ben, and I love it. Just the two of us spend time together. We support each other's work, and I'm even helping him with his scriptwriting. I have so much pleasure from Ben these days—something, I'm sorry to say, I wouldn't have had with Paul around. Paul was like a wedge between Ben and me in his last few years. Now that wedge doesn't exist.

A friend whose son also died said, "It gets softer." And in spite of all the advances I've made in the healing and surviving process, I don't know what "softer" means. Does it mean that the grief is not as painful, that the knife-edges aren't so sharp, that it now feels like a warm fuzzy? I don't think it's softer at all. The sharp edges are still always there for me. I think about what happened to my beautiful first-born son. I think about him every day. The realization that he's dead comes upon me like a punch in my gut without any warning. Or my face begins to shrivel up, my mouth starts to quiver, and my eyes tear at a memory, a thought, or an idea about something he would have loved or something he has missed. We were recently at our annual hometown fair that had a rock climbing and rappelling booth for the youngsters. He would have loved that. Even Bob said recently after we very much enjoyed a one-man show about the composer and conductor Leonard Bernstein that Paul might have liked it too.

But now I consider myself a true survivor. I'm thoroughly liking my life now. That's the main thing. I rejoice that I'm still here. Like an old friend said the other day, "Keep smiling." Yes, I am able to smile again. I can do things that make me happy. And I don't stop myself like I used to. I used to feel so guilty for feeling good, feeling happy, laughing, and smiling. Now when people ask me how I am, I say, "Good." I used to say "Okay." I've gotten beyond okay to good. Not bad.

I've gotten through the worst experience any mother could ever have. I've gotten through seven years of Paul's bipolar illness and more than eleven years since his death. Of course there were times when I thought I wasn't going to make it. But, here I am eighteen years since Paul was first diagnosed with bipolar disorder, still alive, still viable, and still productive. Also I've found out how compulsively—to myself and others—I want to prove I could live on after his death. Unfortunately, I haven't learned to let myself relax and just let what happens happen. I have to take control, be in control. Perhaps that is because with Paul I felt so out of control.

Writing this book has enabled me to know myself better. I know that I'm hard on myself and hard on Bob. But, writing all this down has given me a greater appreciation for Bob. It's bad enough that he lost Paul and Eric in these last years, but he's had to take care of me during my worst days throughout this experience.

Dealing with this grief thing is still a process. It won't be over until I die. What I've gone through is with me every day. I live with it. I live around it. All the diversions that I've created for myself have definitely helped, but I'm not over Paul's death. I don't expect I'll ever get "over" it. Nothing takes this loss away. There is no recovering from a loss of this kind. I could punch him out over and over again, and I would still see his face on that punching bag. I still see him facing me during the last few minutes we had together as if it were yesterday. I remember how he looked as he stood there and then leaned his face down for my kiss as if he is here with me right now. And that's good. My goal to never forget him has been met.

And my goal of finding a balance between keeping his memory alive and moving on and living, not just participating in diversions to get me through the day, has also been met.

Yes… you are right. I've finally turned the hall light off.

Tonglen Practice

It's the mothers and fathers I care about.

When my son died, I grieved for him
and all mothers and fathers
who ever lost a child.
I breathed in pain
and with each exhalation asked
that no parent
would have to feel
the pain of such a loss again.

But I can't do it alone.
The mothers
and fathers
over all the world
must practice Tonglen with me.

We must take the pain into our bodies,
into our souls, into our hearts,
and cleanse it with our healing breath.
Then with our collective breathing out
give this world a chance
to be safe for all our children—
all our sons and daughters.

Breathe in, breathe out
now, forever,
breathe.

EPILOGUE

O n a cool Saturday evening in August, 2010, Bob and I each held one of Ben's hands in ours as we walked with him down the white rose petal-lined gravel path in our garden. Marissa and her mother and father followed. Debussy's "Claire de Lune" played quietly in the background.

Tom, a teacher Ben and Marissa have known since their ninth grade at Crossroads School, waited for them under the tall palm trees to perform their marriage ceremony. Family and friends stood close in tight looking on.

The garden looked magical that night. The lush greenery accented with red, pink, and yellow flowering plants and the simple round gurgling water fountain twinkled with overhead lights and dangling crystals. And, after a day of gray skies, the sun shone bright and warm over the bridal couple—Ben in a black suit with white shirt and cream-colored tie to match the off-white shade of Marissa's strapless gown. Ben had a white rose in his lapel, and Marissa wore a single jeweled feather in her pulled back dark hair. She carried a bouquet of white roses and peonies. A Buddha stood laughing in the background as if to make sure everything went without a hitch.

The ceremony was short and simple yet touching with symbolism. At the beginning, Tom lit a white candle anchored in a round, glass bowl to create a sacred space and signify the oneness of all gathered together for the event. The bridal couple sipped from the same bowl of water, a symbol of connection and sharing of the fundamental essence of life together, while Tom spoke the words of Tao Te Ching:

> *Your love is a great mystery. It is like an eternal lake whose waters are always still and clear like glass. Looking into it you can see the truth about your life. It is like a deep well whose waters are cool and pure. Drinking from it you can be reborn. You do not have to stir the waters or dig the well. Merely see yourself clearly and drink deeply.*

Tom later wrapped a blanket around the couple to typify the union of two lives through cuddling.

Before Ben and Marissa exchanged rings, Tom asked every one of the guests to hold them in their fist and bless them. And at the end Ben broke the glass, a ritual typical in Jewish weddings. Tom told us a broken glass is forever changed into a new form, as is the newly married couple. The breaking of the glass also reminds us that the marriage should last beyond the time it would take to put the shards of glass together again.

Even though our loved ones both living and dead were honored in the ceremony Paul's presence was virtually non-existent that night—at least for me. I had worried that I would miss having him there so much that it would ruin the evening for me, but that didn't happen. This was truly Ben and Marissa's night. I had lost my oldest son one month short of eleven years before Ben's wedding date, and his memory did not interfere with the happiness I felt at the prospect of a new daughter in my life.

I also marveled at the decisions we made along the way that allowed us to make this evening possible. That we decided not to sell our house was foremost. After all it was the place where Ben had grown up, and that he and his bride wanted to have their wedding in his family home meant so much to me. He had avoided being in our house for so long because of the bad memories. His choice to be married there showed how much recovered he is.

I also created the setting from whole cloth when I decided to transform Paul's room into my office. The laughing Buddha and the gurgling pond and plant assortments that I can see outside the office bay window were integral to the wedding ceremony. And whenever I sit at my desk writing now, I can look out and remember this happy time. It's as though I've made no space in my life for the bad memories. It's as though with the breaking of the glass, my life and that of my family have forever changed as well.

Wedding in the Garden

I never would have suspected
that the gravel path
weaving its way through our narrow garden
would become the wedding aisle.
Nor did I think the palm trees that grew
from babies would serve
as the backdrop for the ceremony.

And when all was said and done
every inch of our home
inside and out
the place where our sons grew up
the place of good memories
and bad
served as the perfect wedding venue.

Food displayed in the dining room
eating in the family and living rooms
and out on the deck,
dancing on the patio.
I am so glad I didn't listen
to the folks who said
you have to move
after Paul died.

I knew our house had more
joy to give.
After all,
it's the welcoming family home
where we've all come to grieve,
to laugh, to cry,
and to wipe our tears of happiness
after Ben and Marissa's beautiful wedding
in the garden.

August 2010, Ben and Marissa's wedding (Guru Thapar photo)

Reading Group Guide for Leaving the Hall Light On

1. What does the title of the book mean?

2. What is your reaction to Madeline's story about her son? Did you have any unexpected feelings or responses?

3. Have you known anyone (a friend, a relative, etc.) who has/had mental illness? In your experience, how have people dealt with mental illness?

4. Would you be able to recognize the signs of mental illness or suicidal tendencies? Do you know any support services in your community that could be of help in such a situation?

5. When Madeline and Bob see Paul in a manic state for the first time, they essentially do an "intervention" on the spot and take him to a hospital for a psychiatric evaluation. Would you have taken the same action? Why or why not?

6. What would you do if you suspected a friend or family member was a danger to himself/herself or to others?

7. After Paul is diagnosed with bipolar disorder, he is emotionally distant from Madeline and Bob and sometimes seems hostile. (He frequently tells Bob to "Leave me alone!") How do you give support and comfort to a person who doesn't want support or comfort?

8. Paul doesn't take his medications as prescribed. One of the reasons he cites is that it interferes with his creative work (in his case, composing and playing music). If a medication inhibits an artist's creativity, should the artist give up his/her art?

9. Have you known anyone who committed suicide? What was the impact on people who were close to the suicide victim? How did people deal with the suicide?

326 ~ MADELINE SHARPLES

10. Does the stigma of mental illness and suicide still exist? If so, how can we help erase it?

11. What could you do to help and comfort a family that has experienced a suicide or other tragedy (besides bringing over a casserole)? What kind of friend would you be during a time like this?

12. Madeline and Bob grieved differently. How were their experiences different? What are the pros and cons of their reactions to Paul's suicide?

13. In Chapter Nine "Surviving the First Year (and Beyond)," Madeline talks about "diversions" – reading, going to movies, etc., – all the things she does to keep her mind off of Paul's suicide. What do you think of Madeline's list? Is there anything you would add or do differently?

14. What role does storytelling play when it comes to death? Does it make a difference to survivors to be able to remember a person in stories?

15. Do you think that writing this story was helpful/cathartic to the author? How does writing aid healing? How do you deal with trauma in your life?

16. Do you think the poetry and photos enhanced or detracted from the story? What role does the poetry play in the memoir?

RESOURCES

Books

Anne Brener: *Mourning & Mitzvah—A Guided Journal for Walking the Mourner's Path Through Grief to Healing*, Jewish Lights Publishing (1993)

Pema Chodron, *When Things Fall Apart: Heart Advice for Difficult Times*, Shambala Publications (2000)

Joan Didion: *The Year of Magical Thinking*, Alfred A. Knopf (2005)

Marya Hornbacher: *Madness—A Bipolar Life*, Houghton Mifflin Co. (2008)

Kay Redfield Jamison: *An Unquiet Mind—A Memoir of Moods and Madness*, Alfred A. Knopf (1995)

Kay Redfield Jamison: *Night Falls Fast—Understanding Suicide*, Alfred A. Knopf (1999)

Susanna Kaysen: *Girl Interrupted*, Vintage Books (A Division of Random House, Inc.) (1993)

Alice and Richard Matzkin, *The Art of Aging*, Sentient Press (2009)

Elyn R. Saks: *The Center Cannot Hold*, Hyperion (2007)

Eleanor Vincent, *Swimming with Maya: A Mother's Story*, Captial Books, Inc. (2004)

MAGAZINE

BP Magazine
http://www.bphope.com
374 Delaware Avenue, Buffalo, NY 14202
716-614-4673

ORGANIZATIONS

American Foundation for Suicide Prevention—national not-for-profit organization exclusively dedicated to understanding and preventing suicide through research, education and advocacy, and to reaching out to people with mental disorders and those impacted by suicide
http://www.afsp.org
800-273-TALK

Didi Hirsch Mental Health Services—transforms lives by providing quality mental health and substance abuse services in communities where stigma or poverty limits access
http://www.didihirsch.org
4760 S. Sepulveda Boulevard
Culver City, CA 90230
310-390-6612

Esalen Institute—a center for experimental education
http://www.esalen.org/
55000 Highway 1
Big Sur, CA 93920
831-667-3000

National Alliance on Mental Illness (NAMI)—dedicated to improving the lives of individuals and families affected by mental illness
http://www.nami.org
3803 N. Fairfax Drive, Suite 100, Arlington VA 22203

Our House Grief Support Center—believes that grieving children and adults deserve the opportunity to begin the healing process in a safe, warm, nurturing environment
http://www.ourhouse-grief.org/
1663 Sawtelle Blvd., Suite 300
Los Angeles, CA 90025
310-473-1511
21860 Burbank Blvd., Suite 195
Woodland Hills, CA 91367
818-222-3344

The Compassionate Friends—for bereaved families and the people who care about them, following the death of a child
http://www.compassionatefriends.org
900 Jorie Boulevard
P.O. Box 3696
Oak Brook, IL 60522-3696
877-969-0010

Valley Village—Residential and day programs that protect, foster, develop, and advance the rights and interests of people with developmental disabilities.
http://www.valleyvillage.org/
20830 Sherman Way, Winnetka, CA 91306
818-587-9451

ADDENDUM

TERMS USED IN THIS BOOK

Bipolar Disorder—a person with bipolar disorder experiences mood swings between mania and depression that are sometimes very rapid and that sometimes occur over weeks and months

> *Bipolar I*—a person with bipolar I experiences debilitating manic episodes often accompanied by feelings of paranoia and psychotic hallucinations. This person cannot function fully on a daily basis. Long-term treatment is rarely successful and those with bipolar I are at risk of suicide.

> *Bipolar II*—a person with bipolar II experiences mild mania and is able to function relatively well on a daily basis. Bipolar II is often characterized by impaired social behaviors and occupational challenges.

Schizoaffective Disorder—a person with schizoaffective disorder has the psychotic loss of contact with reality and the mood swings typical of those with bipolar I. However, this person can be expected to go back to their normal life with treatment.

Hypomania—an altered mood state with mild to severe symptoms of mania that may last from a few days to many months. Mania typically causes obvious problems in daily functioning and often leads to serious problems with a person's relationships or ability to function at work. However, hypomania does not cause problems to such an extent.

RECENT FACTS ABOUT SUICIDE AND BIPOLAR DISORDER

1) Rise in Suicide Rates in the Armed Forces

In 2009*:

* Three hundred thirty-four suicides in the armed forces, more than killed in Afghanistan or in Iraq.
* Two hundred twenty-one suicides in the Army, National Guard and Army Reserve.
* Forty-seven suicides of active duty personnel in the Navy, thirty-four in the Air Force, and thirty-four in the Marine Corp.
* For every military death by suicide five military personnel are hospitalized for attempting suicide.
* Twenty to thirty percent of veterans suffer some degree of Post Traumatic Stress Disorder (PTSD).
* Hundreds of veterans die each year in auto accidents from fast driving or driving under the influence of alcohol.
* Three hundred sixty thousand veterans have had some brain injuries because of bomb blasts while in Iraq or Afghanistan.
* Rate of suicide doubled in the military between the years 2004 and 2009.
* Sixty-four percent increase in military discharges because of mental disorders from 2005 to 2009.
* One hundred twenty suicide deaths by September 2010 in the U.S. Army; thirty-two committed in the month of June.

Eighty-six non-active-duty Guard soldiers killed themselves in the first ten months of 2010 compared to forty-eight suicide deaths total in 2009.

In December 2010 the *Psychiatric Services* journal published results of the first large-scale study of suicide among female veterans. In comparing the rate of suicide among female civilians to the rate of suicide among female veterans, Mark Kaplan, a Portland State University researcher, says, "Female veterans—age eighteen to thirty-four—are three times as likely as their civilian peers to die by suicide." As a result, Kaplan wants people to take suicide among female vets more seriously. Because more women will work on the frontlines of war, an increase in female suicides is likely to follow.

A June 2012 Department of Defense report stated military suicides are occurring at a rate of one per day—up 18 percent from the same period in 2011.

2) *Rise in Suicide Rates in the General U.S. Population Aged Eighteen or Older***

- In 2009, 45,132 took their lives—a number greater than a normal population increase for the year; 29,350 people committed suicide in 1999 (the year Paul died).
- In the twenty to twenty-nine age group (Paul committed suicide at age twenty-seven), 5,028 took their lives in 2004 (last data available for that age group), and 4,684 people committed suicide in 1999.
- Suicide was the eleventh leading cause of death in the United States in 1999.
- A person dies by suicide about every fifteen minutes in the United States.
- Every day, approximately ninety Americans take their own life.
- Ninety percent of all people who die by suicide have a diagnosable psychiatric disorder at the time of their death.
- Four male suicides are successful for every female suicide, but three times as many females as males attempt suicide.
- Eight million people had serious thoughts of suicide and one million attempted it in 2009.
- An estimated eight to twenty-five suicides are attempted for every suicide death.

3) *Recent Bipolar Facts****
    - Approximately three percent of adults in the population have bipolar disorder. In the United States alone, approximately ten million people have bipolar disorder.
    - Bipolar disorder can occur at any time, but usually begins before age thirty-five. People between the ages of fifteen and twenty-five years have the highest risk of developing this disorder. The median age of onset for bipolar disorders is twenty-five years. (Paul was twenty-one when he was diagnosed as bipolar I.)
    - Bipolar disorder results in an over nine-year reduction in expected life span, and as many as one in five patients with bipolar disorder completes suicide.
    - Thirty percent of people with untreated bipolar disorder commit suicide.

4) *Change in Mental Health Insurance Coverage*
    The Paul Wellstone and Pete Domenici Mental Health Parity and Addiction Equity Act was passed in 2008. This act declared that patients being treated for mental illnesses cannot be charged more out of pocket than they would be for general medical care. It also declared that mentally ill patients could not have their benefits limited for mental health and substance abuse services. The act protects consumers from insurance discrimination to the greatest extent possible.

5) *Warning labels on Selective Serotonin Reuptake Inhibitor (SSRI) Prescription Labels*
    After a study of children, adolescents, and young adults age eighteen to twenty-four (Paul was twenty-one when his doctors started prescribing these drugs) warning labels indicated "Clinical Worsening and Suicide Risk" in a Black Box on the label. Medication guides underneath the Black Box lists the following risks of these drugs:

- Thoughts about suicide or dying
- Attempts to commit suicide
- New or worse depression
- New or worse anxiety
- Feeling very agitated or restless
- Panic attacks
- Trouble sleeping (insomnia)
- New or worse irritability
- Acting aggressive, being angry, or violent
- Acting on dangerous impulses
- An extreme increase in activity and talking (mania)
- Other unusual changes in behavior or mood.

In particular, the drugs that Paul took (although it is unknown about how much or for how long he took them) with these risks are:

-Fluoxetine (Prozac)
-Citalopram (Celexa)
-Escitalopram (Lexapro)
-Venlafaxine (Effexor)
-Bupropion (Wellbutrin or Zyban).

---

* "Suicide claims more US military lives than Afghan war," by James Cogan, 06 January 2010

** Sources: Substance Abuse and Mental Health Services Administration, American Foundation for Suicide Prevention, National Vital Statistics Reports

***National Institute of Mental Health

Madeline Sharples

Photograph by Paul Blieden

ABOUT THE AUTHOR

Although Madeline Sharples worked most of her professional life as a technical writer and editor, grant writer, and proposal manager, she fell in love with poetry and creative writing in grade school. She pursued her writing interests to high school while studying journalism and writing for the high school newspaper, and she studied journalism in college. However, she only began to fulfill her dream to be a professional writer late in her life.

She co-authored a book about women in nontraditional professions called *Blue-Collar Women: Trailblazing Women Take on Men-Only Jobs* (New Horizon Press, 1994) and co-edited the poetry anthology, *The Great American Poetry Show*, Volumes 1 (Muse Media, 2004) and 2 (August 2010). She wrote the poems for two photography books, *The Emerging Goddess* and *Intimacy* (Paul Blieden, photographer). She is pleased that many of her poems have appeared online and in print magazines in the last few years.

Madeline and her husband of forty plus years live in Manhattan Beach, California, a small beach community south of Los Angeles. Her younger son Ben lives in Santa Monica, California with his wife Marissa.